EVA GORE-BOOTH:
COLLECTED POEMS

Sonja Tiernan
Editor

Eva Gore-Booth:
Collected Poems

Foreword by President Michael D. Higgins

ARLEN
HOUSE

Eva Gore-Booth:
Collected Poems

is published in 2018 by
ARLEN HOUSE
42 Grange Abbey Road
Baldoyle
Dublin 13
Ireland
Phone: 353 86 8360236
Email: arlenhouse@gmail.com
arlenhouse.blogspot.com

Distributed internationally by
SYRACUSE UNIVERSITY PRESS
621 Skytop Road, Suite 110
Syracuse, NY 13244–5290
Phone: 315–443–5534/Fax: 315–443–5545
Email: supress@syr.edu

978–1–85132–169–8, paperback

Typesetting by Arlen House

Cover image by Joy Ní Dhomhnaill

CONTENTS

For Marc, Conor, Lorcan, Eva and Molly Tiernan
with love and admiration

FOREWORD BY PRESIDENT MICHAEL D. HIGGINS

In his poem 'In Memory of Eva Gore-Booth and Con Markiewicz', a poem that is capable of more than one reading, Yeats described the great humanitarian work of suffragist, artist and poet Eva Gore-Booth a dream 'of some vague Utopia'. The reading depends on where the stress lies. Eva's life, however you read the poem, was driven by an uncompromising ethical drive; and her radical vision for a better world, that included gender and class equality, would see her become a unique and revolutionary figure in the social history of our Islands.

Born into Ireland's landed gentry she devoted her adult life to fighting for the rights of the disenfranchised and the emancipation of the poor. She became a trade-union founder and a passionate campaigner for women's suffrage and for gender equality in an age still ruled by patriarchal values.

A pacifist at heart, who regarded war as the destruction of everything that was of value to human life, she was thus a supporter of Conscientious Objectors throughout the heightened militarism of World War I. She nevertheless steadfastly defended the reputation and motivations of her friends who were involved in the Easter Rising, embracing the cause of Irish independence and the call for an end to Empire and the undoing of the consequences of Imperialism.

The rights of workers, particularly those of women workers, was a cause to which Eva Gore-Booth dedicated herself with energy, skill and humanity. During the many years she lived in Manchester with her life partner Esther Roper she advocated for women's access to education and financial independence and she dedicated herself to combating attempts at restricting women's employment. Convinced that the position of women, both in the home and in the workplace, would not improve until they received the right to vote, Eva Gore-Booth made the vital connection between women's industrial struggles and the political battle for women's suffrage.

Her contribution to social reform was unique. She was an imaginative and brave revolutionary; who refused to be bound by the conventions of her time, sex and class and whose emancipatory instinct was remarkable. Indeed we can take much inspiration from Eva Gore-Booth's constant questioning of the status quo, and her willingness to refute much of the prevailing and distorting discourse of the established powers of her day.

Although she did not live long enough to witness the fruits of her many pioneering battles, Eva Gore-Booth's legacy is unique and her imprint on our social landscape has been profound and lasting.

Like so many women, however, Eva Gore-Booth's role in seeking emancipatory change has not always earned her due recognition. Ireland's centenary celebrations in 2016 enabled us to undo to some degree this exclusion, to reclaim the memory of some of those women. In my speeches at commemorative state ceremonies and community events alike, I have been seeking to do a belated justice to the role of women in the struggle for Irish freedom. It remained of particular importance to me that adequate tribute be paid to Eva Gore-Booth as a remarkable, indeed quite extra-ordinary, figure, not just in Ireland's Revolution, but also in the international trade-union, suffrage and peace movements of the last century. When I spoke in London to the British Trades Union Congress I recalled her passionate fight against injustice and suggested that her extraordinary path of engagement is one that remains deeply inspiring to us today, and greatly relevant in a world in which we continue to meet new and significant challenges.

Eva, throughout her relatively short but very productive life created another great legacy through the large body of writing she has left behind. As well as philosophical prose and plays, she also wrote nineteen volumes of poetry. As a key member of the vibrant Irish Revival, Eva Gore-Booth was part of a group of artists and thinkers who were generous and committed to the life of the public and the life of the community.

Eva Gore-Booth's offered her poetry as weapons for peace in the many causes for justice and equality which she promoted and fought for throughout her life. The themes of social change and liberation for women, as well as her pacifist beliefs recur throughout her work, which includes many references to powerful historical female figures such as Cleopatra and Sheba.

Much of her poetry is inspired too by Ireland's ancient mythological figures, most notably Maeve, Queen of Connaught, whose burial ground, Knocknarea's flat-top cairn, overlooked the estate of Lissadell where Eva was born.

Eva Gore-Booth has not been accorded a sufficient recognition amongst those poets writing during that most seismic period of Ireland's history – poets who did not simply yearn for a romanticised Ireland of Celtic myth and legend, but sought to achieve a recovery of intellectual and applied energy for the achievement of a cultural and political autonomy. This is despite the fact that her work was favourably received in Ireland, the United Kingdom and America. She was held in the highest regard by many of her contemporaries, but has been largely neglected and overlooked in the intervening years.

We are already indebted to the work of Sonja Tiernan, who has produced the first biography dedicated entirely to Eva Gore-Booth, as well as an excellent edition of Gore-Booth's *Political Writings*, many of which were out of print and scattered across a variety of archival collections.

We can now also be deeply grateful to Sonja Tiernan for introducing a new generation of scholars, critics and readers to the poetry of Eva Gore-Booth. It is my sincere hope that this collection will restore to Eva Gore-Booth her rightful place in the literary history of our Islands, where she envisioned and worked to fashion alternative and better societies.

THE POETIC LIFE OF EVA GORE-BOOTH

In spite of the fact that Eva Gore-Booth actively engaged with the project of the Celtic Literary Revival, she makes her most famous appearance in this literature as 'withered old and skeleton-gaunt', in Yeats' poem 'In Memory of Eva Gore-Booth and Con Markievicz'.[1] Gore-Booth published a large amount of literature which often involved intense study and commitment. In contrast, she wrote occasional poetry to express her feelings in relation to events as they occurred in her life. The key points in Gore-Booth's life, such as meeting her life-long partner, Esther Roper, her extreme anxiety after the events of the Easter Rising, her work on women's rights, pacifism, theology, theosophy and her final path towards death, are all expressed in her poetry. For this reason poetry is the most personal of all her writings. Esther Roper wrote that 'to follow the procession of her poems is to see and understand the story of her inner life'.[2] The celebrated theologian and mystic, Evelyn Underhill, who composed the introduction to Gore-Booth's final poetry collection, notes how poems 'constitute in themselves a chronicle of her inner development'.[3]

Gore-Booth's poetry is mainly out of print since 1929 and sadly often only available through university and research libraries. To date only small samples of Gore-Booth's poetry have been republished. Éilís Ní Dhuibhne republished twenty of her poems in a compilation, *Voices on the Wind: Women Poets of the Celtic Twilight*.[4] The *Field Day Anthology* included three poems by Gore-Booth in the 'Lesbian Encounters' section of the volume.[5] The continuing importance of Gore-Booth's poetry is apparent in more recent volumes. In her 2012 anthology, *Poetry by Women in Ireland*, Lucy Collins includes a small collection of poems by Gore-Booth. Collins notes how,

> in keeping with the extraordinarily uncompromising life she chose, Gore-Booth's writing became less conventional as her poetic career progressed and her late poems in particular bear the marks of an independent mind with strong capability for abstract thought and precise use of form and language.[6]

Most recently a small selection of Gore-Booth's poetry was included in a compilation of poems of the Easter Rising and also in Declan Kiberd and P.J. Mathews' *Handbook of the Irish Revival*, testifying to Gore-Booth's position in the Irish Revival movement.[7]

Due to the fact that Gore-Booth's poetry is mainly out of print, there are very few critical assessments of her poetic work. Ní Dhuibhne's book is a valuable and well-received volume, yet as it was meant to regenerate mainstream interest in female Irish poets it does not provide a textual analysis. As Ní Dhuibhne declares in her introduction 'the poems and writers in this anthology are presented in the spirit of adventure and exploration'.[8] To date, Emma Donoghue's article in *Sex, Nation, and Dissent in Irish Writing* is the only full-length critical essay dedicated to Gore-Booth's poetry.[9] However, Donoghue points out that Gore-Booth's body of work is 'too extensive to cover in one essay'.[10] For this reason Donoghue focuses her essay on one aspect of the poetry 'how Gore-Booth appropriated linguistic and poetic conventions, as well as Celtic mythology, to feminise and lesbianise the stories handed down to her'.[11] More recently scholars, most notably Maureen O'Connor, are focusing on new examinations of Gore-Booth's literature.[12]

This volume is the first publication of Gore-Booth's entire collection of poetry. On the rare occasions that Gore-Booth is remembered in her own right and not as the younger sister of Countess Markievicz or as a muse of Yeats, she is remembered as a poet. Gore-Booth is however often referred to as a minor poet, which evokes the idea that either she wrote a small amount of poetry or that she was not perceived as a noteworthy author in her era. Gore-Booth wrote and published a large collection of poetry, nearly four hundred and fifty poems in total. She published eight volumes of poetry collections and further compilations were published alongside two of her plays. *Unseen Kings* contains a number of poems, while a large collection of poems entitled *The Three Resurrections* was published with her play *The Triumph of Maeve*.[13] Roper posthumously published a comprehensive edition of Gore-Booth's poetry in 1929. During her life, Gore-Booth was a successful poet, though she was rarely classed as exceptional. Many reviews of her poetry appeared in prestigious Irish periodicals.[14]

Her writing was applauded in theosophical journals, especially *The Occult Review* and her poetry gained the respect of many highly-esteemed contemporary poets.[15] The Lancashire-born poet Francis Thompson much-admired Gore-Booth's poetry.[16] Thompson wrote that,

> she displays, indeed, a true imagination, a poetic gift of her own. Her style and diction are choice and finished, while she has considerable power of imagery, and that imagery is really imaginative.[17]

Æ was so impressed by Gore-Booth's poetry that he included her work in his anthology, *New Songs*, in 1904.

The collection includes poetry by Padraic Colum, Thomas Keohler, Alice Milligan, Susan Mitchell, Seumas O'Sullivan, George Roberts and Ella Young.[18] Mark Sutton notes that *New Songs* became 'famous for the one name whose work was pointedly excluded from its covers. For James Joyce in *Ulysses*, bitterly recalling the incident, his exclusion was based on Anglo-Irish snobbery'.[19] Gore-Booth achieved a certain measure of fame for her poem 'The Little Waves of Breffny' which was published in *New Songs*. In 1910 the composer of popular music, Graham Peel, set the poem to music. Peel published a compilation of five poems by Irish and English authors, as songs. His book of music, *The Country Lover*, includes poems by William Watson, Yeats, Hillaire Belloc, Gerald Gould, along with Gore-Booth.[20] Roper later recalled that Gore-Booth's poems were also set to music by Max Mayer of the Royal College of Music and sung by his wife.[21]

At the time of publication 'The Little Waves of Breffny' was described by the *Manchester Guardian* as 'one of the most beautiful things any writer ... in the new Irish movement has produced'.[22] The Irish author Katharine Tynan further described how Gore-Booth,

> has written ... beautiful poetry, and her 'Little Waves of Breffny' will go singing in the human heart so long as the heart answers to poetry. It is a small masterpiece.[23]

Yeats took an interest in the early poetic career of Gore-Booth. He wrote to his sister Lily that 'Miss Eva Gore-Booth shows some promise as a writer of verse'.[24] Yeats acknowledged that Gore-Booth had natural talent but he observed a flaw in her writing technique. He later wrote to his friend Olivia Shakespeare that Gore-Booth 'needs however, like all literary people, a proper respect for craftsmanship and that she must get in England'.[25] The journalist and historian, R.M. Fox, ranked the quality of Gore-Booth's poetry 'next to W.B. Yeats'. Fox declared that 'critics have written of the magic, glamour, distinction, melody, classic quality and dramatic intensity of her poetry'.[26] Frederick Lapisardi notes that this assessment 'may be overblown, but certainly she is a literary figure whose life and work demands a far better fate than it has known to date'.[27]

Gore-Booth published her first volume of poetry, simply entitled *Poems*, in 1898 shortly after her move to Manchester.[28] She dedicated the book to Julian Sturgis, a close friend who encouraged her publishing career. This volume constitutes one of Gore-Booth's largest compilations, consisting of seventy-two poems. The style of her early work is haunted. In his short biographical entry on Gore-Booth, Mark Sutton maintains that this dark, melancholic style is prevalent because Gore-Booth missed her aristocratic lifestyle in Lissadell. Sutton maintains that,

> unsurprisingly, life in an industrial city proved a shock for Gore-Booth, who had spent all her privileged early life amongst rural beauty, and her first poetry collection *Poems* remains a testament to her nostalgia and longing for her former life.[29]

However, most of the poems contained in this volume must have been written while she was living in Lissadell. Gore-Booth only moved to Manchester in 1897, months before her collection was published. It is unlikely that she wrote seventy-two frequently long poems in a matter of months. A reading of the poems suggests that only a minority were actually penned after her move to Manchester. The forward to *Poems* is a comic expression of the inadequacies of Gore-Booth's own poetry. The first page is addressed to the reader and contains an apology for the weakness of her writing:

> If, Reader, for these poems you should lack
> All sense of gratitude, all words of praise,
> At least you might be thankful for the lays
> That I kept back.

Throughout *Poems* Gore-Booth presents an almost obsessive focus on death. The fact that she witnessed famine in the area surrounding Lissadell during the winter of 1879–80 at a young age may have influenced this dark obsession. Death is expressed as divine and peaceful escape. This negative preoccupation with death is clear in the poem 'In Praise of Liberty'. Her early poems such as this one show that she did not have a spiritual belief in life after physical death, rather 'the dying have desire to live', while in 'Dead Leaves', Gore-Booth questions the fate of death and wonders if it is like the fate of a dead leaf. She describes the leaf soaring high above the land only to end up on the ground. Gore-Booth's early poetry was imbued with questions relating to death which logically progressed to the study of theology and theosophy. Her preoccupation is apparent in her choice of terminology. Terms familiar with death reoccur, such as 'An Epitaph', 'The Abbot's Epitaph', 'La Mort est le baiser de Dieu', (Death is the kiss of God). While funeral imagery persists such as 'rosemary and rue', plants which were burned at funerals in the sixteenth century and 'white lily flower', the flower associated with funerals, appear in lines of 'To May'. May is a time normally associated with spring and rejuvenation while in Gore-Booth's poems May reaps death and destruction.

Gore-Booth's writing style in *Poems* may not fall naturally into the Celtic Literary Revival style adopted by authors such as Yeats and Æ. Their poetry was imbued with an idea of Celticism, which the *Oxford Dictionary of Literary Terms* describes as 'an idea of Irishness based on fanciful notions of an innate racial character'.[30] This notion of innate Irishness stemmed broadly from the writings of the literary critic Matthew Arnold in his 1867 volume, *On the Study of Celtic Literature*.[31] Both Yeats and Æ embraced this impression of Irishness in an attempt to construct distinctively Irish literature in the English language. Ní Dhuibhne maintains that Gore-Booth,

> wrote comparatively few poems which draw on the typical Celtic Twilight raw material of mythology and folklore, but … did draw on it occasionally … and wrote about the Irish Landscape and way of life.[32]

Ní Dhuibhne's assessment is possibly based on a reading of Gore-Booth's early poetry in which Irish mythological figures are not a prominent feature. In contrast with Ní Dhuibhne's assertion, Gore-Booth's poetic terminology does point to a Celtic Revival sentiment.[33] Indeed, Sutton refers to Gore-Booth as having a 'Celtic Twilight style'.[34]

Yeats first published his prose work *The Celtic Twilight* in 1893 and in it he explored the ancient stories that connected the people of Ireland and the inhabitants of the land of Fairy.[35] This became Yeats' most celebrated prose work and he republished an extended version in 1902. The final poem in the Yeats collection was entitled 'Into the Twilight' which inspired the title of his book. The text was such a success that the Irish Literary Revival, to which Yeats played an intrinsic role, is now often referred to as the Celtic Twilight. James Joyce famously mocked this term in *Finnegans Wake* by calling it the 'cultic twalette'.[36] From her earliest poetry publication the term 'twilight' is used almost monotonously throughout Gore-Booth's poems. There are just over four hundred and forty poems in Roper's edition of her poetry and the term twilight appears eighty-three times in sixty-two of these poems.

Similar to much Celtic Revival poetry, a preoccupation with national identity and political independence is a dominant theme throughout Gore-Booth's work. In *Poems* this is presented through a reoccurring theme of liberty. Gore-Booth's focus is republican and revolutionary contrasting with her later pacifism. 'In Praise of Liberty' establishes this revolutionary theme. There are five verses in this poem and each verse ends with the same two lines,

'I know that Liberty is best/and no man sadder than a slave'. While in 'Prayer of the Modern Greek' the Byronic style poem concluded with a description of the liberty cap reminiscent of the French Revolution.

'The Exile's Return', also a five-verse poem, focused explicitly on the French Revolution. The third last line of each verse portrays France: 'For the sun shines fair in France/Though all flowers are dead in France/Golden oranges of France/Back to liberty and France/Splendid fleur-de-lys of France'. Gore-Booth concludes that 'Life and liberty are one'. Liberty appears as a radiant state in 'An Epitaph', 'Hymn', 'A Soldier' and 'To Certain Reformers'. This theme undoubtedly expressed Gore-Booth's own nationalism as the French Revolution had a significant impact on the development of an organised Irish nationalist rebellion. Historian Kevin Whelan concurs noting how,

> the impact of the French Revolution on Ireland was to release the sectarian stalemate. The leading Catholic power in Europe had, astonishingly, produced a revolution more radical than the much vaunted Glorious (and Protestant) Revolution of 1688.[37]

The formation of the United Irishmen was inspired by the success of the French rebellion. Wolfe Tone advocated the principles of the French Revolution in his pamphlet *Argument on behalf of the Catholics of Ireland*.[38]

Tone depicted the French Revolution as 'the morning star of liberty' for Ireland.[39] An important element of the United Irishmen was that they comprised of an equal balance of Catholic and Protestant members. A short poem by Gore-Booth entitled 'Tricolor' elucidates this opinion. The tricolour flag was first used in Ireland in 1848 at a Young Ireland rally in celebration of yet another French Revolution. The tricolour emerged as the flag of the French Revolution with a simple design of blue, white and red. The colours of the flag, expressed the radical changes being introduced into social, political, and economic life. This flag was seen to embody all the principles of the revolution – liberty, equality, fraternity, democracy, secularism, and modernization.[40]

Other European nations have since adopted this simple tricolour design. Ireland's colours, similar to France, express equal lines for Catholic (green), Protestant (orange), joined by peace (white) in the centre. The Irish tricolour was not popularly adopted in Ireland until after the Easter Rising when it was flown over the GPO. With Gore-Booth's knowledge of history and her support of Irish Home Rule she would have been aware of the Irish tricolour when she published this volume.

Gore-Booth rejected a sectarian related aristocracy in line with both the French Revolution and the Wexford Rebellion. This rejection is played out through the use of unsympathetic imagery in her poem 'A Welcome' which negatively depicts the Anglo-Irish gentry. Here Gore-Booth, as an Anglo-Irish woman, describes her own class background as shallow, materialistic and unfeeling, whose only concern was to amass money and only worshiped the god of materialism. *Poems* is distinctive within Gore-Booth's body of literary work as it expresses her pre-pacifist stage. In the collection she praises a French style revolution complete with blood and swords which is at odds with her later pacifist beliefs. In her later poetry we see that she held the same ideals for Irish independence but dramatically changed her opinion in relation to the methods she advocated to achieve this.

The theme of liberty continues in this collection and not just in relation to Irish independence, but also in relation to women's suffrage. A key poem in this anthology is 'To Certain Reformers'. This is the first time in Gore-Booth's poetry that she makes a rallying call for women to unite and fight their oppression. The middle section of the poem calls on women of ancient times, heroines of the past and holy women:

> Yet, take your swords in hand,
> And fight for the light to be,
> And the spirit's promised land
> Of Truth and Liberty.
> White-souled women of the past,
> Heard ye not the trumpet blast?
> Were your spirits less pure then,
> Feebler than the souls of men?
> Holy, it be understood,
> And yet neither strong nor wise –
> May the spirit purge your eyes
> And teach the foolish world at length
> That purity is always strength.
> Right divine to rule ye feel,
> Strong in you the stronger born, –
> Then your right divine reveal,
> Lest your claims be met with scorn.

These lines express how women were presumed weaker than men and viewed as the source of temptation.

Female imagery is a dominant aspect of Gore-Booth's *Poems* as Donoghue notes that,

> when Gore-Booth came to write about nature, she was inheriting traditions of gender polarity. For centuries male poets had cast themselves as suitors in relation to a feminine personification of nature. Simply fitting herself into this tradition, Eva lesbianised the couple.[41]

This can be seen in poems such as 'A Love Song'. Here Gore-Booth expresses her love in feminine terms. She does not hide behind male pronouns, rather, as a female poet she conveys love towards a female muse. Describing the glory of nature as female, 'My Lady of the spring/My Lady of the Hills', the poem concludes:

> All the strength, and the hope, and the gladness of living are hers,
> And her voice is the voice of the wind in a forest of firs.

These poems may be read as clandestine love poems to women or simply as poems celebrating the beauty of nature. Certainly some of these nature poems can easily be identified as erotic, especially 'February at Adare'. Here Gore-Booth personifies spring as a beautiful sleepy woman complete with sexual imagery:

> She seemed as one about to wake, who lingers
> Yet on the blessed borderland of consciousness,
> Her hair streamed down between her claspèd fingers,
> And fell upon the stream like a caress,
> To make a little passing stir and shiver
> In the cool surface of the lazy river.
> You might have thought her dead, so still she lay,
> This sleeping beauty, whom the tyrannous time
> Had left to dream the ice-bound hours away

Donoghue describes this extract as a 'precise and erotic description of coming across spring in the form of a woman of a somewhat Pre-Raphelite appearance dozing beside a river'.[42] Poetry celebrating spring as seductive was familiar among Gore-Booth's female contemporaries such as in Ella Young's poem 'My Lady of the Dreams' and Alice Furlong's 'To Spring'.[43] Katharine Tynan's 'The Dead Spring' depicts spring as lifeless because her male suitor has abandoned her, choosing summer instead.[44] In this regard Gore-Booth's poetry stands out because she avoids the customary heterosexual storylines.

Gore-Booth predominantly employs feminine imagery and casts several female goddesses, religious, historical and mythological figures in her poems. She was moved to write 'The Repentenance of Eve' after viewing a picture with the same title painted by her sister Constance Markievicz. There is a strong feminist theme in this poem. Gore-Booth reminds us that Eve 'ate but half the fruit, sinned half the sin', yet 'Eternal hunger is her punishment'. At the time of writing this poem Gore-Booth had not begun studying Eastern religions and still focussed on Christian doctrines. Within these doctrines the

Old Testament story of Adam and Eve has always emphasised that it was Eve who first ate the apple in the Garden of Eden, thus tempting Adam to sin. This poem explains that the female race is not entirely to blame for the sins of man and the human expulsion from the Garden of Eden. Ultimately, she concludes that it was the fault of 'the wily snake', the devil.

In a poem dedicated to the French heroine of battle, 'Joan of Arc', Gore-Booth pays tribute to the strong female character, probably also influenced by another of Markievicz's paintings in which she depicted herself as Joan of Arc. This was painted in the 1890s and now hangs in the Kilmainham Gaol Museum in Dublin.[45] According to Amanda Sebestyn, Constance,

> had a penchant for drag. Not only was there her Citizens' Army uniform, but she made herself with great care some fifteenth-century armour as Joan of Arc in a suffrage pageant in the year before the First World War.[46]

In contemporary terms Countess Markievicz is often referred to as Ireland's Joan of Arc.[47] The theme of Gore-Booth's poem again exhibits her pre-pacifist stage with expressions of admiration for the female soldier Joan of Arc, 'She whose spirit was strong in strife'.

Gore-Booth's next publication, *Unseen Kings*, was a verse play about Cú Chulainn. This publication includes a short compilation of eleven poems and it was received with much praise from many quarters at the time of publication.[48] A review in the *Literary World* described how 'Miss Gore-Booth is undoubtedly one upon whom the spirit of poetry has fallen from heaven'.[49] These poems mark a change in Gore-Booth's spiritual interests as they include her first references to Eastern religions. In 'From East to West' Gore-Booth portrays Ireland as the West and India as the East. The poem declares that Eastern mysticism can find an appreciative home in Ireland. The poem in story form describes the dreams and stories of the

East searching for a home in the West. Travelling by sea in 'the ships of the gods', the gods were 'aghast' to discover that the West was armed by materialism. 'They saw the earth an iron fort/The air a silver citadel/the sky a fortress built of solid gold'. Gore-Booth uses the term Prāni, a Hindu term that depicts a living, breathing force possessed of vital air. The ship continued its journey until it came to a land perfect for their home. The land is strikingly presented as Ireland by the use of strong Irish imagery. It is a 'twilight land in the west' where even the wind carried 'a song with a golden lilt'. The land is described as a place 'Where old unquiet mysteries/And pale discrowned spirits dwell'. Gore-Booth describes Ireland as a land dispossessed of mythology and history, yet here the doctrines of the East find an ideal home, where they build 'An ivory castle for their dreams'.

Eastern imagery is interlinked with Celtic mythology in this collection and, similar to her plays, the warrior queen Maeve is again a prominent figure in this collection. 'A Hermit's Lament for Maeve' is simply a hermit's expression of grief for the death of Maeve. After the two opening verses which describe Maeve's 'lonely grave on the haunted mountain side', the theme changes to a pacifist tone, the first time it is seen in Gore-Booth's poetry. The hermit declares 'I could have been brave to fight for Maeve/Now I pray that all war may cease'. This contrasts her earlier poems which simply praise the brave fighting women. The poem concludes with the lines 'I care no more for peace or war/But I pray for a little rest/Where the golden soul of silence rises out of the West'. Here we see Gore-Booth's struggle with the dichotomy of war and peace. The next poem is also a tribute to Maeve purely entitled 'To Maeve'. This time Gore-Booth addresses a feminist theme, describing how brave Irish women have been misrepresented in history. The opening verse describes how men have rewritten the history of Maeve.

'For men put lies on thy lips, and treason, and shrieking far/Because thou wert brave, they say thou wert bitter and false of tongue'.

The theme of feminist re-visioning continues in 'Lament of the Daughters of Ireland'. In a footnote Gore-Booth shows that,

> by a law passed at the Council of Drumcreat, 590, the women of Ireland were exempted from military service. Over 100 years later the law had to be renewed as it had become inoperative.[50]

Gore-Booth establishes in this footnote that there was actually a legal attempt to exclude women from participation in fighting in sixth-century Ireland. During this era the control of lands and kingdoms was decided through battle, therefore excluding women from such participation also excluded them from political power. Even though the law became 'inoperative', in the opening line of the poem Gore-Booth illustrated how women's deeds have still been forgotten. 'Now is the day of the daughters of Éireann passed and gone/Forgotten are their deeds, and their fame has faded away'. The poem continues with an account of all the heroines of Irish culture and history who have now been erased from the record books and forgotten within Irish heritage. The poem represents a roll call of these women, including, Maeve, 'Lavarcam the Wise, and Fand, and the Faery-woman Feithleen', to highlight how many women actively participated in Irish history. The poem can be described as a feminist attempt to rewrite lost and ignored history. In it Gore-Booth stresses that we are still connected to these women, 'Our mothers went forth to the battle strong-armed and eager to dare'. Those women were not ruled by a patriarchal system for 'Their souls were fierce with freedom, they loved, and they called no man lord'.

The feminist theme continues with 'The Queen's Flight' which is an account of Gore-Booth's rejection of her privileged aristocratic birth but it includes a moral in relation to class. The poem is presented as a story in which a King falls in love with a beggar maid. In the beginning of the poem the beggar maid wore a dress of 'washed out blue' and walked barefoot. The beggar maid fell in love with the King and when she became his Queen, her life was radically changed which is reflected in what she wore, 'In flowing garments of velvet and vair/With a crown of gold on her golden hair'. Gore-Booth describes how the beggar maid's life then revolved around materialistic things, 'Throned in vanity over the vain'.

Gore-Booth's description of the privileged lifestyle afforded to royalty is harsh and critical. She portrays the privileged life as monotonous and materialistic in comparison to a life of poverty, which she describes as fun and full of possibilities amongst nature. This portrayal is summed up in one short line of the poem when the Queen realises that 'The palace is narrow, the world is wide'. The Queen swaps her robes of velvet for her 'gown of washed-out blue', and returns to her life in the forest. Instantly the beggar maid 'laughed aloud as she used to do'. Even though 'Her dress was faded and ravelled and torn/But her heart was gay as a summer morn'. The comparison between the two lifestyles continued throughout the poem as the beggar maid says 'The King's hall is guarded by bolt and bar-/Behold, I am free as the wild things are'. This poem symbolises Gore-Booth's own choice in life to reject her own privileged background and instead to live in the working-class district of Manchester.

Donoghue notes that Gore-Booth's poetry reflects,

> her polarised images of masculinity and femininity [which] seem to show an essential view of gender, yet she founded a magazine to help men and women escape from the prison of sex roles.[51]

In her poems, Gore-Booth exposes the bad aspects of masculinity and positions femininity as divine, incorporating the ideal characteristics for one gender. She exhibits the categories of male and female as a false binary that could and should be collapsed. Gore-Booth portrays the materialistic in terms of male in 'The Queen's Flight'. As Donoghue observes in this way Gore-Booth suggests that 'the worst things about human society are male'.[52]

The theme of 'The Queen's Flight' is reminiscent of an earlier poem by Lord Alfred Tennyson entitled 'The Beggar Maid' published in 1842. 'The Beggar Maid' details the same story and Gore-Booth almost replicates Tennyson's image, 'Bare-footed came the beggar maid ... She in her poor attire was seen'.[53] In contrast, Tennyson's poem concludes with a marriage between the King and the beggar maid as a positive development, rather than Gore-Booth's negative union. Tennyson's poem inspired Sir Edward Coley Burne-Jones to paint King Cophetua and the Beggar Maid in 1884, an oil on canvas which is housed at the Tate Gallery in London. Gore-Booth was inspired by Burne-Jones' paintings for her plays The Sorrowful Princess and The Sword of Justice and the influence of Burne-Jones is unmistakable in her poetry. The imagery used for both Tennyson's poem and Burne-Jones' painting has resonant feminist significance. According to Breanna Byecroft, the story of King Cophetua and the Beggar Maid is about possession of a woman, by a man:

> The King recreates the beggar maid in the image of his choice. The King falls in love with the beggar maid who sits unnervingly still and appears drained of emotion like the sculpted image of Galatea. Like the artist who creates life out of inanimate material, it is the role of the King to bring the passive woman to life ... the female heroines are never allowed to assert their own image and significance. Each story depicts a power relation in which the woman depends on the man to free her and animate her. In each myth, the man strives for possession and completion.[54]

In Burne-Jones' painting the characters are animated except for the pale and gaunt beggar maid who sits without movement or emotion on her face. The King, who has descended from his throne, has removed his crown and worships at the feet of the beggar maid. Although in adoration of the woman, the King dominates her, he carries a sword and his body blocks her possible retreat from the scene. Gore-Booth subverts both Tennyson and Burne-Jones' imagery by endowing her beggar maid with strong characteristics such as assertiveness and independence.[55] In her poem the King wished to possess the beggar maid and recreate her image, however she rejects the King's possessiveness and ultimately asserts her own presence. It is clear that Gore-Booth was inspired by the paintings of the Pre-Raphaelites, a group of English artists who emulated the art of Italian painters before Raphael. Dante Gabriel Rossetti and Edward Burne-Jones were both prominent artists of this movement. Pre-Raphaelite art influenced many poets at the turn of the twentieth century including Yeats and Oscar Wilde. Gore-Booth was inspired by the portrayal of the female form in this art. Pre-Raphaelite women were depicted as beefy, masculine and statuesque, but essentially female forms.

This strong feminist theme continues in the next poem in the collection, 'The Waters of Life'. The poem includes a quotation after the title,

> Nor deemed I that thy decrees were of such force, that a mortal could over-ride the unwritten and unfailing laws of Heaven. For that life is not of to-day or yesterday but from all time.[56]

Gore-Booth references this as a line spoken by Antigone to the King. In Greek mythology Antigone was a fearless woman who defied a powerful King, a story which has an ongoing significance for feminists. Catherine Holland points out that the heroine,

> Antigone, occupies a prominent position within contemporary feminist thought, a figure around whom feminists have recast the relation of women to political action by contesting and

reconfiguring relations between household and polis posed by the western theoretical tradition.[57]

Indeed, many feminist articles examine the significance of Antigone's story in relation to political inclusion. Judith Butler observes that,

> the legacy of Antigone's defiance appeared to be lost in the contemporary efforts to recast political opposition as legal plaint and to seek the legitimacy of the state in the espousal of feminist claims.[58]

In the same year that *Unseen Kings* was published, Gore-Booth published forty-five poems in a collection entitled *The One and the Many*.[59] Sutton describes how in his opinion this collection 'bears witness to a young woman fired with anger and commitment to social change'.[60] This reading may be too simple an assessment. Throughout *The One and the Many* there are single lines expressing various messages printed alone on two pages in between the poetry, which hold key messages. The title page contains a quote from Porphyry, 'The Soul, being Wingèd, governs the World'. Porphyry was a Neoplatonist philosopher – his basic philosophical view was that there is a gap between the sensible and the intelligible realm. The pursuit of the 'One' is the basic theme of *The One and the Many*. Gore-Booth pursued The One through a merging together of Celtic and Eastern mysticisms. *The Journal of Education* reviewed this collection when it was first published. The reviewer praised this aspect to Gore-Booth's work,

> This book brims over with the mystery and poetry of the East and of the ancient religions, as well as with the sweet lilting melody so often characteristic of the songs of the Western Gael. The over-long crooning lines of some of the chants – Whitman-like and fascinating – have a certain rune-like charm … Miss Gore-Booth is a poet for poets.[61]

Amongst the mystical poems in this collection Gore-Booth presents perhaps her most harsh criticism of British rule over Ireland. She portrays her total rejection of landownership and of her own heritage in 'The Land to the Landlord'. The opening verse launches directly into an attack on the landed elite:

> You hug to your soul a handful of dust,
> And you think the round world your sacred trust –
> But the sun shines, and the wind blows,
> And nobody cares and nobody knows.
> O the braken waves and the foxgloves flame,
> And none of them ever has heard your name –
> Near and dear is the curlew's cry,
> You are merely a stranger passing by.

The message here is all the more effective because it is written by the daughter of a prominent Anglo-Irish landlord. The language is harsh and unsympathetic, employing the term twilight effectively to show how the Celtic Twilight, this rejuvenation of the ancient Irish culture and religion, has left the landlords on the outside. Once again Gore-Booth uses male pronouns to represent negative aspects of human nature. The poem clearly notes how the landlord thinks he is 'king', he is 'lord', while nature, with female pronouns, 'the hemlock bows not her head as you pass', remains uncontrollable and independent. Significantly hemlock is a poisonous plant and it was used in ancient Greece to execute people. Socrates was poisoned to death by hemlock. Gore-Booth was born into an aristocratic family and therefore she had the security of a privileged life. However, in her poetry she not only rejected her privileged background, she seemed embarrassed by her heritage. It is clear in her poems that Gore-Booth felt equal to the women she lived and worked amongst in the working class district of Manchester. This comradeship was not idealised by Gore-Booth, rather it was the ideal for her.

Feminist imagery continues throughout this collection. Donoghue remarks that certain female characters persist in Gore-Booth's poetry to portray an 'abstract representation of womanhood'.[62] An important figure for Gore-Booth is Proserpine who features prominently in Gore-Booth's early poetry, such as 'An Idyll', where she imagines 'jewels rich and rare, on the breast of Proserpine'. In 'Finger Posts' 'Content at last, and glad to enter in Despair's abode, and rest with Proserpine' and in 'Visions of Solitude' she pleads to 'worship now Divine Poppy crownèd Proserpine?' In *The One and the Many*, the titles of many of the poems reflect Gore-Booth's admiration for Proserpine; 'From the Garden of Proserpine', 'Proserpine in Hades' and 'Proserpine Enthroned'. Proserpine is the Roman equivalent to the Greek Persephone, however it is apparent that although Gore-Booth adopts the Roman spelling of the goddess of spring, she actually refers to the Greek myth.[63] In the Homeric *Hymn to Demeter*, the story is told that Proserpine was gathering flowers in the Vale of Nysa when she was abducted by Hades and brought to the underworld.[64] She became the wife of Hades and consequently the Queen of the Underworld. Proserpine's mother, Demeter, became unconcerned with the harvest of the earth and widespread famine followed. Zeus intervened and commanded Hades to release Proserpine to her mother. This myth has been appropriated by a number of artists and poets. Milton alludes to the story of Proserpine in *Paradise Lost IV*. Rossetti painted *The Abduction of Proserpine* in 1874. 'The Garden of Proserpine', a poem written by Algernon Charles Swinburn, is reminiscent of Gore-Booth's later poem, 'From the Garden of Proserpine'. Proserpine symbolises one of the few feminist aspects in Roman and Greek mythology as Helene Foley points out,[65]

> In contrast to the Homeric epics, the Hymn puts female experience at the centre of the narrative by giving the privileged place to the point of view of the divine mother and daughter on their shared catastrophe. The (nevertheless critical) actions of the gods Zeus, Helios, and Hades occur at

the periphery of the narrative and receive relatively little attention or sympathy.[66]

Greek mythology played a significant role among Gore-Booth's circle of literary friends and sexual reform activists. The homosexual rights activist, Edward Carpenter, dedicated years of his life to the study and translation of ancient Greek texts. He translated *The Story of Eros and Psyche from Apuleius, and the first book of the Iliad of Homer* and he wrote poetry dedicated to mythological figures, including Prosephone.[67] His epic poem 'Prosephone' concludes,

> ... Eaten the seeds of life, Persephone,
> Obedient to love's unexpressed decree,
> Each year went earthward to renew her might
> And bless returning summer with the sight
> Of Night's conception. So while winds blew chill,
> She dwelt with Hades and the land was still.[68]

Ultimately Carpenter published a detailed study entitled *Pagan and Christian Creeds: Their Origin and Meaning.*[69] This aspect of pagan mythology connected directly into Gore-Booth's interest in theology, theosophy and gender/sexuality debates. Greek mythology inspired much nineteenth and twentieth century homosexual literature. In her study of gay historiography from 1870 to the present, the novelist Sarah Waters notes that Greek mythological characters 'figured at the turn of the century as a particular sensitive register of homosexual desire and cultural anxiety'.[70] Additionally, interest in the classical past found a strong expression within Anglo-Irish Literature. Literary critic Elizabeth Butler Cullingford remarks that,

> Marx noted the reliance of the French revolutionaries on historical models supplied by republican Rome, their need to deck their radical enterprise in the retro fancy dress of togas and laurel wreaths. During the same historical period, the first Celtic revivalists also looked back to the classical world for dynamic comparisons, but they constructed Irish identity in

opposition to imperial Rome, which to them looked uncomfortably like the British Empire.[71]

Gore-Booth can be seen to focus specifically on female characters from Greek mythology in order to present the inequalities of gender relations, which can be further read as anti-colonial expressions.

Gore-Booth further reacts to the paintings of Burne-Jones and wrote another poem based on his work, 'The Soul Attains'. Burne-Jones worked on a series of drawings which resulted in a sequence of four paintings that made up his *Pygmalion and the Image* collection, depicting the story of Pygmalion. *The Soul Attains* is the final painting in this collection, following *The Heart Desires*, *The Hand Refrains* and *The Godhead Fires*. Christopher Newall best describes the meaning behind the Burne-Jones series of paintings,

> The Pygmalion series was again a deliberate or unconscious commentary on the artist's love affair with Maria Zambaco … In the first place he imagines what it might be for an artist to make a woman, as Pygmalion created Galatea, who would be the fulfilment of all desires and who would be under the absolute control of her creator … The neurotic aspect of the series is that they describe both his longing for and his dread of submission to a woman of sexual authority during these years of turbulence and crisis.[72]

Breanna Byecroft points out that, similar to the submissive female in his *King Cophetua and the Beggar Maid*, Burne-Jones' 'women belong to another category of enigmatic females endowed with a deliberate sense of abstraction and removal from everyday life'.[73]

In *The Soul Attains*, the sculptor kneels before his now mortal love. Akin to many other female figures in Burne-Jones' paintings, the newly-created woman is devoid of any emotion as she gazes past the sculptor. The woman stands naked and submissive before the artist who grasps both her hands in an almost controlling grip. In Gore-

Booth's 'The Soul Attains' she alludes to the story expressed in this painting with the line 'Deep in the artist's soul the flame burns cold'. Yet, Gore-Booth concludes 'He who attains, remembers, and grows old', for 'Joy dwells in the austere deeds, the perilous climb'.

Gore-Booth includes imagery of the Celtic landscape in this collection. Her poem 'Lis-An-Doill', is footnoted with a translation of the Irish placename as meaning 'The Fort of the Blind Man'. The biographer Gifford Lewis provides a background explanation of this name. According to Lewis the,

> legend had it that the blind man was Muireadhach Albanach (Scots) O'Daly, brother of the poet Donnchadh Mór O'Daly, ancestor of the ... famous line of bards who later flourished in Scotland.[74]

While Gore-Booth's older sister Countess Markievicz was imprisoned after the Easter Rising she wrote letters to Gore-Booth about Lissadell as the home place of the poet O'Daly. The fact that Gore-Booth uses the old Irish place name of Lissadell is indicative of the literature of the Celtic Revival. The title also suggests that Gore-Booth missed her home place as the poet O'Daly wrote about his yearning to return to Lissadell. Some of the poems he wrote after fleeing Ireland around 1217 still survive. In them he describes 'How peaceful would my slumbers be ... A poet in good company/Couched upon Eire's rushes green'.[75]

Gore-Booth's most famous poem about Irish landscape, 'The Little Waves of Breffny', is included in this collection. The Sligo library which houses some of Gore-Booth's artefacts maintains that she 'is known chiefly as the writer of "The Little Waves of Breffny"'.[76] The poem was later set to music by Max Myer and the song version has more recently been re-recorded by Brian McDonagh and sung by Cathy Jordan. The style of this poem contrasts Gore-Booth's other poetry as it presents a Hiberno-English syntax. The opening two lines of the first verse highlight this: 'The grand road from the mountain goes shining to the sea/And there is traffic in it and many a horse and cart'. Though she did include two uses of her favoured term 'twilight'. 'But the haunted air of the twilight is very strange and still/And the little winds of twilight are dearer to my mind'. Gore-Booth chose the ancient Irish place name Breffny for her title, which was an old Irish territory covering modern Cavan and West Leitrim which were under Anglo-Norman rule in 1300.

Perhaps the most significant poem in *The One and the Many* is 'The Travellers' dedicated 'To E.G.R.' (Esther Gertrude Roper) in which Gore-Booth immortalises meeting Roper. This is one of only two poems that are dedicated to her partner. This poem encapsulates how Gore-Booth experienced their meeting, an encounter so dramatic that even the course of nature was disrupted, the tide ceased, as did those meaningless events of their own lives, 'the jar and hurry'. Describing the love between her and Roper as 'the world's great song', music as a symbol of their love continues throughout the poem. It would appear from the second verse that their lives, and possibly their relationship, underwent some difficult times, when Peace left them to their 'fretful days'. However, through it all 'the great song chimes and rings'. The second verse concludes that their love will survive till death, however in the next verse Gore-Booth is saddened by the thought that their love will die after their physical death. The sad and desperate question continues 'shall life go down in silence at the end/All our love and dreams of no avail?' Gore-Booth describes Roper in the final verse, as 'You whose Love's melody makes glad the gloom' and concludes on a positive note that their love, 'that music', is surely greater than life and will 'outlast that doom' of death.

Gore-Booth's next collection of poetry entitled *The Three Resurrections* was published alongside her play *The Triumph of Maeve* in 1905.[77] A review in the esteemed literary magazine *Pall Mall Gazette*, describes the work as 'full of beautiful things'.[78] This collection includes thirty-six poems. The text opens with two quotations, the first from Paracelus: 'The three magic powers are Imagination, Will, and Love'. Paracelus (c. 1493–1541), was a Swiss physician who created a radical approach to medicine. He condemned,

> medical teaching that was not based on observation and experience. Paracelus saw illness as having a specific external cause rather than being caused by an imbalance of the humours in the body.[79]

Theosophical studies praised the work of Paracelus. Theosophists claimed that he 'was renowned for his remarkable cures' and according to a medical doctor, Franz Hartmann, Paracelus 'traced diseases to both visible and invisible causes'.[80] The second quotation, 'Thine is the Kingdom, the Power, and the Glory', is the concluding line of 'The Lord's Prayer'. The fact that Gore-Booth placed these two quotations together on the title page is significant. Through this she joined together the basic principles of Theosophy and Christianity, which became her final intellectual project in life.

The poetry collection opened with the title poems comprising *The Three Resurrections*: 'I Lazarus', 'II The Return of Alcestis' and 'III Psyche in Hades'. This title is suggestive of the three resurrections in the Christian bible. It was believed that after Christ's Crucifixion he visited Hades and it is from here that he was resurrected.[81] Although Hades is generally assumed as the underworld in Greek mythology, the term was appropriated by the scribes of the Old Testament as a place where spirits went after death (Eccles. 9:10).[82] David Leeming notes that 'resurrection is a mythic theme related to the heroic monomythic archetype of rebirth and return'.[83] Gore-Booth's choice of 'three resurrections' is the key to this mystical compilation of poetry.[84] The poems in the tryptic are cleverly linked as they all involve resurrections from Hades and on their return each resurrected person carries their soul with them in the form of the 'unseen light'. This link is subtle and only apparent after several readings. The first poem, 'Lazarus', is possibly Gore-Booth's longest poem, comprising twenty-one verses in total. The story of the resurrection of Lazarus is told in the Gospel of John 11: 41–44. Gore-Booth's poem relates to the relationship between the body and the soul 'till the soul trembled at the body's name', describes how the soul is superior and immortal while the body is a fixed mortal state. Gore-Booth depicted Lazarus' soul with female pronouns 'drove the soul back to her patient toil/and bid the slave rebuild her broken towers'. It was believed in Christian doctrine that Lazarus, like Christ, went to Hades when he died.

In the next poem, 'The Return of Alcestis', it is another female heroine of Greek mythology who is resurrected from Hades. In Greek mythology Alcestis was the wife of King Admetus. Alcestis gave her life to save her husband. After her death she was sent to Hades where Hercules eventually rescued her.[85] In Gore-Booth's poem she portrayed Alcestis as 'the proud Queen', while Admetus she termed as 'the coward King'. Once again Gore-Booth portrays a strong female protagonist who defied the negative aspects of the male, in this case cowardice and punishment. The final poem of the three is entitled 'Psyche in Hades'. Psyche is the Hellenistic personification of the soul as female, which is aligned with Gore-Booth's poetic descriptions of the soul. Ultimately Aphrodite sent Psyche to the underworld to ask Proserpine for a piece of her beauty. Psyche had to be careful not to eat anything in Hades or, like Proserpine, she would be trapped there forever. Gore-Booth alludes to this story in her poem:

When Psyche staggered through the darkness dense,
And stood in Hades, still feared to taste
The feast of the dark gods of clay and sense,

But dry bread with tears and fled in haste.
Yet did she bear a gift from Proserpine
To Aphrodite in the spheres of light,
A casket holding the lost dream divine,
The perilous beauty of the Infinite ...

These three poems contain a uniform imagery in that they all refer to the 'unseen light' in some context. In 'Lazarus' when Christ called him from Hades he stood 'silent, thine eyes fixed on the Light Unseen'. In 'The Return of Alcestis' when Alcestis rose from Hades she was portrayed 'bright with the radiant breath of the Unseen'. In 'Psyche in Hades' while Psyche journeyed home from Hades, 'the Unseen Light lay clasped against her breast'. This is the key point of these poems that the soul, the 'unseen light' will prevail from the death of the body. In this collection these three poems interconnect mythology and Christianity in a new and interesting way which is carried throughout this collection.

A significant poem in this poetry collection is 'The Caduceus'. The inclusion of this poem provides an insight into why Roper chose to have the symbol of the caduceus embossed on the front cover of Gore-Booth's collection of poetry which she edited and why Gore-Booth herself chose the image for the covers of two of her volumes; *The Three Resurrections and The Triumph of Maeve* and *The Agate Lamp*. The caduceus, otherwise referred to in Greek mythology as the staff of Hermes, was embossed on the covers of books in the sixteenth and seventeenth centuries. It was believed that the staff of Hermes would ensure the delivery of information as Hermes was the messenger god. Although this compilation of poetry was published alongside Gore-Booth's play, *The Triumph of Maeve,* recounting the tale of a female icon of Celtic mythology, there is scarce evidence of Celtic imagery in the poetry.

The only obvious reference to Celtic imagery is contained in the final poem 'Immortalities'. The title contains a quotation from Gregory Nazianzen, a religious character from the fourth century. According to John McGuckin, Saint Gregory of Nazianzus (329–389) was 'a classically trained speaker and philosopher he infused Hellenism into the early church, establishing the paradigm of Byzantine theologians and church officials'.[86] Gregory is worshipped as a saint in both Eastern and Western Christianity, which encapsulates Gore-Booth's theme within this collection to combine the religions of both the East and the West. In the poem Gore-Booth connects images from Greek and Irish mythology:

Now do men say that though the gods be fair
Phoebus who moulded beauty into rhyme
And Irish Niamh of the wind-blown hair
Are but the children not the lords of time.

It is not true, still does Apollo hide
In little songs the world's great mysteries,
And the white beckoning hands of Niamh guide
The hero-hearted over pathless seas.

The Egyptian Pillar was published next in 1907 by the Dublin publishing company Maunsel & Co for their 'Tower Press Series'. Gore-Booth dedicated this book to her sister. The inscription reads 'To my Sister, Constance De Markievicz, *in remembrance of November 10th, 1906, and some dreams we hold in common'*. This collection of poetry is one of two books that Gore-Booth published through Maunsel & Company, Dublin, founded in 1905.

Maunsel was dedicated to publishing Irish works. David Gardiner notes that this was 'the only publisher of Irish writing at the time, Maunsel *was* Irish literature'.[87] Although no book length research has yet been conducted on the Maunsel Press, an article by Gardiner describes the press as an intrinsic part of the Celtic Literary Revival. This can be confirmed through a list of their published authors which includes Lady Gregory, Padraic Colum, J.M Synge, Douglas Hyde, Patrick Pearse, Austin Clarke, Æ and

Stephen Gwynn. Significantly both the editor and sub-editor of the *Irish Homestead*, Æ and Susan Mitchell, published with Maunsel. Gardiner further notes that,

in the Maunsel poetry list, not only were women a shaping element, but the issues raised there – nationalism, socialism, and women's suffrage – were embraced by both the women and men who were published by Maunsel.[88]

Gardiner distinguishes the list of female Irish poets published by Maunsel as the 'most established', including Katharine Tynan, Dora Sigerson Shorter, Alice Milligan, Susan Mitchell, Ella Young and Eva Gore-Booth. Indeed, Gardiner proposes that the inclusion of these women actually provided the Maunsel Press with financial security.[89] Of this list Gardiner further distinguishes Sigerson Shorter and Gore-Booth because of the many repeat editions of their works printed by Maunsel, which he claims 'indicate that [these] works also provided a financial basis for the press'.[90] This fact highlights that Gore-Booth was both a respected and a successful poet of her time 'converting the Celtic romantic of much of the Literary Revival into social commentary, Gore-Booth is an overlooked influence'.[91]

Gore-Booth's social commentary is noticeable for the first time in *The Egyptian Pillar* volume. This book was a short compilation of twenty-two poems that focus on women's work, gender differences and Gore-Booth's own experiences working for equality for women workers. *The Egyptian Pillar* represents yet another change in Gore-Booth's poetic style and theme. Roper describes this collection as a glimpse of Gore-Booth's working life.[92] Indeed 'The Street Orator' is undoubtedly a description of the poet rallying women through a public address. In the first verse we can imagine Gore-Booth amongst the crowd in a busy street, fired up with emotion:

At Clitheroe from the Market Square
I saw rose-lit the mountain's gleam,

I stood before the people there
And spake as in a dream.

The poem acts as a catalogue of her busy campaigning schedule, in it she details places visited. 'At Oldham ... the folks were kind/At Ashton town the rain came down/over little Clitheroe, the sky was bright'. It is obvious in the poem that Gore-Booth worked tirelessly in a place that was, at times, alien to her. She longs for her home of Lissadell, framed by mountains and overlooking the sea:

At Clitheroe through the sunset hour
My soul was very far away:
I saw Ben Bulben's rose and fire
Shining afar o'er Sligo Bay.

Many of the poems in the collection describe Gore-Booth's personal recollections of her political campaigns. Roper observes that one poem from the collection, 'A Lost Opportunity', describes Gore-Booth's depression after speaking at a great deputation of working women to the Prime Minister (Sir Henry Campbell-Bannerman) on 19 May 1906.[93] Interestingly the title of this poem is taken from the concluding line of 'The Repentance of Eve', a poem from her first published collection. By connecting these two poems Gore-Booth suggests that women have been oppressed since the dawn of time at the Garden of Eden.

This poem reflects Gore-Booth's self-criticism, although she acknowledges her passion and insight into the working woman's issues, the reader is shown her own disappointment with her speaking ability on the day. Roper clearly disagrees with this assessment, describing Gore-Booth's speech that day 'when the depth and intensity of her feelings, little as she knew it, lent her words wings'.[94] The Prime Minister listened to the women's speeches but did not make any promises to enforce legislative changes to improve the conditions for women workers. This lack of government action propelled

Gore-Booth to write another poem, 'Women's Trades on the Embankment'. The poem is subtitled with a quote supposedly from Campbell-Bannerman who advised the women on the day to 'have patience!' The last verse of the five verse poem shows that Gore-Booth was not content to simply be patient:

> Long has submission played a traitor's part –
> Oh human soul, no patience any more
> Shall break your wings and harden Pharaoh's heart,
> And keep you lingering on the Red Sea shore.

In 'Women's Rights' Gore-Booth continues to express her negative view of masculinity, while she portrays women as superior and connected with nature. The poem ends as such:

> Oh, whatever men may say
> Ours is the wide and open way.
>
> Oh, whatever men may dream
> We have the blue air and the stream.
>
> Men have got their towers and walls,
> We have cliffs and waterfalls.
>
> Oh, whatever men may do
> Ours is the gold air and the blue.
>
> Men have got their pomp and pride –
> All the green world is on our side.

After publication of *The Egyptian Pillar*, Gore-Booth took a rest from publishing poetry and plays. During this time she became submerged in many political campaigns for the rights of women workers. Her next publication did not appear until 1912. For this publication of *The Agate Lamp* Gore-Booth returned to her original publishers, Longman's Green & Co.[95] The volume includes twenty-eight poems and ten sonnets. Æ praised this collection in *The Irish Homestead* stating that 'the poems breathe the same eager adventure of the mind that inspires all Eva Gore-Booth's work'.[96] The title poem begins with a verse reminiscent of the sentiment expressed in 'The Travellers, to E.G.R.'

> How is it doomed to end?
> Shall I, when I come again,
> Watch the old sun in a new eclipse,
> Breathe the same air with different lips,
> Think the same thoughts with a different brain,
> With a new heart love the same old friend?

This relates to Gore-Booth's belief that only physical bodies will die and souls will be reincarnated into a new body with a 'different brain' and 'different lips'. Here Gore-Booth's concern is whether she will have the chance to love the 'same old friend' in her next incarnation, easily identified as Roper. Gore-Booth concludes 'The Travellers' on a positive note deciding that surely their love would 'outlast that doom'. Here we see that Gore-Booth is still concerned by whether or not she will meet Roper in their next incarnations.

The rest of this compilation of poetry is made up of tributes to particular artists, individual paintings and sculptures. In 'Leonardo Da Vinci' Gore-Booth pays homage to Da Vinci who 'lit the soul of John' in his painting of *The Last Supper*.[97] 'San Di Pietro (Siena)' is a tribute to the Italian Renaissance artist Francesco di Giorgio e di Lorenzo who is known as Lorenzo di Pietro (1412–1480) and whose works remain mainly in Siena. 'Rodin's Caryatides' depicts the plight of the caryatides sculpted by Rodin. Rodin's caryatides were all female and therefore this poem could be interpreted as the plight of women. The following poem 'Adoration of the Shepherds' refers to a painting by Italian artist Domenico Ghirlandajo (1449–1494.) 'David' and 'The Dawn' represent paintings by Michelangelo. 'Angels of the Incarnation' painted by Botticelli and 'Athene (restored)' is a giant sculpture of the Greek goddess Athena by Phidias. The list of tributes continues throughout this collection, honouring the great artists of mainly the Italian Renaissance.

A series of ten sonnets broke the theme of artistry and Gore-Booth concludes this series with a mixture of poetry relating to reincarnation, mythology and women's rights. Perhaps one of the most intriguing poems in this collection is 'A Vision of Niamh'. Gore-Booth includes a note under the title stating 'Niamh was perhaps the Uranian Aphrodite of Irish legend – the goddess of remote and spiritual beauty'. This is an interesting description of Niamh as the poem itself depicts strong lesbian imagery. Consider the final three verses,

... For thee Maeve left her kingdom and her throne,
And all the gilded wisdom of the wise,
And dwelt among the hazel trees alone
So that she might look into Niamh's eyes.

No sorrow of lost battles any more
In her enchanted spirit could abide;
Straight she forgot the long and desolate war,
And how Fionavar for pity died.

Ah, Niamh, still the starry lamp burns bright,
I can see through the darkness of the grave,
How long ago thy soul of starry light
Was very dear to the brave soul of Maeve.

The intriguing aspect of this poem is that in classic Celtic mythology the paths of Queen Maeve of Knocknarea and Niamh, the goddess of spiritual beauty, never cross. Maeve is a central figure throughout Gore-Booth's Celtic literature and she became a focus in both *Unseen Kings* and *The Triumph of Maeve*. Gore-Booth manipulates classic mythological stories to create her own feminist variation of events in her plays and she continues similar manipulation in her poetry. In T.W Rolleston's account, Maeve retired to an island and was killed by a Cuculain sympathiser with a slingshot. However, in Gore-Booth's account Maeve travelled to Tír na nÓg and on finding the land, her desperation and grief was healed by a simple 'Vision of Niamh'. It is this account that provides the focus for the poem. A poem further into this collection concluded Gore-Booth's version of the Maeve story. In 'The Romance of Maeve' Gore-Booth marvelled at the strength of Maeve's love for Niamh which instilled Maeve to forfeit her kingdom and her pride.

Gore-Booth's next volume of poetry, *The Perilous Light*, was published by Longman's Green & Co in 1915.[98] All twenty-one of these poems had been previously published in other volumes. This volume is a re-publication of her most popular poems, including 'The Little Waves of Breffny' and 'The Land to the Landlord'. She also includes a selection of poems from *The Triumph of Maeve* and *Unseen Kings*. In 1918 Gore-Booth published *Broken Glory*, again through the Maunsel Press.[99] This volume fit naturally into Maunsel's catalogue of Irish literature. Gore-Booth dedicated *Broken Glory* to the 'memory of August 3rd, 1916. "For Love and the Voice on the Wind"'. The date was the day of Roger Casement's execution. These twenty-seven poems focus specifically on the atrocities of the Easter Rising and the First World War. The introductory poem, 'The Age of Gold', sets the precedent for this collection, confirming that even though this collection of poetry was an attack on the powers that govern, particularly the British Empire, the poems are written from a pacifist perspective.

Her poem 'Government' however sets an angry tone describing how God's good work is now destroyed. She describes governments that rule the earth as 'savage and blind', they have 'dug Gethsemane for all mankind'. The garden of Gethsemane is depicted in the New Testament as the place to which Jesus and his disciples retreat before his crucifixion. Here Gore-Booth predicts a looming disaster for all mankind. The poem is a clear attack on the British authorities and their government of Ireland. It is significant that in this poem she equates the killing of Christ with the execution of Roger Casement. Gore-Booth describes the execution of the leaders of the Rising and states that this has 'Buried, the broken dreams of Ireland lie'. However, she singles out Casement:

No cairn-heaped mound on a high windy hill
With Irish earth the hero's heart enfolds,
But a burning grave at Pentonville,
The broken heart of Ireland holds.

In her poem 'Roger Casement' Gore-Booth's empathy for Casement is most obvious. When she originally wrote this poem she sent a copy to her friend R.M. Fox. The copy of that poem is now held in the National Library of Ireland. Written on the reverse side of the page in Gore-Booth's hand is a chilling account of Casement's execution:

As he was walking out of the cell to the scaffolds, dear little Fr McCarroll whispered to him: 'now Roger for God and Kathleen Ní Houlihan'. He answered, 'Yes Father,' and threw back his proud head with such a beautiful smile. Hanging as a rule distorts all the features. Yet, at the inquest he had that same beautiful smile and looked so kingly as Síofra kissed his dear dead brow.[100]

The poem is a tribute to Casement's life. The second verse praises his humanitarian work in the Congo and Peru:

I dream of him wandering in a far land,
I dream of him bringing hope to the hopeless,
I dream of him bringing light to the blind.

In the fourth verse Gore-Booth alludes to his trial for treason and the rumours about his personal life:

I dream of the hatred of men,
Their lies against him who knew nothing of lying,
Nor was there fear in his mind.

The feminist and pacifist Francis Sheehy Skeffington also features prominently throughout *Broken Glory*. Gore-Booth refers to Sheehy Skeffington as one of 'the noble dead' in her poem 'Easter Week'. She pays tribute to him in a further poem simply entitled 'Francis Sheehy-Skeffington' which is subtitled with the date and place of his murder, 'Dublin, April 26, 1916'. Gore-Booth describes how 'unarmed he stood in ruthless Empire's way'. Similar to Casement's poem, Gore-Booth uses religious imagery to equate Sheehy Skeffington with Christ. 'Who in the Olive Garden agonized', here we get a sense of Sheehy Skeffington agonising before Captain J.C. Bowen Colthurst ordered his unlawful execution.

Three poems in this collection are addressed to Markievicz while she was imprisoned for her part in the rebellion. The first, 'To Constance – in Prison', pleads with Constance to remember the beauty of Lissadell and the wonder of nature in order to surpass her time in prison 'outcast from joy and beauty'. She tells Constance to remember that 'yours is that inner Ireland beyond green fields and brown'. 'Christmas Eve in Prison' provides a comfort to Constance 'not to be lonely, dear, nor grieve'. The final poem to Constance is entitled 'To C. M. on Her Birthday', the date 'February 1917' is included under the title.

> What has time to do with thee,
> Who hast found the victor's way
> To be rich in poverty,
> Without sunshine to be gay,
> To be free in a prison cell?
> Nay on that undreamed judgment day,
> When on the old world's scrap-heap flung,
> Powers and empires pass away,
> Radiant and unconquerable
> Thou shalt be young.

Amusingly in this poem Gore-Booth appears to comfort Constance about the fact that she has got one year older – the fact that she is in prison is not the primary focus. This aspect provides us with a glimpse of the personalities of the two women and their close relationship. This also illuminates why there is a discrepancy regarding the date of Constance's birth on her prison committal form. Her date of birth is noted as 1873, when in fact she was born in 1868. It now seems probable that Constance lied about her age when she was first arrested.

Donoghue claims that 'Gore-Booth was a fervent pacifist, yet many of her poems award a heroine status to military leaders, including her own sister Con'.[101] Gore-Booth expresses admiration for many female military leaders in her poems. However this is another feature of her feminist re-visioning of history. Gore-Booth was a fervent pacifist, yet she was also a nationalist. Through her poetry Gore-Booth's progression towards pacifism can be mapped, it is only her early poetry that asserts a revolutionary style. Gore-Booth reflects her pacifism in her anti-establishment poetry and her dedication to fellow pacifists such as Francis Sheehy Skeffington. She was convinced that Irish independence could be achieved constitutionally through pacifist methods. Gore-Booth did award Markievicz a heroine status in many of her poems, not because she took up arms in battle but because she loved and admired her sister. In Gore-Booth's poems to Markievicz in prison she focuses not on killing or violence but on positive themes of nature and love. Additionally, Gore-Booth sent Markievicz a copy of her play, the *Death of Fionavar*, while Constance was imprisoned for her military part in the Easter Rising.[102] The play had a strong pacifist message and may well have been an attempt to convince Markievicz that pacifist methods were the best course of action to achieve Irish independence. This is borne out in a letter Markievicz wrote to Roper after her sister's death. Markievicz discusses the influence Gore-Booth had over her in this respect: 'her gentleness prevented me getting very brutal, and one does get very callous in War. I once held out and stopped a man being shot because of her'.[103]

The only other person mentioned directly in *Broken*

Glory is fellow poet, Dora Sigerson Shorter. Gardiner remarks that 'both Eva Gore-Booth's partner, Esther Roper, and Katharine Tynan popularised the notion that Sigerson Shorter died of a broken heart following the 1916 executions'.[104] I suggest that this belief was instigated by Gore-Booth herself, along with Tynan. A poem dedicated 'To Dora Sigerson Shorter' and subtitled 'The Sad Years' is the final poem in *Broken Glory*. *The Sad Years* was a volume of poetry published the same year as Sigerson Shorter's death, which includes a memoir by Tynan.[105] Although Roper stated that the effects of the Easter Rising 'caused the death of … Dora Sigerson', this claim was made as an explanation of Gore-Booth's poem.[106] In the first of the two-verse poem Gore-Booth describes how she felt a connection with Sigerson Shorter whom she had never met. The poem clearly blames the atrocities of the Rising for causing the poet's death:

> You whom I never knew,
> Who lived remote, afar,
> Yet died of the grief that tore my heart,
> Shall we live through the ages alone, apart,
> Or meet where the souls of the sorrowful are
> Telling the tale on some secret star,
> How your death from the root of my sorrow grew –
> You whom I never knew?

Gore-Booth did not publish any more poetry until *The Shepherd of Eternity* in 1925, which was her last poetry publication while she was alive.[107] According to Mark Sutton this collection and *House of Three Windows* published posthumously by Roper in 1926 'both advanced her increasingly religious blend of pantheism and Christian Platonism'.[108] Gore-Booth spent her final years engrossed in study and contemplation for *The Psychological and Poetic Approach to the Study of Christ in the Fourth Gospel*. The final two poetry compilations here are deeply connected with this work. These two collections are the largest, *The Shepherd of Eternity* includes ninety-seven poems and *House of Three Windows* has eighty-eight poems in total.

'The Logos of Life' focuses on Martha's relationship with Christ and 'Apostles of Eternity' reiterates Gore-Booth's belief that some of Jesus' apostles were female. The poem is subtitled 'Certain women of our company' and includes references to Mary, poet and seer; a Samaritan woman; Martha; Mary of Bethany and Mary Magdalene. The titles of many of the following poems relate to specific instances in John's Gospel; 'The Divine Messenger', 'The Inner Trinity', 'In the Temple', 'The Angel in the Garden' and 'The Gospel of John'.

A number of poems in *The Shepherd of Eternity* are noteworthy. 'In Praise of Life' is an elegy to the lesbian poet Sappho. The poem opens with the proclamation that 'Sappho said long ago/"If Death be good/Why do the Gods not die?"/Sappho was wise'. This poem was obviously significant to both Gore-Booth and Roper as an extract from the conclusion was chosen as the inscription for their joint headstone:

> Sappho was right:
> Life that is Love is God, and Mercy wise
> Is that which never dies –
> Life, Love and Light.

The House of Three Windows was published with an introduction by Evelyn Underhill and is similar in style and content to *The Shepherd of Eternity*.[109] It is striking in Underhill's introduction that she refers to Gore-Booth as not just a mystical poet but as a mystic:

> She was both a mystic and an artist; a combination of qualities more rare than is sometimes supposed, for many of those whom we regard as mystical poets are not mystics, but poets who have chosen as their subject-matter that hazily Platonic conception of the world which is often called 'mystical.' Miss Gore-Booth was not a poet of this type. She was a true mystic.[110]

The poems in this volume are apparently the final poems ever written by Gore-Booth and, as such, they provide a glimpse into her final journey. Included in this religious volume are poems which relate to very intimate experiences, such as 'New Year (1926)' which Gore-Booth wrote after she survived a particularly traumatic night during her final illness. The second poem that is dedicated to Roper is also included in this volume entitled simply, 'To E.G.R.' which ends simply 'Sit by this window, let us watch awhile'. Gore-Booth dedicated two poems to Roper, which describe a deep and committed love between the two women. Gore-Booth's contemporaries regularly expressed their lesbianism through coded language. Even the most adventurous of authors, such as Gertrude Stein, rarely left a recorded comment on lesbian sexuality in their literature.[111]

This publication of Gore-Booth's poetry is intended to help reclaim Gore-Booth as an important figure in Irish literary and cultural heritage. For perhaps it is only now in this post-modern globalised era that Gore-Booth's radical literature and political campaigns can be best appreciated. The final poem in the last publication by Gore-Booth is a fitting end to this introduction.

Suddenly everywhere
  Clouds and waves are one,
The storm has cleared the air,
  The sea holds the sun
  And the blue sky –
There is no under, no above,
  All is light, all is love –
Is it like this when you die?[112]

NOTES
1   W.B. Yeats, 'In Memory of Eva Gore-Booth and Con Markievicz', *Collected Poems*, edited by Augustine Martin (London, Arena, 1990).
2   Esther Roper, 'Introduction', *Poems of Eva-Gore-Booth: Complete Edition* (London, Longmans, 1929), p. 31.

3   Evelyn Underhill, 'Introduction', *The House of Three Windows* by Eva Gore-Booth (London, Longmans Green & Co, 1926), p. vii.

4   Éilís Ní Dhuibhne, *Voices on the Wind: Women Poets of the Celtic Twilight* (Dublin, New Island, 1995).

5   Emma Donoghue, 'Lesbian Encounters: 1745–1997', *Field Day Anthology Vol IV Irish Women's Writing and Traditions*, edited by Angela Bourke, Siobhan Kilfeather, Maria Luddy *et al* (Cork, Cork University Press, 2002), pp 1107–9.

6   Lucy Collins, *Poetry by Women in Ireland: A Critical Anthology 1870–1970* (Liverpool, Liverpool University Press, 2014), p. 118.

7   Mairéad Ashe FitzGerald (ed.), *A Terrible Beauty: Poetry of 1916* (Dublin, O'Brien Press, 2015); Declan Kiberd and P.J. Mathews (eds), *Handbook of the Irish Revival: An Anthology of Irish Cultural and Political Writings 1891–1922* (Dublin, Abbey Theatre Press, 2015).

8   Ní Dhuibhne, p. 14.

9   Donoghue, Emma, 'How Could I Fear and Hold Thee by the Hand? The Poetry of Eva Gore-Booth', *Sex, Nation, and Dissent in Irish Writing*, edited by Eibhear Walsh (Cork, Cork University Press, 1997), pp 16–42.

10   Donoghue, 'The Poetry of Eva Gore-Booth', p. 17.

11   *Ibid.*

12   Maureen O'Connor, 'Vegetable Love: The Syncretic Nation in the Writings of Margaret Cousins and Eva Gore-Booth', *Journal of Irish Studies*, 28 (2013), pp 18–33.

13   Eva Gore-Booth, *Unseen Kings* (London, Longmans, 1904); Gore-Booth, *The Three Resurrections and the Triumph of Maeve* (London, Longmans, 1905).

14   Rev George O'Neill, 'Review of Three Pretty Volumes of Verse, including *Poems* by Eva Gore-Booth', *New Ireland Review*, Vol XI (March 1899), pp 63–5. 'Review of Eva Gore-Booth's *Agate Lamp*', *Irish Review*, Vol II (Feb 1913), pp 667–8. George O'Neill, 'Review of *Broken Glory*', *Studies*, Vol VIII, No 30 (June 1919), pp 336–7. 'Review of *Poems*', *Irish Book Lover*, Vol XVIII (Nov-Dec 1930), p. 182.

15   Meridith Starr, '*The Shepherds of Eternity*: A Review', *The Occult Review*, Vol 42 (1925), p. 127.

16   R.M. Fox described Thompson as the author of the 'haunting mystical poem, "The Hound of Heaven,"' which 'enriched English thought and language'. R.M. Fox, *Rebel Irishwomen* (Dublin, Talbot Press, 1935; Dublin, Progress House, 1967), p. 27. For more information on this poet see Brigid M. Boardman,

Between Heaven and Charing Cross: The Life of Francis Thompson (Yale, Yale University Press, 1988).

17   As cited in Fox, p. 27.

18   Æ, *New Songs* (Dublin, H. Bullen, 1904).

19   Mark Sutton, 'Eva Gore-Booth', *Literature Online Biography*, (Cambridge, Cambridge University Press, 2006).

20   Graham Peel, *The Country Lover: Album of Five Songs* (Chappell & Co. Ltd, 1910). The songs were as follows: 1. Eva Gore-Booth, 'Little Waves of Breffny': 2. William Warson, 'April': 3. W.B. Yeats, 'Lake Isle of Inisfree': 4. Hillaire Belloc, 'Early Morning': 5. Gerald Gould, 'Wander Thirst'.

21   Esther Roper, 'Eva Gore-Booth: An Address given at the Unveiling of a Window Placed in her Memory in the Round House' (Manchester, Manchester University Settlement Papers, 1928), pp 4–5.

22   As cited in Declan Foley with Janis Londraville, 'Eva Gore-Booth', *John Quinn: Selected Irish Writers from His Library* (West Cornwall, Locust Hill Press, 2001), p. 158.

23   Katharine Tynan, cited in Roper, introduction, *Poems of Eva Gore-Booth*, p. 18.

24   John Kelly and Eric Domville (eds), *The Collected Letters of W.B. Yeats: Vol. I, 1865–1895* (Oxford, Oxford University Press, 1986), p. 239.

25   Kelly and Domville, pp 256–7.

26   Fox, p. 28.

27   Frederick Lapisardi, (ed.), *The Plays of Eva Gore-Booth* (California, Mellen Research University Press, 1991), p. x.

28   Eva Gore-Booth, *Poems* (London, Longmans, 1898).

29   Sutton, 'Eva Gore-Booth'.

30   Christopher Baldick, 'Celtic Revival', *The Concise Oxford Dictionary of Literary Terms* (Oxford University Press, 2004).

31   Matthew Arnold, *On the Study of Celtic Literature* (London, Smith, Elder, 1867).

32   Ní Dhuibhne, p. 10.

33   'Celtic Revival, a term sometimes applied to the period of Irish literature in English (c. 1885–1939) now more often referred to as the Irish Literary Revival or Renaissance. There are other similar terms: Celtic Renaissance, Celtic Dawn, and Celtic Twilight'. Baldick, 'Celtic Revival'.

34   Sutton, 'Eva Gore-Booth'.

35   W.B. Yeats, *The Celtic Twilight: Men and Women, Dhouls and Faeries* (London, Lawrence and Bullen, 1893).

36 James Joyce, *Finnegans Wake* (New York, Viking, 1939), 344: 12. Marian Eide analyses this term to show that Joyce's pun 'resonates on a number of levels. With this phrase, he signals the cult influence of Irish nationalism, a label that would indicate both the unexamined adherence of its members and the movement's transience. The French toilette gestures toward the hypocritical purism of the movement'. Marian Eide, 'The Woman of the Ballyhoura Hills: James Joyce and the Politics of Creativity', *Twentieth Century Literature*, Vol. 44, No. 4 (Winter, 1998), p. 391.

37 Kevin Whelan, *Fellowship of Freedom: The United Irishmen and 1798* (Cork, Cork University Press, 1998), p. 22.

38 Wolfe Tone, *Argument on behalf of the Catholics of Ireland* (1791, British and Irish Communist Organisation, 1969).

39 Whelan, p. 23.

40 Whitney Smith, 'Flag of Ireland', *Encyclopedia Britannica Online*, vers. 2007.

41 Donoghue, 'The Poetry of Eva Gore-Booth', p. 18.

42 *Ibid*, p. 19.

43 Alice Furlong, 'To Spring', *Roses and Rue* (London, Elkin Mathews, 1899), p. 38. Ella Young, 'My Lady of Dreams', *Poems* (Dublin, Maunsel, 1906), p. 9.

44 Katharine Tynan, 'The Dead Spring', *Louise de la Vallière and other Poems* (London, Kegan Paul, 1885), pp 13–20.

45 Lisa Weihman, 'Doing My Bit for Ireland: Transgressing Gender in the Easter Rising', *Éire-Ireland* Vol 39: No 3 & 4 (2004), p. 237.

46 Amanda Sebestyn, 'Introduction', *The Prison Letters of Constance Markievicz*, edited by Esther Roper (London, Virago Press, 1987), p. xxxiv.

47 Emer Mullins, 'Ireland's Joan of Arc', *Irish Voice*, 4 May 1994. The term 'Ireland's Joan of Arc' is intermittently used to describe both Constance Markievicz and Maud Gonne. See Margaret Ward, *Maud Gonne: Ireland's Joan of Arc* (London, Pandora, 1990).

48 Francis Thompson wrote that 'she displays indeed a true imagination, a poetic gift of her own. Her style and diction are choice and finished; while she has considerable power of imagery, and that imagery is really imaginative'. Francis Thompson, 'Review of *Unseen Kings*', *The Academy*, cited in Eva Gore-Booth, *The Perilous Light* (London, Erskine Macdonald, 1915), p. 8.

49   'Review of *Unseen Kings*', *Literary World*, cited in Eva Gore-Booth, *The Perilous Light*, p. 8.

50   Gore-Booth refers to Douglas Hyde, *A Literary History of Ireland* (London, T. Fisher Unwin, 1899). This text was later reprinted with revisions by Brian Ó Cuív (London, Benn, 1967).

51   Donoghue, 'The Poetry of Eva Gore-Booth', p. 17.

52   *Ibid*, p. 23.

53   Lord Alfred Tennyson, 'The Beggar Maid', *The Works of Tennyson*, edited by Hallam Tennyson (London, 1907–08).

54   Breanna Byecroft, 'Rescue and Creation Myths: Expressions of Gender and Power in the Works of Burne-Jones', *English and History of Art*, Vol 151 (Brown University, 2004), p. 114.

55   The original reference for this story was taken from Shakespeare's *Romeo and Juliet*: 'Young Adam Cupid, he that shot so trim, When King Cophetua loved the beggar-maid'. *Rom. and Jul*. Act II. Scene i. 14 (1594–96).

56   The ancient Greek playwright Sophocles wrote of the story of Antigone in his plays *Oedipus the King* and *Oedipus at Colonus*.

57   Catherine Holland, 'After Antigone: Women, the Past, and the Future of Feminist Political Thought', *American Journal of Political Science*, Vol 42, No. 4 (Oct, 1998), p. 1108.

58   Judith Butler, *Antigone's Claim: Kinship between Life and Death* (New York, Columbia University Press, 2002), p. 2.

59   Eva Gore-Booth, *The One and the Many* (London, Longmans, 1904).

60   Sutton, 'Eva Gore-Booth'.

61   'The One and the Many Review', *Journal of Education* cited in Eva Gore-Booth, *The Perilous Light*, p. 7.

62   Donoghue, 'The Poetry of Eva Gore-Booth', p. 18.

63   This is evident in the interpretation of *The Death of Fionavar* when Gore-Booth refers to the 'old Greek myths, such as the stories of Proserpine or Psyche'. Eva Gore-Booth, 'An Interpretation', *The Death of Fionavar from the Triumph of Maeve* (London, Erskine Macdonald, 1916), p. ii.

64   N.J. Richardson, *The Homeric Hymn to Demeter* (Oxford: Clarendon Press, 1974).

65   This feminist aspect was appropriated by early female poets such as Elizabeth Barrett Browning (1806–1861), whose poem 'Psyche and Proserpine' was posthumously published in 1890. Elizabeth Barrett Browning, 'Psyche and Proserpine', *The Poetical Works of Elizabeth Barrett Browning in six volumes* (London, Smith, Elder & Co, 1890).

66 Helene Foley, *The Homeric Hymn to Demeter: Translation, Commentary and Interpretive Essays* (Princeton, Princeton University Press, 1994), p. 80.

67 Edward Carpenter, (trans.), *The Story of Eros and Psyche from Apuleius, and the first book of the Iliad of Homer* (London, Sonnenschein, 1900).

68 Edward Carpenter, 'Persephone', *Narcissus and Other Poems* (London, Henry S. King & Co, 1873).

69 Edward Carpenter, *Pagan and Christian Creeds: Their Origin and Meaning* (London, George Allen & Unwin, 1920).

70 Sarah Waters, 'Wolfskins and Togas: Lesbian and Gay Historical Fictions 1870 to the Present', PhD (Arts) 1995 Thesis. Queen Mary University of London/Classmark ZTH3194 Thesis.

71 Elizabeth Butler Cullingford, *Ireland's Others: Gender and Ethnicity in Irish Literature and Popular Culture* (Cork, Cork University Press, 2001), p. 99.

72 Christopher Newall, 'Sir Edward Coley Burne-Jones', *Oxford Dictionary of National Biography Online* (Oxford, Oxford University Press, 2004).

73 Byecroft, p. 116.

74 Lewis, p. 15.

75 *Ibid.*

76 Sligo Library web site, 'Eva Gore-Booth', Accessed 6 June 2016. http://www.askaboutireland.ie/reading-room/arts-literature/irish-writes/eva-gore-booth/index.xml

77 Eva Gore-Booth, *The Three Resurrections and the Triumph of Maeve* (London, Longmans, 1905).

78 'Review of The Three Resurrections', *Pall Mall Gazette,* cited in Eva Gore-Booth, *The Perilous Light*, p. 8.

79 Tony Deverson, 'Paracelsus', *The New Zealand Oxford Dictionary Online* (Oxford, 2006).

80 Franz Hartmann, cited in *Sunrise Magazine,* April/May (Theosophical UP, 1989).

81 E.A. Livingstone (ed.), 'Hades', *The Concise Oxford Dictionary of the Christian Church Online* (Oxford, Oxford University Press, 2006).

82 According to W.R.F. Browning 'there was a legend (Isa. 38:10; Matt. 16:18) that entry into Hades was through gates, and Christians supposed that the keys were in the possession of the risen Christ (Rev. 1:18)'. Hades was mentioned in the *New Testament* as a place of torment in Luke 16:23 and Mark 9:48, where it was described as a place where sinners were sent.

W.R.F. Browning, 'Hades', *A Dictionary of the Bible* (Oxford, Oxford University Press, 1997).

83 David Leeming, 'Resurrection', *The Oxford Companion to World Mythology Online* (Oxford, Oxford University Press, 2004).

84 The rebirth and return aspect of resurrection also became important to Yeats' literature. Years after Gore-Booth's death he published a prose play entitled *The Resurrection* which involved three characters: a Greek, a Hebrew and a Syrian who witness the events of Christ's resurrection. W.B. Yeats, *Stories of Michael Robartes and his friends: an extract from a record made by his pupils and a play in prose the Resurrection* (Dundrum, 1931).

85 Elizabeth Knowles (ed.), 'Alcestis', *A Dictionary of Phrase and Fable Online* (Oxford, Oxford Universty Press, 2006), UCD Lib, 27 June 2007.

86 John McGuckin, *Saint Gregory of Nazianzus: An Intellectual Biography* (New York, Crestwood, 2001), p. xxi.

87 David Gardiner, 'The Other Irish Renaissance: The Maunsel Poets', *New Hibernia Review* 8:1 (Spring, 2004), p. 56.

88 *Ibid*, p. 66.

89 *Ibid*, p. 67.

90 *Ibid*.

91 *Ibid*, p. 71.

92 Roper, 'Introduction', p. 20.

93 *Ibid*, p. 21.

94 Roper, 'Introduction', p. 21.

95 Eva Gore-Booth, *The Agate Lamp* (London, Longmans, 1912).

96 Æ, 'Review of *The Agate Lamp*', *The Irish Homestead*, cited in Eva Gore-Booth, *The Perilous Light*, p. 8.

97 *The Last Supper* (1498) is held in the Convent of Santa Maria delle Grazie, Milan.

98 Eva Gore-Booth, *The Perilous Light* (London, Erskine MacDonald, 1915).

99 Eva Gore-Booth, *Broken Glory* (Dublin, Maunsel, 1917).

100 Eva Gore-Booth, Letter to R.M. Fox and Patricia Lynch, August 1916. Fox and Lynch Papers, National Library of Ireland: MS 40, 327/6.

101 Donoghue, 'Poetry of Eva Gore-Booth', p. 17.

102 Maureen O'Connor led a project, 'Eva Gore-Booth and Constance Markievicz's Art of War: Sisters in Arms', which culminated in a staged reading of *The Death of Fionavar* in Cork City Gaol on 2 November 2015, where Markievicz was imprisoned in 1919.

103 Esther Roper (ed.), *Prison Letters of Countess Markievicz* (1934: London, Virago Press, 1987), p. 311.
104 Gardiner, p. 68.
105 Dora Sigerson Shorter, *The Sad Years and Other Poems*, with port. and memoir by Katharine Tynan (London, Constable, 1918).
106 Roper, 'Introduction', p. 25.
107 Eva Gore-Booth, *The Shepherd of Eternity* (London, Longmans, 1925).
108 Sutton, 'Eva Gore-Booth'.
109 Eva Gore-Booth, *The House of Three Windows* (London, Longmans, 1926).
110 Underhill, p. vi.
111 Gertrude Stein played with terminology such as her famous use of the then underground term gay, in her short story 'Miss Furr and Miss Skeene', *Geography and Plays*, 1922.
112 Roper footnoted that 'Another and apparently an earlier version of this poem has been found: *The storm has cleared the air, The sea holds the sun and the blue sky, Suddenly, everywhere, shining, all things are one ... Is it like this when you die?*'

EVA GORE-BOOTH:
COLLECTED POEMS

Poems
(1898)

FROM THE GERMAN
(Lessing)

If, Reader, for these poems you should lack
All sense of gratitude, all words of praise,
At least you might be thankful for the lays
That I kept back.

A LOVE SONG

Like a wave that roams the sea,
So lonely and so free,
Like a cloud that haunts the sky,
So distant and so high,
Like the fragrant summer wind,
So gentle and so kind,
Like a castle in the air,
So joyous and so fair,
Like a lily by the wall,
So golden and so tall,
Gay as any flower that blows,
Splendid as a sun-lit rose,
Bright and bravely blossoming,
Is my Lady of the Spring.
Fair of face, and clear of sight,
Living always in the light,
Valorous and free and strong
As the wind's courageous song,
All of magic sunshine made,
Secret as a forest glade,
Silver-lit beneath dark trees
By pale-starred anemones,
Fair as that white dawn that gleams
Through the ivory gate of dreams,

Glorious to gaze upon,
With strange lights of summers gone,
Silver of bright daisies stored,
Smallest change in summer's hoard,
Gold of vanished daffodils,
Is my Lady of the Hills.

The grace of all things gay,
The joy of a swallow's flight,
The light of a summer's day,
The peace of a moon-lit night,
All the strength, and the hope, and the gladness of living
are hers,
And her voice is the voice of the wind in a forest of firs.

IN PRAISE OF LIBERTY

Some care for glory, some for peace,
    The dying have desire to live;
Sad spirits pray for death's release,
    The rest that sleep alone can give;
But peace, or strife, or toil, or rest,
    The stir of life, the silent grave –
I know that Liberty is best,
    And no man sadder than a slave.

And some would see their wealth increase,
    And some would hoard, and some would give,
And each man has his own caprice,
    And all delight is fugitive;
A silken robe, a ragged vest,
    For prince or beggar, fool or knave –
I know that Liberty is best,
    And no man sadder than a slave.

True lovers, when their kisses cease
    Cannot forget, will not forgive,
That Love has but a mortal lease,
    A little time to strive and live;
They cannot stay the parting guest,
    They can but curse the joy they crave.
I know that Liberty is best,
    And no man sadder than a slave.

For Love is not life's masterpiece,
    And Hope has nothing much to give,
And they who find the golden fleece
    Do not so greatly care to live;
Though rich men smile, and saints are blest,
    And kings rejoice, and lovers rave,
I know that Liberty is best,
    And no man sadder than a slave.

Slave, Love is but a passing jest,
    And Life the herald of the grave;
Of these three Liberty is best,
    And no man sadder than a slave.

ATTAINMENT

I left the brazen tower on the plain,
    And climbed up here through the rain and cold,
But now I'll never believe again
    The rainbow's promise of faery gold.
Oh, better the glad earth's golden green
    Than the fading rainbow's fickle light,
And better the seen than the unseen,
    The sunny day than the starry night.
For there's storm and sorrow and little mirth
On the hill where the rainbow touches the earth.

Green was the hill from the distant plain,
   The grass was covered with Mary's gold,
In the brazen tower again and again
   The song was sung and the tale was told;
Wonderful songs of the Rainbow Queen
   And her treasure hid from mortal sight,
The gold deep buried beneath the green,
   And watched by the goblins day and night.
For there's gold and glamour and light and mirth
On the hill where the rainbow touches the earth.

Vain were the words and the warnings vain
   Of those phantom faces pale and cold,
Faces of dead men lost or slain
   On the bitter quest of the rainbow gold.
How can one fight with a foe unseen?
   So near the sky should one want for light?
Where an angel's footstep once has been
   A star shines out on the darkest night –
For there's light and hope and the shadow of mirth
On the hill where the rainbow touches the earth.

The sun burns low, on the marshy plain
   White fogs hang heavily, dank and cold,
And the brazen tower gleams through the rain,
   It gleams and glitters and looks like gold.
Yet here there's nothing but gray and green,
   A barren hill on a windy night,
Not a sight or sound of the Faery Queen,
   Or the buried gold, or the mystic light:
No gladness, nor glory, nor joy, nor mirth,
On the hill where the rainbow touches the earth.

A WELCOME

I, the ancient King, and guardian of the city,
Crave your justice, noble friend, and trust your pity;
When you ride triumphant down the streets at last,
As you trample under foot the gardens of the past,
Be the grass untrodden where the cypress waves,
Leave some roses blooming on your fathers' sombre
graves;
Cast no flaming torch to burn a house that falls,
Let the ivy hang unhindered from the ruins of its walls;
And although you crown your brows, as victors should,
with bays,
Leave the laurels in the churchyard, for the dead have
naught but praise.

PRAYER OF THE MODERN GREEK

Heroes, from the fields of light,
Will ye watch the unequal fight?
Souls who urged the battle on
To victory at Marathon,
Gods who bent from heaven to see
Earth's valley of Thermopylæ,
Laurel-crowned and throned in state,
Free spirits, ye who fought of late
A fight as glorious as this
By sea-surrounded Salamis;
See the incense of our prayer
Dulls the bright Elysian air,
Whilst echoes of our grief and wrong
Still ring across the fields of song.
Hasten, help us, Strong and True,
Surely we have need of you;
Rest no more by lonely streams,

Where Peace amongst her olives dreams,
Go forth, nor linger as you pass,
To gather poppies in the grass,
But grasp your rusty swords again,
Ye peaceful ones, for peace is slain.
Placid-browed, indifferent-eyed,
Cast your laurel wreaths aside;
Let each man take his victor's crown
And fling it down, oh, fling it down,
Let Liberty's coarse cap of red
Flame out athwart your brows instead,
Ye souls of heroes long since dead.

DISILLUSION

When I was young,
　The Sirens were most fair;
Golden harps and golden hair;
　In a strange golden tongue
Their songs were sung.

Now I am old,
　The Muse is all my care;
She is more fair
　Than Sirens manifold,
When one is old.

AN EPITAPH

'Alas that every flower is dead'
These words a smiling angel read
Carven on an ancient stone,
By wild roses overgrown.

REST

All day the city's din
Must hem me in,
And thus sublime
At evening time
Comes my release,
Where daisies, white
In the sun's bright light,
All silver pure
The moon endure,
And Heaven allows the stars caprice,
Under grey olive boughs I seek for peace.

THE PILGRIM

Thus did she follow Art,
   Like a starved sparrow,
Picking up every crumb
Dropped on life's muddy road.
   Meanwhile an arrow
Sharp pointed from the gods' abode
   Did quickly come,
And struck her to the heart.

A CRITIC

His was the voice
That – when the morning stars together sang
In their first rapture of awakened life
And God's own angels held their breath for joy,
Whilst heaven, by that new harmony entranced,
Was wrapped in awful silence – broke the charm,

Serenely speaking in cold accents thus –
'I know not, yet methinks 'twas Jupiter
Went out of tune and spoilt the whole effect.'

THE MUSICIAN TO HIS LADY

Behold this life's a glorious thing.
Belovèd, for thy joyous sake,
I'll write such music as shall make
    Sad angels sing.

FROM A FAR COUNTRY

I have such longing to be home again,
'Tis lucky that the Muse
Doth still refuse
To visit me on wingèd Pegasus,
For if she came to see me riding thus
I might be tempted with prosaic force
To steal her horse.

    Drudgery itself is a sort of goddess. Symonds

Goddess of Drudgery, to thee
I dedicate my hopes and all my days,
Knowing that labour brings no earthly praise
Nor heavenly bliss for guerdon,

Only this:
The promise of a higher life, to be –
The lightening of life's burden
Of satiety.

THE REPENTANCE OF EVE
(A picture by Con Gore-Booth)

This is our Mother Eve, who shall not win
Respite or peace; in vain she makes lament
She ate but half the fruit, sinned half the sin,
Eternal hunger is her punishment.

She weeps and mourns for that sweet apple's sake
Whilst high above her in the sacred tree,
Coiled round its withered boughs, the wily snake
Smiles over her lost opportunity.

JOAN OF ARC

The treasure of age and the hope of youth
    And the hidden light of the dreamer's heart,
A treacherous word in the ear of Truth,
    The breath of fools on the mirror of Art;
Honour and glory and slander and shame,
    These are the golden gifts of Fame.

And the soul that fought for a laurel crown
    Shall flaunt it aloft in the victor's car,
But his golden fancies must dwindle down
    Like the flames that kindled a burnt out star;
Indolence, safety, a glorious name,
    These are the golden gifts of Fame.

But she whose spirit was strong in the strife
    Has gained the guerdon that was her due –
The torture of death and the height of life,
    The blackness of Hell and the Heaven's blue,
Strength and rapture and sword and flame,
    These are the golden gifts of Fame.

A STORM

From the jasmine on the wall
Such thick showers of white stars fall,
That the violet at her feet
Shivers in her safe retreat,
Looking upwards, blue with fright,
Shudders at the dreadful sight,
Folds her leaves and crouches low,
Hiding from such early snow;
Nay, it is not Winter yet,
Only Autumn, Violet.

TRIOLET
('l'amitie est l' amour sans ailes')

If love has lost a wing
    He shall not fly away,
For life has lost a sting
If love has lost a wing,
Though, idly wandering,
    He yet may go astray;
If love has lost a wing
    He shall not fly away.

TO –

In lines thus narrow
Your mind can harrow
    The fields of thought,
But never the wheat
Shall grow at your feet;
You don't know how

To drive the plough,
   You won't be taught;
You'll find to-morrow,
With heavy sorrow,
   Your harvest naught.

A FABLE

When restless Psyche of the radiant wings
In pity on a drooping lily lit,
She meant to rest a while and gladden it
With light and life and faery flutterings.
This was the sorrow of a summer's morn:
Just then, a laughing child, half mad with play
And sunshine, chased the butterfly away,
And the poor flower was left for aye forlorn.

TO THE PEOPLE ON EARTH

Ye tortured mortals, cease your cries,
   Ye are but fools who thus forget
That in the centre of your Bridge of Sighs
   There is an oubliette.

A SPIRIT IN PRISON

At midnight on the high sea
A strange voice spoke to me,
Strange eyes gleamed through the blast,
A strange form stood by the mast.
These are the words the phantom spoke:

'I was the Dryad of an ancient oak,
My house was deep in the forest glade,
Strong were the walls, green was the shade.
Oh for the life so bright and good,
The long cool grass, the sun-lit wood,
The dear delight of mother earth,
The gladness of her summer mirth,
Beneath my feet her greenery spread,
And great boughs rustling overhead.

Oh for the sheets of shining blue,
Down by the stream where the hyacinths grew.
Now the Naiads dream alone,
And the laurel's overgrown,
Strangling ivy free to choke
Every unprotected oak;
Nettles growing long and rank
Straggle up the river bank;
Unmourned, neglected utterly,
Sweet flowers shed their leaves and die.
Great Phoebus, I would rather now
Be the poor wretch who drives the plough
From morn till even, toiling thus,
In long straight lines monotonous,
Whose feet have never learnt to stray
From drudgery's most narrow way,
Than wander up and down the earth
Bereft of freedom, void of mirth,
No strife well fought, no battle won,
No sweet rest earned, no labour done,
The ghost of a nymph thus fettered fast
To this ghost of a tree men call a mast,
Tossing always to and fro
Wherever you mortals choose to go,
Thus I live on the wild sea,
Misery, ah misery.'

WEARINESS

Amid the glare of light and song
    And talk that knows not when to cease,
The sullen voices of the throng,
    My weary soul cries out for peace,
Peace and the quietness of death;
    The wash of waters deep and cool,
The wind too faint for any breath
    To stir oblivion's silent pool,
When all who swim against the stream,
    And they that laugh, and they that weep,
Shall change like flowers in a dream
    That wither on the brows of sleep.

For silence is the song sublime,
    And every voice at last must cease,
And all the world at evening time
    Floats downwards through the gates of peace,
Beyond the gloom of shadowy caves
    Where water washes on the stones,
And breaks with quiet foamless waves
    The night's persistent monotones;
The stars are what the flowers seem,
    And where the sea of thought is deep,
The moonlight glitters like a dream,
    On weary waters gone to sleep.

PROMISES

Snowdrops pushing through the snow
    Already bring,
From nature's quiet grave below
The cold and darkness whence they grow,
    White thoughts of Spring.

A STUDENT

I am well learned in all the weary lore
  Of all the ancients, and my brain is tired;
Each day I seem to wonder more and more,
  Is this great knowledge much to be desired?
But just two things I'd really like to know –
  These childish questions haunt me day and night –
'Where do the spirits of dead people go?
  And, in the darkness, what becomes of light?'

JANE CLERMONT TO BYRON

Your words are vain.
You wounded me; the pain was fierce,
  But now at last
  Your power is past,
For, like a wasp, you left your sting
In my sore sorrow festering;
And thus you lost the means to pierce
  My heart again.

PREOCCUPATION

Thus did our swift boat past the islands glide,
The pleasant islands of Delight and Youth,
Where dwell the Sirens; as it sped along
He did not even hear their fatal song,
For Orpheus was standing by his side,
Making sweet music of an unknown truth.

ASPIRATIONS

Eels in the mud of the garden pond,
Do you ever think of a life beyond,
Do you ever see that the sky is blue,
And wish that the moon was nearer you?
Do you ever sigh when the skylark sings,
And dream of wings?

AN AUTHOR

He wrote all day, he could not think,
His very blood was turned to ink,
He burned with endless patient toil
Whole gallons full of midnight oil –
A sort of Paper Chase sublime
    He ran with Time.

Methinks he strewed the scent too thick,
Time caught him, he grew old and sick;
He ran too fast, he lost his breath
And fell an easy prey to death.

AN OLD STORY

A maiden loved Diogenes,
Well she thought the sage to please,
But he did not understand her,
Treated her like Alexander;
To all her blandishments replied,
'Gracious Maiden, stand aside,
When your pleasant talk is done
I would see the blessed sun.'

After such cross words as these,
Still she loved Diogenes.

TRICOLOR

In liberty of thought,
  Equality of life,
The generations sought
  A rest from hate and strife.

Hard work on common ground,
  Strong arms and spirits free,
In these at last they found
  Fraternity.

DIE RHEINBAHN

Als sie beendet war,
Ein junger Fischer sah,
Im hellen Mondenschein,
Von ihrem Fels, mit wild Geschrei,
Das schönste Mädchen Lorelei
Sich toll hinunter stürzen in den Rhein.

A POLITICIAN

'Oh, Sisyphus, a weary life is yours
Of endless toil and unrewarded pain.'
'Not so, my friend,' said he;
'I toil to push my stone uphill, of course,
But then I rest, and there's a sight to see:

Each time, with right good will,
The stone turns slowly on the hill,
Although I rolled it up with all my force,
The little impish schoolboy in my brain
Chuckles to watch it rattling down again.'

DEAD LEAVES

Is this what it means to die –
Free and fair, powers of the air,
On the wings of the wind to fly –
Bold and bright, in sheets of light
Out of the shaken sky;
Over the wold in showers of gold
Stricken of colours manifold,
Shattered and scattered left to lie –
Is this what it means to die?

Is this what it means to die –
Round and round, down to the ground,
Floating and falling helplessly,
Gold in the dust as dead things must,
Wet and sodden, or hard and dry,
Footsteps drowned in a rustling sound,

Sweet to the feet of the passer-by;
To soar like gods for a space, and then
To be trodden underfoot of men,
Prostrate thus in the dust to lie –
Is this what it means to die?

MORNING GLORY

Perfectly pure and pale, a thing apart,
  Where long rank grass and common hedge flowers
grow,
Most like a star cast down from Heaven thou art,
  Here, by the dusty wayside, lying low
With one brown earth stain at thy radiant heart.

A NIGHTMARE

I wrote eight verses late last night,
And slept, and lo! a wondrous sight,
There came eight funerals instead
Marching slowly past my bed.
As they went each nodding plume
Swayed and rhymed across the gloom.
  In the twinkling of an eye,
The whole procession passed me by,
And every verse – became a hearse
  To carry murdered poetry.

TO A POET

No voices speak to thee –
No visions shalt thou see –
The very sunset thou shalt know
But in its fading afterglow.
In thy mind's secret place
Is neither light, nor song, nor grace –
Foolish echoes, void of sound,
Wander o'er the stony ground.
In such an arid desert set,

Music doth her truth forget;
And in her highest rapture croons
But snatches of remembered tunes.
Think'st thou that life shall cast divine
Pearls before such feet as thine?
Strive as well thou mayest strive –
Thou art only half alive.
Ah, God, the sounds unheard,
The whispered word,
The songs unsung
By mortal tongue,
The shaft of light
Straight from the low sun's golden bow,
No power shall throw
Across thy spirit's night,
Nor any life, nor beauty, shalt thou know,
But endless echoes, and an afterglow.

A SONG

I sing the song of the river,
   That mirrors the shallow stars,
While misty moonbeams shiver
   Behind their cloudy bars;
The stars, in mystic dances,
   Flicker and flash and gleam,
To woo with their burning glances
   The icy-hearted stream.

A voice of siren gladness
   Floats clear across the sky,
And kindles into madness
   The river's melody.

For heaven's fairest daughters
  Are singing like love-sick maids,
To waken the sleepy waters
  With starry serenades.
These cunning, clear-voiced Pleiads
  Shine out so near, they seem
To lie like white-armed Naiads
  On the breast of the loving stream;
The song of the starry seven
  Floats down in waves of light
Across the vaults of heaven
  And through the shades of night.

I sing the song of the showers
  That fall on the river's breast,
Forsaking their cloudy towers
  Away in the gleaming west;
They whisper the secret story
  How fair, on far-off heights,
The stars, in lonely glory,
  Burn cold, deceitful lights.

The river laughs in their faces,
  Despising their fickle play,
Now he knows their airy graces
  Are thousands of miles away;
And they will not leave the beauty
  And light of heaven above,
For a doubtful earthly duty,
  And a humble earthly love.

I sing the song of the rushes,
  That bend o'er the river and pry
To read its heart as it gushes
  In musical gladness by.
It ripples over the shingle,
  And passes in laughter away,

To where its waters mingle
With the ocean of yesterday.

'AN IDYLL'
(A picture by Maurice Greiffenhagen)

In the twilight land of gleams,
    Through the dusky waves of corn,
Where the scarlet sunset dreams
    Languid of the morrow morn;
Where the poppies nod and smile,
    Climbing slowly, one by one,
Past the bank, beyond the stile,
    Up to meet the setting sun,
Let us wander on and on,
    As the dreamy poppies do,
Till the silent night is gone,
    And we meet the morning blue.

If we wander very far,
    We shall find that distant land,
Where the rainbow jewels are
    Buried deep beneath the sand,
Dreamy eyes and gleaming hair,
    Where are gems that flash and shine
Like those jewels rich and rare
    On the breast of Proserpine.
For we toil not, must not weep,
    Cannot feel your scorn,
In the arms of love and sleep,
    Dreaming through the corn.'

So they wandered through the fields,
    Till they came at last to Life,
Holding up two golden shields

And her poisoned sword of strife.
And they would have passed her by,
  But she lifted up her head
With a passing weary sigh,
  And reluctantly she said:

'You must toil and you must weep,
  Bear my love and scorn,'
Far from where the poppies sleep,
  Nodding through the corn.

'Take these heavy golden shields,
  Wake and gird yourselves to fight,
Leave the dreamy poppy fields
  And the dreary shades of night.'
But he flung the shield aside,
  Down the sword of life she cast,
Dreamily he clasped his bride,
  Dreamily they floated past,
Plucked the poppies, rich and red,
  Bound them round the brows of Life;
'Come and rest with us,' they said,
  'Rest from all your barren strife.

So Life followed, poppy crowned,
  Steeped in blissful sleep,
And her eyes, grown strange and round,
  Quite forgot to weep.
Thus they wander on and on,
  As the holy spirits may;
Change is past, and time is gone,
  Till they meet the coming day –
For they toil not, cannot weep,
  Feel not any scorn,
In the arms of love and sleep,
  Dreaming through the corn.

SONG OF THE FAIR EXILE

In this cold country of the seas
    The hills are gray, the mist is white;
My very spirit seems to freeze,
    I shut my eyes on such a sight.

Then all about me everywhere
    Golden lilies float and dance;
My God, I wish that I were there –
    The sun shines joyously in France.

In Scotland, people never smile,
    'Tis months since I have heard a song;
They tell me I am very vile,
    And everything I do is wrong.
There's nothing left but psalms and prayer,
    The folk don't even care to dance;
My God, I wish that I were there –
    Men live so joyously in France.

'Tis true that here I live in state –
    At home I've many foes, they say,
Yet surely 'twere a noble fate
    To die thus free and young and gay;
Death comes to all, why should I care?
    I think I'll go and take my chance,
And if they murder me out there –
    Well, folk die happily in France.

Gold fetters bind my hands and feet,
    Men bow before me very low,
And soldiers stand behind my seat,
    They follow me where'er I go.
My guards take such unceasing care
    To save me from each evil chance,

I often think in blank despair –
    I'll never get to Heaven, or France.

Yet sometimes, for long hours, I stand
    And gaze and wonder at the sea;
And think of that fair distant land,
    The only Paradise for me.
Among the vines and olives there
    In sunshine all my spirits dance,
My God, the South is very fair,
    Some day, I shall go back to France.

Yon golden lilies, flowers of light,
    Still folded in the dark away,
Shall flaunt yet in a nation's sight,
    Sun-gilded on that glorious day
When all about us everywhere
    The people laugh and sing and dance;
My God, I wish that I were there –
    Safe home at last in sunny France.

THE EXILE'S RETURN

You are old and I am young,
    Fling high the golden ball,
Bells of joy for all are rung,
    The sun shines on us all.
Rain fell heavily last night,
Ah, but now the world is bright.
Let us laugh and sing and dance,
For the sun shines fair in France.
    And the rainy night is done, –
    Forward, Children of the Sun.

Though the orange blossom's dead
  And withered petals fall,
Filing gold oranges instead,
  The sun shines on us all.
Here we are at home again,
Past is our long dream of pain;
Let us laugh and sing and dance
Though all flowers are dead in France;
  Yet the day of death is done
  For the Children of the Sun.

Though you people cannot sing,
  Yet catch the golden ball,
There's a skylark on the wing,
  The sun shines on us all,

Shines athwart the flitting breeze,
On green vines and olive trees.
Clasp your hands, my friends, and dance,
Golden oranges of France,
  Life and liberty are won
  By the Children of the Sun.
Scotland may be gray with cold,
  Let hail or snowstorms fall,
Here the world is green and gold,
  The sun shines on us all.
Wave the flags and ring the bells,
Out of Scottish dungeon cells
Here we come to sing and dance,
Back to liberty and France.
  Joy and freedom should be one
  To the Children of the Sun.

Though the roses all are dead,
  Fling high the golden ball,
Golden lilies bloom instead,
  The sun shines on us all.

Earth shall echo with the shout
As we shake the banner out;
Round the flag of Freedom dance,
Splendid fleur-de-lys of France.
  Life and liberty are one
  For the Children of the Sun.

CLOUDS

Drooping over Ireland, veiled in sombre gray,
See the sky is weeping all its light away,
Heedless of the magic music of the spheres,
Drooping over Ireland, land of falling tears.

Land of falling tears and broken promises,
Land of idle slaves and famine and distress,
Land of crime and struggle, and of futile strife,
Land of acquiescence, land without a life.

See amid the shadows where dead Ireland lies,
Justice stands, the future flashes from her eyes:
After thy new birth of travail and of pain,
Rise, she says, dead nation, live and hope again.

Nay, not dead but sleeping; surely she shall wake,
In her mighty hands her life and honour take,
Drink the wine of courage, break the bread of life,
Bear the sword of Freedom foremost in the strife.

Soon above those mountains clothed in sombre gray
Joyous winds shall scatter clouds and mists away;
Ireland's sun is shining, strong and free again,
And her fields are all the greener for the rain.

A TRAITOR

You think that I was false for guerdon or for gold.
  Nay, friends, I was not bought by such a base reward,
Whose fingers smote and rang out fearlessly, of old,
  Steel music, and the clashing rhythms of the sword.
Nay, how could I have cared for any golden chain
  Beneath that hateful medal shining on my breast?
My conquered heart beats on in sobs of smothered pain,
  I mourn for my lost faith, I cannot sleep nor rest.
They did not try a bribe, they were too wise for that,
  They said, 'It's only just to hear the other side.'
I wish that they had turned and stabbed me where I sat:
  No traitor, your true friend I should have lived and
died.
And now that I have left you, your young men have dared
  Their fickle friend and leader daily to revile –
I am 'he whose avarice all his soul ensnared,'
  'Who feigned to love, like Judas, hating all the while.'
Nay, friends, can you not fancy, did you never find
  The foe that slays and spares not all you hold most dear,
Your enemy, your heart's worst traitor, your own mind?
  For this is life's last strife, that all men born must fear;

With reason for a sword the mind goes forth to fight,
  The Heart's fair citadel is guarded by love's wall,
Strange thoughts fly thick and fast, winged arrows swift as
light,
  The feelings yield, the fight is o'er, the towers fall,
And death, death, death, to those who flee or yield,
  Death to the vanquished, mercy is not there;
Cold lies the dead heart on the battle-field,
  Food for that bitter worm men call Despair.
'Tis death, death, death, and this is death indeed.
  Lay the slain powers in a soldier's grave –
Now is the martial mind for ever freed;
  See o'er the dead her glorious standard wave –

Fair flag of freedom, splendid star of Truth,
    I will follow ever where thy beams are shed;
Yea, though they light me to the grave of youth,
    And shine athwart pale faces newly dead –
Hope for the morrow, faith in what shall be,
    Trust in the spirit's striving that ascends
To hard-earned life, far stronger and more free
    Than all your long lost love, my scornful friends.
'Tis life, life, life, the battle on the height –
    The wand'rer groping through the pathless wood –
The patient following of a far-off light –
    The fight for freedom and for brotherhood.
And if the darkness ever fades away,
    And in fair light we friends together stand,
I think that I can promise in that day
    You shall not scorn to wring a traitor's hand;
For light, light, light is all we want on earth,
    Hearts were not hard if only eyes could see,
We who are blind and selfish from our birth
    Are wrapped about with clouds and mystery.
But light, light, light, we pray for all mankind,
    A ray of sunshine on the churchyard sod,
Fire in each heart – a torch in every mind,
    A star among the shadows veiling God.

AN EPITAPH

God , I thank Thee that all things must end,
    That soon pale life shall strive and cry no more,
That Death tears down the veil Faith cannot rend,
    And wide before me stands an open door:
That Thou hast given to pain a potent sword,
    And, building all the mansions of the Blest,
Hast still created in Thy mercy, Lord,
    Before the House of Death, a Gate of Rest.

And thou, my friend and comrade, hold my hand,
  Here on the threshold in the fading light
Watch by my side, together let us stand
  And hearken to the voices of the night.
Write thou these words in ashes, nay, embroider them
  In gold and purple, a phylactery
Of pious thoughts, sewn round the vesture's hem
  Of that pale ghost, fast-fading Memory:
'He was a slave, fast bound to Fortune's wheel,
  A saint, who strove in vain to serve the Lord –
A sufferer whom no human art could heal –
  A soldier fighting with a broken sword –
He was a sinner, whom may God forgive
  In pity on his life-long misery;
By his own heart betrayed he feared to live,
  By his own hand destroyed he dared not die.'
Oh, listen, ye who stand upon the higher slope,
  And strain against the world's low prison bars,
And climb the rugged mountain tops of Hope
  Seeking for Joy amongst the barren stars.
Ye, who would probe the secrets of the night –
  Fret not yourselves, ye go but whence ye came;
Climb ye by faith who have no clearer light,
  Back to the silent land without a name.
Thus be assured that Peace shall come at last
  Though Hope be dead, and Faith grow cold and strange,
And all your years of endless life be past –
  Bow yourselves to the changeless law of change.
Nay, when the wind's voice in the wilderness
  Prepares the way for winter, scattering
Sweet memories of summer's long caress,
  And all the broken promises of Spring,
Have ye not felt the first faint shudder pass
  Right through the garden; seen the daisies sink
Their blushing faces deeper in the grass,
  Whilst high above them stricken lilies shrink,
Each white-faced martyr bound upon a stake.

The coward wind may stab them as it will,
They know not how to bend, they cannot break,
　They can but wither slowly and be still.
See where the hollyhocks, a gaudy row,
　Stand up erect against the darkening sky,
Flaunting so bravely lest the wind should know
　The secret of their burnt-up agony;
They too can bear their burden, undismayed,
　The hidden anguish and the secret stain,
It is not only lilies that must fade
　Or chastened martyrs who can suffer pain;
Sinner and saint still languish side by side –
　Virgin and harlot must alike endure –
To what man's life is misery denied?
　Few can be martyrs, Death is always sure.
Think ye that Christ alone in torment died,
　Whilst all the careless world stood round to see?
What of the thieves so justly crucified,
　One at each side of him on Calvary?
Who does not suffer, who shall enter in
　The narrow path that leadeth unto life
Without the knowledge gained through death and sin,
　Unsanctified by grief and bitter strife?
Has not for man's salvation pain sufficed?
　Those who with Him in torture drew their breath,
Stand now for ever face to face with Christ,
　Ennobled thus and glorified by death,

Thus bound together by a common woe,
　Scorn of despair and loss, contempt of gain,
The only Christian brotherhood we know
　Is Christ's eternal brotherhood of Pain.
All men are equal, yet in this alone
　The spirit lives, the body perisheth;
Amid the darkness of the blind unknown
　We feel the austere equality of death.
Freedom is fair, yet is no spirit free,

Bound and constrained by every linkèd nerve
Of this great chain of flesh; for liberty
  Is but the power to labour and to serve
Unlimited, unfettered, unrestrained
  By the heart's weakness and the failing breath;
Only through pain is perfect peace attained,
  And life's ideal reached at last by death.
Who are ye, then, that ye should stand alone
  Above the grovelling crowd serene and high,
In the calm cloudland of the fair unknown,
  Building your golden stair to scale the sky?
Can ye throw back the sunset gates of flame,
  And gaze deep down into the Heaven's blue,
And write across the sky God's Holy Name,
  So that all men may know that He is true?
Nay, then, come down from these your lonely heights,
  Give up the holy joys of solitude,
And stars and storms, and all divine delights;
  Now the coarse faces of the multitude
Must be to you as once was nature's face,
  For the unfailing good, the changeless law of right,
Do battle in the crowded market place –
  I, the dead coward, bid you heroes fight;
And ye who dwell among the valleys, glad
  With the earth's gladness and the youth of things,
Care not, though youth shall fail and all the joys ye had
  Fly from the rustling of death's might wings;

Though love be very fair and deep your life's delight,
  Yet rest is fairer, and the grave as deep;
Hearken unto the voices of the night,
  Shall there be any bliss like this of sleep?

FINGER POSTS

This is the way of Heaven: you may kneel
   And beat your breast for hours in futile prayer.
   No faint light flickers on the golden stair,
No hand draws back the curtains that conceal
   That land of shadows men imagine fair,
   And the belovèd shade who wanders there
Invisible, no power shall reveal.
Men talk of all the strength of love and faith;
   Vain words and false, it is an idle boast
   To dream we hold communion with a ghost,
Or bring to earth again a vanished wraith.
No shadow answers to a shadow's call,
This is the way of all things spiritual.

II

This is the way of Nature, as of old,
   When from the primal darkness first there grew
   Flowers, and the sun shone and all the sky was blue,
And life's bright promises were manifold,
Her hidden wealth is now as then untold;
   He who digs deep enough shall find her true,
   Each miner gains at last his honest due
Of her great buried store of gems and gold.
This is the way of Earth: she hears the call
   Of every ploughman's prayer; the labourer,
   If he be worthy, has his will of her.
From the deep furrows where the good seeds fall,
She brings forth hope, and all the life that clings
Round the strong patience of material things.

III

This is the way of Sorrow: wearily
   Should one set out with such a weary guide;

The path is narrow and the world is wide,
And no man knoweth any reason why.
And yet 'tis foolishness to strive or cry,
  The doom must fall on whom the gods decide,
  They walk with pain for ever at their side,
Through her long wilderness of mystery.
Yet though sweet sorrow hath few words to say,
  A dull companion on a lonely road;
Yea, though she hath not faith enough to pray;
  And on life's shoulders binds a heavy load,
Her heart is true, her footsteps shall not stray.
She leads at last unto the gods' abode.

IV

This is the way of Joy: the artist knows
  The secret that makes all things fresh and fair.
  She gives a fragrance to the summer air,
And, flashing by where life's dull river flows,
She shakes the languor of its slow repose,
  And drives it, scattering music everywhere,
  Up to the foot of Heaven's golden stair,
Through the wild tangles of the mystic rose;
There, in the shade beside the river's bed,
  She rests awhile, and dabbles in the stream –
  Till down the giddy mazes of her dream
She finds the little peaceful hour has fled.
Then forth into the startled sky she springs
With swift wet feet, and shining golden wings.

V

This is the way of life when Joy has fled:
  She passes through a wilderness of cloud,
  And, wrapped in music for a mimic shroud,
She comes unto the dwellings of the Dead.
No river now, a mournful nymph instead,

By Joy's short sojourn with a soul endowed,
  She seeks for her among the nameless crowd
That throng the gateway of the Halls of Dread –
Seeks for the long-lost Joy, the light divine,
  The Paradise that she shall never win –
  Content at last, and glad to enter in
Despair's abode, and rest with Proserpine,
Sorrow, whose eyes are dark with unshed tears,
And all the ghostly company of fears.

VI

This is the way of Love: a ray of light
  In the mid forest through the foliage shines,
  And makes green shadows of the serried pines,
Bringing a secret pathway into sight,
Where two may walk alone in their delight,
  And half in darkness: for the thick set lines
  Of mighty trees their narrow road confines
With the black limits of enshrouding night.
Yet has the forest fortress failed in strength;
  Swift windy beams split through the leafy screen,
  And pierce the heavy shroud of waving green,
Until the narrow pathway feels at length
The strength of sunshine and the light of rain,
And broadens out into the open plain.

VII

This is the road of Hope, that some men call
  The way of Love, far out of human sight,
  Amid strange mansions of austere delight,
A way of shadows, pale, æthereal;
High among stars and storms, outsoaring all
  The silent glories of each lonely height,
  Above the tumult of the windy night,
Beyond the bounds of Heaven's cloudy wall,

Still God's calm splendour shineth overhead,
 The great white way where light and gladness are;
This is the Joy of earth transfigurèd,
 Set high in heaven, very faint and far;
The glorious Highway of the holy Dead,
 The path of Love from star to scattered star.

HYMN
'The wind bloweth where it listeth ... So is everyone
that is born of the Spirit.'

Holy Spirit , force of light,
Soul of beauty out of sight,
Height of light and depth of pain,
Golden sunshine after rain;
Shivering seas and winds that glide,
Shadows on the mountain side,
All things swift and all things strong,
Life and colour, hope and song,
Are Thine, O Lord Divine.
Freedom of the winds that fly
Through waste spaces of the sky,
Freedom of the thoughts that range
On from change to endless change,
Force of life that shall not yield,
Victor on the battle-field,
Lightning winged, and fire shod,
Freedom of the laws of God;
Spirit born of liberty,
If the truth can make us free,
In the power of the whole
Of the world's impatient soul,
Strive with us when we aspire
In the strength of self-restraint,
To the land above desire,

And the life beyond constraint
Of the saint.

SONNET

They who rise satiate from Life's banquet, spread
  With mystic providence of food and wine,
  Would worship something for an outward sign
That they are grateful, being fully fed.
Thus do they reverence golden calves instead
  Of God, and all high thoughts resign,
  Mistake abundance for the life Divine,
Fulfilment for the secret of the dead.
They shall not probe the mysteries of pain,
  The primal truths, whose feet have never trod
Life's barren wilderness of strife and strain,
  Nor learnt among her solitudes that God
Not Satan is the spirit that denies, –
The life and essence of self-sacrifice.

A SOLDIER

'Young knight, go forth and slay
The Dragon while 'tis day,
For soon the sun will set
On your most vain regret,
That no fair deed is done
  Ere set of sun.'

'Nay, rather would I fight
In darkness,' said the knight,
'Than go forth unprepared
Unto my work, ensnared

By reckless vanity,
 To do or die.

My sword not sharp enough,
My armour sorry stuff,
My horse half trained and wild,
Defenceless as a child
And immature,
 Defeat were sure.'

'Yet doth the snake alway
Such harmless people slay,
And work his wicked will,
The while you linger still,
Jousting and throwing spears
 Through youth's best years.

'And all your blows ring hard,
Sham fighting in the yard;
I pray you waste no time,
The battle joy sublime
Is life to men like you.
 Bold hearts are few.'

The soldier answered not,
But still his blows fell hot
And thick; his way he rent
Through the mad tournament;
Long strove he undismayed
 To learn his trade.

But when strong-armed he rode
At last from his abode,
The country people said,
'Behold, the Dragon's dead.
For all your warlike state,
 You are too late.

'A knight unknown to fame,
A braver warrior, came
Across the sea to do
The deed God meant for you.
Thus has a stranger's sword
  Earned your reward.'

He smiled. 'Shall I repine
For fame that is not mine,
And grudge with childish greed
Another man his deed?
Mourn at the sight of this
  Brave brother's bliss?

'Whilst still beneath the sun
There's work for every one,
And never yet was knight
Who found no foe to fight,
No sword did ever lack
  Some skull to hack.

'As long as hearts are wrung,
As long as songs are sung,
Whilst still the Star of Hope
Reigns in Life's horoscope,
The whole world through
  There's work to do.

'Then forth strong armed I go
To meet an unknown foe,
An unknown friend to save,
And fill an unknown grave.
Thank God, the world is wide
  Through which I ride.

'Forward through field and wood,
To some far goal of good,

Content if by the way
Some evil thing I slay;
Dreaming, when life seems hard,
Of Joyous Gard.'

I know not how he fared
Who was so well prepared,
Nor if the tales were true,
Of giants that he slew,
Of deeds of valour done,
And battles won.

Of hardships well endured,
And captives fast immured
He set at liberty –
Such things as these may be –
Right well I know he did his best –
Sweet be his rest.

FEBRUARY AT ADARE

Beneath a mist of dog-wood buried deep,
Here, as I passed along the riverside,
I found the Spring low-laid in blissful sleep,
Entranced she seemed, yet watching open-eyed
The deep brown pools that lie beneath the stream
Like great thoughts hidden in a misty dream,
The shadowy fishes darting to and fro,
And all the wintry sunshine come and go.
She seemed as one about to wake, who lingers
Yet on the blessed borderland of consciousness,
Her hair streamed down between her claspèd fingers,
And fell upon the stream like a caress,
To make a little passing stir and shiver
In the cool surface of the lazy river.

You might have thought her dead, so still she lay,
This sleeping beauty, whom the tyrannous time
Had left to dream the ice-bound hours away
In calm despair or confidence sublime.
The laurel wreathed about her sunken head
Its sickly fragrance through the bower shed;
All round her there had grown a magic ring,
Enchanted snowdrops, whitely blossoming,
Planted by faery hands long time ago,
Perfect alike in beauty and in number,
Bore witness to the pureness of her slumber;
Unstained of sinfulness, undimmed by woe,
Passed by of fear, untouched by joy or sorrow,
Serene she waits life's call and God's divine to-morrow.

A CHOICE

In His Rainbow Garden, God
Made the Spirit of the Spring,
The very sunshine on the sod
Rose to greet her, seemed to sing,
As she openèd her eyes
In the Flower's Paradise.
On the morning of her birth
He gave her leave to pluck a flower
From His Rainbow Garden bower,
To take with her down to earth.
The Spirit chose
No gaudy rose;
She passed where lilies blossomed fair,
Making sweet the fields of air,
Golden sunflowers in vain
Called to her to turn again;
When her scent-compelling feet
Trod violets, she found them sweet,

And passed the fragrant flowers by,
And hurried down the Eastern sky;
Till by Heaven's utmost wall
She met the Dawn, who, as she went,
Scattered blossoms, letting fall
A glory through the firmament.
Down like a faded star she threw,
Laughing softly all the while,
A primrose drenched in light and dew,
The very spirit of her smile.
Then was Spring astonishèd,
She caught the pale delight and fled
To where, on the horizon's verge,
Heaven and earth in dreamland merge,
And the silver April showers
Scatter music through the skies;
There she found no garden flowers,
Nor any bird of Paradise,
But an earthly skylark sang,
And Heaven's weeds were growing wild,
Then through the Rainbow's arch there rang
The laughter of an eager child,
As roaming o'er the Eastern hills,
She gathered common daffodils.

SWEET PEAS
TO MABEL

Sweet peas. The very life of Spring
Stirs each frail wing
To a diviner colour, fair
As the first glimmering
Of moonlight in a spirit's hair.
Sweet with the essence of unfolding flowers,
Fresh with the fragrance of the morning hours,

Bury thy face deep down in dreams of these,
Sweet peas.
Lift up thy heart to the divine delight
Of their frail flight;
Be thy life stirred by subtle airs
Like theirs,
To the faint music of the coloured dream
They seem.
The liquid light that paints the early sky,
Ere in the noonday it grows cold and dry,
Is yours, fair flowers, yours are the sunny ways
Of sweet spring days;
As frozen earth, the while she sleeps below
This cruel sky grown white with thoughts of snow,
Dreaming a dream of colour, seems to see
The glory and the green that soon shall be,
So does my heart, sweet peas,
Though it may freeze,
Long for the sun to warm it through and through,
Dream of the touch of God's own colour blue,
And wandering through Fancies' garden beds,
Where ghosts of blasted rose trees droop their heads
And weep down icicles instead of dew,
Gain gladness from the very thoughts of you.

LAMENT

Oh, the streak of gold in the gray,
    And the sun's first ray of light,
And the fresh cold air of the day
    On the burning cheek of night,
And the winds that shake as they pass
    The glory of piled-up sheaves,
The shadow of wings on the grass,
    And the rustle of autumn leaves,

Are as songs that are out of fashion
   That no man loves or sings,
Since life in the fire of passion
   Has blackened her rainbow wings.

The glory of struggle and strain –
   The joy of the world at morn,
The light of the falling rain,
   The strength of the growing corn,
A smile that transfigures the Truth,
   The sound of a voice that sings,
The glory and gladness of youth,
   And the splendour of obvious things,
The songs that were dear to the singer,
   Dead and devoid of mirth
Are lost to the gods in heaven
   And voices of men upon earth.

For the star of our hope burns faint,
   And the light of the world grows dim,
As the halo that crowns a saint,
   Or the notes of a vesper hymn;
And thoughts are too bitter for words,
   And the silence grows and grows
And there's never a song from the birds,
   Nor a scent from the dying rose;
And fear in the soul of a nation
   Makes dreadful a noble strife,
Whilst death, with a cold negation,
   Has broken the heart of life.
Yet the sun still gladdens the sky,
   And the giddy stars endure,
For the end is not yet nigh,
   The meaning is still obscure;
Doomed spirits, unwilling to die,
   Can murmur still as they pass
Into Silence and Mystery,

'Perhaps,' as well as 'Alas';
For still the delight of colour
Lies blue on the distant hills,
And the air of spring's all golden
With sunshine and daffodils.

LA MORT EST LE BAISER DE DIEU

Pain is the price of freedom we must pay,
    Wrapped in the pride of our most noble birth,
    Cut off from all the brotherhood of earth,
We fret and struggle through our little day,
And senselessly despise the senseless clay,
    Yet in the spring time feel but little mirth,
    And wonder whether what we gain is worth
The gift of peace, so lightly cast away,
The silence and the strange unconscious life
    Of flowers and trees, deep rooted, strongly bound
    Beneath the base dominion of the ground,
So near to nature, calm amid the strife
Of forces, life's degrading fight for breath,
And all the noble quietness of death.

SONNET

Strong spirit, striving upward to the light,
    Soul of the world, half smothered in its dust,
    Breath of the battle, life's despairing trust
In progress and hope's golden wingèd flight.

Where art thou, spirit? Vainly through the night
We call. Thy sword is eaten up with rust –
We know that thou art strong as thou art just,

Why hast thou wholly vanished from our sight?
The Spirit works in darkness, secretly,
Among the hidden depths and roots of things,
Down in those caverns where no skylark sings,
But germs of power and buried forces lie.
Have patience, when all flags of hope are furled,
Still there is courage in the under world.

THE ABBOT'S EPITAPH

'The summary of a good man's life,
The record of his earthly strife,
A holy message to his heirs
Beseeching for their constant prayers;
A voice of warning and of doom
Out of the silence of the tomb,
So deep anon.
Such things as these I mean to write
Ere I go forth into the night,
With my last breath they shall be said
And carved in marble o'er my head,'
Said Father John.
'That every passer-by may see
That Death is Life's epitome
When I am gone.'

The Mass was sung, the prayers were said,
We came about his dying bed,
And prayed the most beloved of men
To tell his mourning children then,
Whilst still he flickered to and fro
'Twixt Life and Death prepared to go,
    Yet lingering on,
What those most sacred words might be
Of the long written Elegy,

The Holy Rede that should be read,
Carved in the marble o'er his head,
    When he was gone.
He turned his face away from us –
    'Miserrimus, miserrimus!'
    Said Father John.

SHUT OUT

'Twas hard to bear,
    For years to wander thus and wait
Amid pale shadows of half real despair
    In the dull road outside the Ivory Gate.
All round my feet the pansies grew
    Nodding their wise heads to and fro,
Mocking faces gold and blue
    Seemed to whisper 'No, No, No,
        No thoroughfare.'

How strange it seems,
    Now round me poppies blossom red,
Low at my feet the river gleams,
    Great beech boughs rustle overhead;
Pansies, you mocked me all in vain,
    Light flowers who did not understand,
Fade on outside, I live again,
    And labour in the magic land
        Of light and Dreams.

PETTY LARCENY

Lived a man was wont to steal
Oysters for his daily meal,

He broke them open with a stone,
And ate them on the shore alone.
One day he had not strength enough,
Or else the shell was very tough,

He struggled till he sprained his wrist,
E'en then the knave did not desist,
But forced the oyster open wide
And found a glorious pearl inside.

MONOTONY

Oh, poor, pale days that pass me by
    Thus one by one,
With neither tempest nor blue sky,
    Nor wind nor sun.
Glad without smiles, and sad without a sigh,
    Beloved of none:
Content to fade away and die
    At set of sun.
With neither stars nor flowers nigh,
Nor evening breeze nor sunset sky
    When day is done.

TRANSMIGRATION – A NIGHTMARE

Down in the darkness of his damp abode
I heard the moaning of the dismal toad:
'I was a princess on a golden chair,
Right joyously I breathed the upper air,
With glory crowned and gladness shod
The polished palace floors I trod;
I smiled to hear my mother say,

'Such shows as these shall pass away.'
Now as I sit where the well is deep,
I weep all day, all night I weep,
For the gladness has gone, and the glory flown,
And here I live in the mud alone.'

FROM BACON

Wings for the feet, not shoulders, poets need,
To grace the motion of the flying deed,
Slowly prepared, accomplishèd with speed.

TO MAY

Through the garden of my dreams
Scantily the sunlight gleams,
And the barren grass plot seems
    Void of grace.

Yea, a wilderness indeed –
Every flower has run to seed,
Dying slowly; every weed
    Grows apace.

In the spring last year there grew
Violets white and violets blue,
But never a dream or a flower for you,
    May, the Queen.

Though your small feet, as you walk,
Hardly bend the cowslip's stalk,
Or disturb the daisies' talk
    On the green;

And your white hands would not mar
The petals of one yellow star,
Where primroses in clusters are,
    In the grass;

Though I know you fear to break
The bluebell's stem, or even shake
Her fragile tower for music's sake,
    As you pass,

Yet methinks 'tis passing strange
To hear the sudden catch and change
In the ringings' airy range
    Of delight.

Such a chilly sobbing breath
Through the sunshine shivereth;
From the open gates of Death,
    And of Night;

Till the music's rapid whim
Groweth very slow and dim,
Dying in a mournful hymn
    Solemnly,

And each heavy purple bell
Seems to ring a funeral knell
For the spirit of the dell
    Doomed to die:

While without the garden rail
Bright anemones turn pale
As the lilies of the vale,
    And the breeze,

Where the sleeping river lies
Underneath the trancèd skies,

In swift gusts of terror flies
  Through the trees.

Seemeth it so small a thing
Clouds and darkness thus to fling
In the sunny face of Spring,
  Striking down

All the thrills and flights of thirds
Of the music of the birds,
With a weight of weary words
  And a frown.

Till the lark in his ascent
Seemeth but to make lament,
That all flowers have lost their scent
  On the earth;

And the tulips talk in Dutch,
Of the little human touch
That makes sadness overmuch
  For their mirth.

Whilst the wild wood Columbine,
Cannot for her life divine
Why the sun has ceased to shine,
  As of old.

Where across the lawn you glide,
Buttercups on every side
Deep among the mosses hide
  All their gold.

At the rustle of your gown
The very sunshine seems to frown,
And the daisies shudder down
  In the grass.

Shall I thank you much for this
That you spare my clematis,
For you blight it with a kiss,
   As you pass.

Ah, the cowslips once were sweet,
Spreading out their golden sheet
In a carpet for your feet,
   Soft and bright.

Yet they faded one by one,
Lying withered in the sun
Till the very thrushes shun
   Such a sight.

Two tall tulips by the gate
Spent the sunny hours of late
In a stately tête-à-tête,
   Growing bold.

Nodding each emphatic head,
Found their petticoats too red,
Wished that they were white instead,
   Trimmed with gold.

Now their petals flutter down,
And the scarlet fades to brown,
As a smile turns to a frown
   In your eyes.

Oh the dead dreams everywhere;
Wingèd hopes that once were fair,
Flitting through the tremulous air,
   Butterflies –

Broken winged and dead they lie,
Where beneath the faded sky

Every flower seems to die,
  In the land.

Blossoms wither where you go,
The very brambles will not grow;
The grass looked yellow as from snow
  Where you stand,

Leaning lightly, lest you fall,
Like a lily white and tall,
With the carven sun-dial
  For a crutch.

Thrilling through his overgrown
And moss-hidden heart of stone,
With the melody unknown
  Of your touch.

You, before whose blighting breath
Every flower withereth,
Have cast your shadow as of Death
  On the green.

In the spring this year there grew
Nothing but rosemary and rue,
And one white lily flower for you,
  May, the Queen.

A WELCOME

Friend , you enter to your heritage at length,
You may pluck your laurels from the ruins of our
strength;
Desecrate our churches, liberate our slaves,
Gather roses even from the gardens of our graves.

But this thing I charge you, nay, beseech you, gracious
lord,
Though you ravage all the city now with fire and the
sword,
Though our lives go down in darkness and our children's
blood is spilt,
Yet respect the gold we toiled for, and the treasury we
built;
You, who know not any worship for things mortal or
divine,
Bow your head and enter humbly, this is Mammon's
inmost shrine.

A LOST MEMORY

Ivory-gated, velvet-lined
Is the cupboard in my mind,
Where I put the things I find
    On the shelves.
There behind the great white door
Lies my precious, piled-up store –
All the things I knew before
    I saw the elves.

Misery, ah misery,
They have made a fool of me,
Stealing thus my golden key
    In the night.
When I tried to break the lock,
The house trembled with the shock,
But the door stood like a rock,
    Firm and white.

For the elves, they understood,
I might curse them if I would,

It was not the slightest good –
　　Waste of breath.
When I meet them on the stairs
They laugh at all my fruitless prayers,
For they say my key is theirs
　　Until Death.

Oh, lock up your dusty shelves,
Lest the little reckless elves,
Seeking what they want themselves,
　　Should invade
The dark cupboards of your mind.
Hide your keys, or you may find
That they leave no hope behind
　　On their raid.

SPRING IN MANCHESTER

The ghost of Twilight seems to dog
　　The feet of golden morning hours,
The sun gleams silver through the fog,
　　And silver frost lies on the flowers.

Poor battered crocus, feebly fair,
　　Smutty and stained and crouching down,
Half stifled by the smoky air
　　And murky coldness of the town.

And snowdrops, dreaming such a dream
　　Of magic sounds too sweet for sight,
And sunlit fields, and streams that seem
　　The very smile of Spring's delight.

When, long ere primroses unfold
　　Their leaves, or birds care much to sing,

Bright crocus flowers with cloth of gold
  Weave faery carpets for the spring,

Where all the earth is fresh and clean,
  In deep still woods the snowdrops grow,
And spread above the struggling green
  Their whiteness like a fall of snow.

First flowers of the Spring to be
  You chosen children of the light;
Was it but inborn purity
  That made you so divinely white?

Nay, rather powers of sun and breeze,
  And fresh sweet air, and scent, and sound,
The sunshine gleaming through the trees,
  The gentle forces of the ground.

Else had you not grown lovelier
  Than these gray ghosts who mourn their loss,
The great beech boughs that shake and stir
  Above green bowers of rain-washed moss.

You flowers who shiver through the gloom,
  Round whom the blighting east wind sighs,
Was it your fault, or Nature's doom,
  That shut you out from Paradise?

Remorselessly she passed you by,
  Poor broken-petalled silver ghosts,
Phantoms of flowers, left to die
  So far from all her sunny hosts.

Her gay-clad hosts, whose light and mirth
  Brings sunshine to the eyes of Truth,

And crowns the ancient brows of earth
  With garlands of eternal youth,

'Twas strange she left you lying there,
  With weeds and bits of broken glass,
You that might once have been so fair –
  Dead flowers on the blackened grass.

And yet not strange, for all her ways
  Are hard and oftentimes unjust,
Yet gently, after many days,
  She mingles always dust with dust.

Dust of bright blossoms, manifold
  Dust of stained petals, glad to fall,
Mixed with the same devouring mould,
  The same stars shine above them all.

Forgotten, yet not all unblest,
  Redeemed from strife, and hope, and fear,
Wrapped in that silent dream of rest,
  Whence springs the life of every year.

Dead flowers. – To the world is lost
  So much of beauty, joy, and light,
Killed by an accidental frost
  Embittering a winter's night.

AFTER THE STORM

How the battle raged last night
Through my garden of delight,
And the east wind carried death
In the terror of its breath.
Broken is each lily's cup

The very moss is withered up,
Where life and light were once outpoured,
One sunbeam, like a dead man's sword,
Lies split and shattered on the grass,
Alas, alas.

DEFEATED

One more defeat – and so we've failed again;
   We can but yield, heart stricken and forlorn;
Our swords are broken and our heroes slain,
   The very flag of freedom stained and torn.

There's none to stand, and not one left to strike,
   And evening veils the flight we call retreat;
The sun goes down on friend and foe alike,
   Their glorious victory and our defeat.

'It is too dark to fight,' a traitor's cry:
   The sky's yet red, the sun's not quite gone down.
Cowards, ye still see well enough to fly;
   Strike now, if any yet would save the town.

One more defeat, you think it's time to yield;
   Nay, we're not conquered, only driven back,
For in the language of the battle-field
   One more defeat means but one more attack.

A desperate hope, by desperation led,
   Shall triumph in the strong name of despair;
For the great cause, in honour of the dead,
   Charge once again, now follow ye who dare.
Oh! comrades, heroes, can you still hang back?
   ''Tis madness.' Nay, can courage not enlarge

The bounds of reason? Is it that you lack
Courage? No – then sound the trumpet. – Charge.

FROM THE FRENCH (of Victor Hugo)

When the fog hangs heavy and chill as death,
   When the moonlight floats where the sunshine stood,
And the evening fills with its shivering breath
   The pallied darkness of field and wood –
We will walk through the green land weeping again,
   We will lean and rest in the dying light,
Our mortal souls opened out by pain,
   On the flowers that are open at night.
Calm night has made such a sombre prayer
   From the rumours of earth and the stars above,
Whilst we, of the darkness of life and despair
   Have made but love.

THE PHILOSOPHER

You think it strange that I resort
To seek Diogenes at Court?
Nay, for he knows he needs material things,
To give them is the privilege of kings:
Whilst the poor king, indeed,
Knows not his own sore need,
Else he would put his empty glory by
And kneel to court divine philosophy.

TO CERTAIN REFORMERS

As long as idols stand
In the holy place, as of old,
And, instead of light through the land,
Shines the tawdry glitter of gold,
So long as the senses reign,
And the spirit is trodden down,
Your desire ye shall not gain,
Ye shall not win your crown;
For the flesh is very strong,
And the spirit is weak in the strife,
And the weak must suffer wrong,
These are the ways of life:
Yet, take your swords in hand,
And fight for the light to be,
And the spirit's promised land
Of Truth and Liberty.
White-souled women of the past,
Heard ye not the trumpet blast?
Were your spirits less pure then,
Feebler than the souls of men?
Men who told you, you are good,
Holy, be it understood,
And yet neither strong nor wise –
May the spirit purge their eyes
And teach the foolish world at length
That purity is always strength.
Right divine to rule ye feel,
Strong in you the stronger born, –
Then your right divine reveal,
Lest your claims be met with scorn;
For whilst the sky shines clear and blue
Above us, these two things are sure,
Who would be wise must first be true,
Who would be strong must first be pure.
Ye who have not learnt your power,

Whose chained spirits shrink and cower
Slavery stunted, idly tame,
Lift your hearts whilst every nerve
Quickens, in the spirit's name
Boldly claim the right to serve.
Band together, fighters you,
Strength and wisdom shall endure,
Who would be wise must first be true,
Who would be strong must first be pure.
Then put your trust
In the spirit's strife;
The body is dust,
And the spirit life,
And take your swords in hand
To fight for the Light to be,
Ye shall reach your promised land,
And the Truth shall make you free.

FALLEN NATURE

What though thick clouds have quenched the moon,
And all the stars must follow soon,
For blind winds groping in the dark
Swiftly blow out each flaring spark,
Whilst the night grows wild and strange
With the voice of change.
What though the room is warm and bright,
And the fire burns gold on a chilly night –
Let us rise up, my soul, and go,
For outside in the wind and the snow
I see a shadowy form,
I hear a voice in the storm –
Oh, Lucifer, through closèd doors
My heart goes out to yours.
Soul of the Universe,

My soul immerse,
In the deep waters of the rolling years,
And all the rainbow light of falling tears.
Son of the morning, art thou fallen indeed
As the good seed,
The life of spring that's lying now
Cold in the furrows of the plough,
In the first glory of the deep
Unconsciousness of blessed sleep,
The wingèd seed that shall arise
To flaunt against the summer skies –
Till God from His mercy seat
Sees the banner of the wheat,
Her brazen yellow flag unfurled,
Waving out across the world.
Thus, Lucifer, from Earth's cold clay
Be thy Resurrection Day,
Fallen Nature reascend,
With the higher forces blend
This hidden human life of thine,
Thy sacrament of bread and wine.
Yet, soul of sin and life and pain,
When thou dost enter heaven again,
Remember that the earth was sweet
To thy naked human feet,
Remember that the sea shone bright,
Spread out before the gates of light;
When thou dost wave thy spirit's wing,
Think of the earth's good spirit, spring,
And how her meadows were more fair
Than any wind-sown field of air;
Remember how her daffodils
Waved vagrant over all the hills –
Nay, long before thy second birth,
Most humble angel of the earth,
Remember, though thou wert not then
Regenerate or fit for men,

Earth spirit, essence of the sod,
Thou wert yet very near to God.

VISIONS OF SOLITUDE

TO CON

I

Who shall venture to intrude
In the dim secluded wood,
Where the birds have hushed their song,
Fearing to do silence wrong,
And the wind's breath scarcely stirs
In the midst of shadowy firs;
Whilst the sunshine, pale and thin,
Hardly dares to enter in,
Such a sombre gloom profound
Hallows the enchanted ground?
Here old Time might end his life,
Rest from all his toil and strife,
Lay his sickle in the grass,
Smile to watch the hours pass,
And the low winds wander by,
Rustling through eternity.
Hush, the silence grows immense,
Soon a shape shall issue thence;
Some fair Goddess white and tall,
Shadowy-limbed, majestical;
Leaning on her bow and spear,
Cynthia's self might venture here;

Satyrs through the bracken glide,
Or the lonely wood nymph hide,
'Twas in such a place that Pan

Last was seen of mortal man.
Have the gods then in derision
Swept away our powers of vision,
Dreams and poems manifold,
Souls of stories never told,
And those sacred fancies, known
Once to Mother Earth alone?
Have they robbed her thus and fled,
Gone to dwell amongst the Dead,
Bringing these good gifts of hers
To their ancient worshippers?
Shadowy Phantoms, wild and gray,
Sweep along the great white way,
Shattering stars and scattering light
In the tumult of their flight,
Seeking high above the sky
In the Halls of Harmony
Light and peace, where lonely fate
Their desire can satiate;
Where no human voices rude
On their silence can intrude,
But the Rainbow's column spread
Joins the living and the dead,
There they dwell alone, afar,
On some vast mysterious star;
Or could time perchance deface
Even Aphrodite's grace,
Cynthia, growing old and wan,
Cease to charm Endymion?
Or the light grow dim that lies
In Athenè's cold gray eyes?
The twilight of the gods began
First when Psyche flouted Pan,
Leaving him alone to dream
By the bulrush-bordered stream,

Forsaking the strange brotherhood
And secrets of the magic wood,
Foregoing all its ecstasies
And half-discovered mysteries
Of shady light and living shade;
The all inconstant careless maid
From her faithful Lover fled,
'Following the Gleam,' she said.
So it is no vision stays
In these dim degenerate days,
To dazzle unaccustomed eyes
With its old world ecstasies.
Who shall wake the music mute
Of Apollo's broken lute?
What strange priestess now can tell
The secrets of his oracle?
Nay, then in this dim and sweet
Shadow of a green retreat
Are the voices of the wood
Clearly known and understood,
Have the rash intruding hours,
Searching out all hidden powers,
Dragged its secret forth to lie
Bare beneath the open sky?
And that song, to Life unknown,
Sung by Mother Earth alone,
Melody no spirit dare
Breathe upon the shrinking air,
Sacred music unconfined,
Born of silence and the wind,
Faintly heard amid the strife
Of Life that crieth out to Life,
Echoed back from sound to sleep,
Deep that answereth to Deep.
Dying with the mutterings
Of those hopeless drowning things,
That strive against the infinite

Dark waters of oblivion's night,
To wake the silence with a cry,
And probe the depths of mystery;
Making a transient flash and gleam
On the dark face of Lethe's stream,
A little shower of foam and light,
Flecking the surface of the night.
Heard by Eros, drowing there
The echoes of unanswered prayer,
Bending o'er the chasm's brink,
Watching life and gladness sink,
Through the skies reflected show,
Down to the dim depths below;
Saved by Love when Hope was gone,
Rescued from oblivion,
Softly sung above the Dead
Sweet with joy rememberèd,
To Eros self grown doubly dear,
When chanted over Psyche's bier,
The North wind heard it passing by
And caught the ancient melody;
Sang it loud along the black
Silence of his nightly track;
Rang it clear across the sky
In great waves of harmony,
Beating up against the white
Glory of the growing light,
Thundering through Heaven above
Love's triumphant call to Love.
Dying when he fails for breath,
Death that answereth to Death!
Is that mighty music past,
Has the world grown old at last?
Does the soul of man desire
Less Prometheus' stolen fire,
Can Tantalus his great thirst slake?
Have weary hearts then ceased to ache?

Do the Hours no longer throng
Round the chariot of song,
When the first swift quenchèd spark
Shudders out into the dark,
Waiting with awe-stricken eyes
For the golden shaft that flies
Suddenly and free and fair
Through great waves of throbbing air,
Down to where all swathed and hid
By oblivion's coverlid
Earth lies sleeping, in her dreams
The sudden flash of fire gleams,
New-born thoughts and feelings start
Into life in her chill heart,
Every Dream becomes a flower,
Deep rooted, waiting for its hour;
In cold and darkness yet unborn,
Striving upwards to the morn?
How the struggling souls resent
The prisons of their punishment,
Beneath the silence and repose
That every peaceful valley knows,
And wintry calmness of the hills,
Deep buried Life and sorrow thrills,
And earth's great heart must throb and ache
For a smothered snowdrop's sake,
Till by the old accustomed pain
She knows herself alive again.

Are no midnight vespers chanted,
No dark caverns vision haunted?
Does no man worship now Divine
Poppy crownèd Proserpine?
Has the laurel ceased to grow?
Do the nymphs no longer know
How to make its foliage stir
Best to charm the wanderer,

That this forest glade can be
Untenanted of mystery?
Hark, a rustle in the grass,
Heard ye not the wood nymph pass?
Nay, she did not pass, but stayed,
Gazed around her unafraid,
Look upon her ye who dare,
Is she not, then, passing fair? –
Mystery of mysteries –
By yonder tree the goddess lies,
And, although its branches spread
Leafy shelter round her head,
Still the sunbeams shiver through
On her coronet of dew,
And strange robes of radiant green,
Faery maiden, Forest Queen
Of the dim enchanted wood,
Phantom haunted Solitude!

II

Let us sail and sail away
Right across the sunny bay,
Leaving far behind the shore
Where the breakers evermore
Toss themselves and foam and fret,
Vainly striving to forget
What the inconstant sea gulls say,
Flashing on them through the spray,
Far beyond the sun's bright gates,
Where the quiet twilight waits,
And no ripples wave and sigh,
But the cold dead waters lie,
And the white sail flaps and falls
Like great flags at festivals.
Round us such a calm is spread
The sea's strange spirit might be dead,

Dead or drifting in a swoon
Through the silent afternoon,
Down to where the great waves are
Breaking on the sandy bar.
Surely we shall find the vision
Of that sunset land Elysian,
Where the clouds and mountains go
In the dreamy afterglow, –
Hush – the silence grows immense
Till a Presence issues thence;
Folded are her rainbow wings,
Softly to herself she sings,
And her white feet may be seen
Dabbling in the waters green,
Whilst the winds on either hand
Seemed to wait her high command,
Chained and silent to fulfil
The mighty maiden's sovereign will.
High she sits, alone, serene,
Holy Universal Queen,
Snowy limbed and white and nude
Ocean Maiden Solitude.

FINIS

The dogwood's dead, and a mantle red
Over the corpse is flung,
Bow down, oh willow, your silver head,
Summer's silver and winter's red
Glory and gray and green have fled,
All winds are silent, all sorrows said,
And all songs sung.

UNSEEN KINGS
(1904)

FROM EAST TO WEST

Great ships glided into the port,
Surely the ships of the gods laden with dreams;
And men said, 'It is well,
They have brought their dreams to us as of old,
And now new tales shall be told.'
But the gods stood on the decks aghast –
They saw the earth an iron fort,
The air a silver citadel,
The sky a fortress built of solid gold.
Then Prani said, 'Here is no place for our dreams.'
So they flung the great sails over the mast,
And sailed out slowly across the seas
Till they came to a twilight land in the west,
Where old unquiet mysteries
And pale discrownèd spirits dwell,
And the world's will is laid to rest;
Where the wind sings a song with a golden lilt
And the air flows by in silver streams,
There in wide wastes of the world they built
An ivory castle for their dreams.

GRASS OF PARNASSUS

Ye who in old days dared to wander far
Beside the haunted springs of Hippocrene,
And ye Wise Men who followèd your Star,
Look down on our pale land of gray and green,
And see by these white tokens in the grass
Here too the footsteps of the gods have been.
Yea, though the black smoke of the world can mar
The Vision sleeping in its magic glass,
Star smitten still the hearts of wanderers are –
The moon sits thronèd in her silver car –

And in her shadow floating, dimly seen,
The pale dreams smile upon us as they pass.

A HERMIT'S LAMENT FOR MAEVE

Now is the High-Queen vanquished, she has cast her
    sword aside,
And the stones are gray on Knocknarea,
That build up the cairn of her pride,
And Maeve lies cold in her lonely grave on the haunted
mountain side.

Stately of earth-encrusted gold the High-King's dun is built.
Yet fairer by far is the gold of a star,
Or a sogn with a golden lilt,
Or the dream-gold of the dead Queen's hair and her
dagger's carven hilt.

My sorrow grows and darkens as the bitter years increase,
I could have been brave to fight for Maeve,
Now I pray that all war may cease –
Now do I mourn for a Queen long dead and passed
through the gates of Peace.

I fear the folk that pass my door to market or to mass,
Dearer to me are the waves of the sea
Than the faces of those that pass;
Better I love the silver mob of daisies that toss in the grass.

I hate the sight of swords that flash in the noonday sun,
I shrink with fear from the battle-cheer
And the clatter of deeds that are done –
My soul grows gray in the silence like the quiet soul of a nun.

The Hood of Darkness on my brow is folded down and pressed;
I care no more for peace or war,
But I pray for a little rest,
Where the golden soul of silence rises out of the West.

TO MAEVE

Not for thee, oh Maeve, is the song of the wandering harper sung,
For men have put lies on thy lips, and treason, and shrieking fear,
Because thou wert brave, they say thou wert bitter and false of tongue,
They mock at thy weakness now – who once fled from thy flaming spear.

Now thou art cold on the mountains – buried and silent and blind –
Dumb as the hills and the stars, blind as the waves of the sea.
A clatter of treacherous tongues goes railing along the wind
And many an evil word is spoken in hatred of thee.

Was it Fergus whose envious breath first cast o'er thy shining name
A poison of venomous words in the midst of the mourning host,
Till thy glory shone before them a wicked and perilous flame,
And thy beauty seemed but a snare, thy valour an empty boast?

They have buried thy golden deeds under the cairn on the
hill,
    And no one shall sing of thy hero soul in the days to
come;
For the sky is blue with silence, and the stars are very still,
    The sea lies dreaming about thee, even the mountains are
dumb.

THE HARPER'S SONG OF SEASONS

The wind that blows among the apple-trees
    Is as a harp of sorrow in the spring,
Piercing the sunshine of sweet melodies
    With the sharp crying of a silver string –
Yet there are white blooms on the apple-trees.

The wind that blows among the apple-trees
    Makes musical the brazen summer hours,
And gladdens the loud hosting of the bees
    With sweet scents torn from many honeyed flowers,
Where the fruit reddens on the apple-trees.

The wind that blows among the apple-trees
    Dies into silence on the wintry air,
And breathes but iron sleep for the world's ease,
    When the leaves fall and every bough is bare,
And sunshine fails among the apple-trees.

The wind that blows among the apple-trees
    Haunts the cold caverns of my frozen mind
With dreams and sorrows and sweet memories,
    What are they but the crying of the wind ...
The wind that blows among the apple-trees?

The wind that blows among the apple-trees
  Of my desire, breaks through the world's control,
And shakes with many secret melodies
  The silver harp-string twisted round my soul ...
Where the stars shine above the apple-trees.

LAMENT OF THE DAUGHTERS OF IRELAND
'In women, too, dwells the Spirit of Battle.'
– Sophocles.

Now is the day of the daughters of Eirinn passed and
gone,
  Forgotten are their great deeds, and their fame has faded
away;
Alas, for one glorious hour, one ray of the sun that shone
  On the gold cathbarr of Maeve, and the might of her
battle array.
As we sit forlorn at the spindle the hours drag slowly on,
  Hour after hour for ever and ever, cold and discoloured
and gray.

Alas, for the deeds of the dead forgotten and out of mind,
  Lavarcam the Wise, and Fand, and the Faery-woman
Feithleen;
Alas, for the sword of Fleeas, red flaming along the wind,
  And Skiah from the Isle of Mists, the dark and terrible
Queen.
Alas, alas, for Bride of the Songs grown feeble and old and
blind,
  Who weeps in the darkness in vain, for the change that
her soul has seen.

We are the daughters of crownèd Queens, the children of
the sword,
  Our mothers went forth to the battle strong-armed and

eager to dare,
Their souls were fierce with freedom, they loved, and they
called no man lord,
   Freely the winds of Eirinn could tangle their loose-
flowing hair.
We who sit by the fireside spinning, gain peace for our
soul's reward,
   And the sword slips out of the grasp of hands grown
white and feeble and fair.

Alas, for the camp, and the great watch-fires, and the
battle-song,
   And the line of glittering cars that thundered over the
plain,
And the grapple hand to hand in the midst of the
maddened throng,
   The swift delight of the sword, the joy that is fiercer than
pain –
Here in the sunny grianan the days are weary and long,
   Weary are we of the sunshine and the cry of the wind
and the rain.

THE QUEEN'S FLIGHT

When the world was young and foolish and fair,
And gold was as nothing to golden hair,

Two mortals met in a forest glade,
A King fell in love with a Beggarmaid.

Dried by the wind and drenched with the dew,
Her dress was a wonderful washed-out blue,

Her shadowy face was pallid and thin,
But gold was the frame that it glimmered in.

Her little bare feet were as hard as stone,
But her hands were the hands of a queen on a throne.

Her hair was loose and her garments were torn,
But her heart was gay as a summer morn.

When the sunlight glittered through serried trees
And the bracken rustled about her knees,

In the thick wood far away from the town
She gathered great heaps of the fir-cones brown;

She carried them down to the city square
And sold them for bread to the people there,

Whilst the idle folk in the market-place
Gave alms for the joy of her lovely face.

When the world was young and golden and green
The Beggarmaid loved and became a Queen.

With never a sigh for the forest shades
Nor a tear for its dim-lit colonnades,

She went forth to live amongst men and reign
Thronèd in vanity over the vain;

In flowing garments of velvet and vair,
With a crown of gold on her golden hair,

She sat on an ivory throne all day
Till the world grew weary and old and gray.

She sat on her ivory throne and sighed,
'The palace is narrow, the world is wide.'

On golden dishes the feast was spread,
But she longed for a wayside crust of bread;

Her robe was of velvet through and through,
But she sighed for a gown of the washed-out blue.

Her heart was sore when she thought of the King,
'This life that he praised is a bitter thing,

Alas!' she said, 'and I would I were free,
For love is but dust and ashes to me.'

She tore off her robe of velvet and vair,
And she took the crown from her golden hair;

Then she put on her gown of washed-out blue,
And she laughed aloud as she used to do.

She went to the King in her rags arrayed,
'Ah, the Queen is dead,' said the Beggarmaid.

And away she fled in the night alone,
Her little bare feet were as hard as stone;

Her shadowy face was shrunken and pale,
But her eyes were as bright as a fairy-tale;

Her dress was faded and ravelled and torn,
But her heart was gay as a summer morn.

Through the long soaking grass she hurried down,
She paused when she came to the sleeping town.

'Good people,' she said, 'sleep on, take your rest,
But you shall not be blest as I am blest.

'Behold, I am free, that was once a Queen,
I will seek my hut in the forest green –

'The walls of the city are narrow and strong,
Bringing great peace to the cowardly throng:

'When the battle raged in the plain outside
And many a patriot fought and died,

'The walls of the city the foe withstood –
Better I love the green walls of the wood;

'The gates of the city are carven fair,
All gateless stands the blue arch of the air;

'The castle ramparts are stately and high,
No fort defends the free dome of the sky;

'The King's hall is guarded by bolt and bar –
Behold, I am free as the wild things are.

'Alas, for all souls bound fast with a chain
To the wheel of fortune – the wheel of pain –

'At the heart of the city the goddess stands
Turning and turning with bloodstained hands.

'My soul grows weary, my senses reel
At the giddy round of the whirling wheel.

'The people rejoice that the wheel flies fast,
But all men are ground in the dust at last.

'The voice of the forest is low and sweet,
I will tread the dead leaves under my feet;

'Where great boughs shiver and sway in the breeze,
The bracken shall rustle about my knees.

'Though I eat my bread with labour and tears,
Sounds of the forest shall ring in my ears.

'Though I grow old and weary and wise,
Sights of the forest shall gladden my eyes.

'I have little delight in human words,
My heart goes out to the song of the birds;

'I care not at all for sceptre or crown –
But I love the smell of the fir-cones brown.

'The world grows old and its sorrows increase,
But the forest's soul is the soul of peace.'

Her feet were frozen and drenched with the dew,
And her dress was soaking through and through.

But she laughed aloud in her youth and mirth,
Her eyes were bright with the joy of the earth.

Then away she wandered over the plain –
For the Queen was a Beggarmaid again.

THE WATERS OF LIFE

'Nor deemed I that thy decrees were of such force, that
a mortal could over-ride the unwritten and unfailing
laws of Heaven. For that life is not of to-day or
yesterday but from all time.'
– *Antigone to the King*

Forth from her lofty spirit the wild deed
    Rushed like a torrent from the mountain height
Unswerving to its end, a rapture freed
    By the swift tumult of its giddy flight
From the long narrow channel down the hill,
    Fierce with the stored-up force of streams that rise
In the deep waters of a Rebel Will,
    The hidden waters of the Brave and Wise,
That move the earth's heart with strange secret powers
    Stirring the idle slumbers of the wheat,
They soak the bitter roots of the wild flowers –
    The buried springs that keep the whole world sweet.

THE WISE HERMIT

A hermit dwells alone by the lost stream
    Of living waters long since sunk and dried,
Where the brown lark once bathed her broken wing,
    He mourns the silent voices of the tide.

Once, like night birds drawn by a lighthouse flame,
    From jungle cave and lair and secret den,
The fierce-eyed dreamers of the forest came
    To seek the stream lost now to gods and men.

The thirsty tiger left her bloodstained cave,
    And of the waters of the well drank deep;
Wolves slew no more, among wild deer grown brave
    The lion and the lamb lay down to sleep.

Now do all wild things follow their wild prey,
    Death out of death and war from war has grown;
And the pale hermit, weeping night and day,
    Mourns by the dead stream broken and alone.

Once, long ago, clear water from the well
  Gleamed in the hollow of his outstretched hand,
His soul shrank back afraid, the great drops fell,
  Lost in devouring waves of the gray sand.

Now here he dwells in a long, patient dream,
  For he has fashioned a great golden cup
Ready to plunge into the living stream,
  And gather all her flowing sweetness up.

Faithful he waits beside the buried spring
  Until the fountain of clear water flows;
Then to the world his golden cup he'll bring,
  And we shall know what the wise hermit knows.

A MOMENT'S INSIGHT

Beyond the smoke there burns a veilèd fire,
  Behind the horizon sails a ship of dreams,
Yet in the night of deeds and dull desire
  The earth that blinds our eyes our Mother seems.

Lo, now the smoke rolls her thick cloud away,
  And white sails gleam on the horizon line;
Fierce Pity whispers in the ears of clay,
  And broken gods still know themselves divine.

THE ONE AND THE MANY
(1904)

THE ONE AND THE MANY

Peaceful as evening, white as hawthorn boughs,
Dark as the sea, tumultuous from of old,
Beauty has built her shrine on many brows,
And her dreams are manifold.

White hawthorn boughs make heaven of the blue sky,
White daisies mob the green ways of the ground,
White waves at twilight, breaking sigh on sigh,
Pass beyond sight or sound.

We who have seen the spirit of the spring
Die downward to the lowly life of grass,
Whilst the dark earth holds fast each soaring wing –
Dream that all dreams must pass.

Yet Beauty, robed in silence and white Peace,
Leans from the stars and fills not any grave,
Nor ceases when the daisies fade and cease,
Nor breaks with the broken wave.

Deeper than twilight, whiter than the may,
Lo, she hath built her house of wind and sun,
Her coloured robe may change from day to day,
But the soul of Beauty is One.

IN THE PINEWOODS

Here the white stars brood high above the austere pines,
And the long pine stems seem to gather up the shadowy
stream
Of the earth's beauty, all her flowing curves and rapturous
lines,
Folded together and lifted up in a long ecstatic dream.

Here in the silent wood Beauty and Peace join hands at
last,
And all the wars of the world have shrivelled and fallen
away,
For the winds of an Unknown Will are blowing out of the
Vast,
And the soul of the world grows one with the lips that pity
and pray.

THE EYES OF THE BLIND

Through the wise books that trouble the world
Ye seek but ye shall not find,
For no scroll that was ever unfurled
Can open the eyes of the blind.

The open-hearted Mystery
Still slumbers among the hills,
And her thoughts are the stars of the sky,
But her dreams are daffodils.

Her moods are the light of running streams
That break into foam and pass,
Where the sunset of her sorrow gleams
The dew lies hoar on the grass.

Her pity softens the twilight wind,
Her hands that are cool with dew,
Shall open at last the eyes of the blind –
And her love is the heaven's blue.

OCTOBER

The sleepless light of morning drives every cloud away,
Shining on a garden space of blue and sunny hours,
But the dreaming twilight holds the secret of the day,
Forgotten by its sunshine and hidden from its flowers.

The rainbow-coloured robe of spring is delicate and dear,
And bright with the unfolding of many eager wings,
But the wise October is the Dreamer of the Year,
And the Autumn twilight holds the secret of all things.

PEACE

The long and waving line of the blue hills
Makes rhythmical the twilight, no sharp peak
Pierces the kind air with a rough-hewn will
To storm the sky, no soaring mountains seek
To break the melody of the flowing line,
But the hills wander on in a long wave,
And all the while invisible stars shine
Over the sea and the white cairn of Maeve.

THE QUEST

For years I sought the Many in the One,
I thought to find lost waves and broken rays,
The rainbow's faded colours in the sun –
The dawns and twilights of forgotten days.

But now I seek the One in every form,
Scorning no vision that a dewdrop holds,

The gentle Light that shines behind the storm,
The Dream that many a twilight hour enfolds.

SYMBOLS

I have seen the dreams of the world in a rose that the
winds have slain,
And the flower of Life flaming gold in the blue shrine of
the Light,
The cry of a mystical harp shudders clear through the cold
spring rain,
And the twilight is folded in round a dream of the Infinite.

For a moonray has slipped from my soul to the mirror of
my mind,
And lights up the shows of the world, changing its
diamonds to dew –
But the words and the deeds of men are as smoke that
darkens the wind –
Black smoke from the mills of the world blown across the
unfaltering blue.

THE REVOLT AGAINST ART

The earth bends to her will, the obdurate marble serves
Her dream, flowing about her soul in gracious lines,
Rose white as sunlit waves – a mystery of pale curves
Flung up in palace towers or dreaming over shrines.

One Beauty moulds the fragile clay in many forms,
Till men who build seem but the shadow of strange
powers,

And the wild southern sea with all her clouds and storms,
Bends low beneath the yoke of a white host of towers.

So doth the round arch of the blue air Byzantine
Seem but the jewelled slave of her enthroned desire,
Yet far from the unfolding of her loveliest line,
Burn the free spiral flames and cones of wind-blown fire.

I have seen broken vails of twilight folded round
A purer mystery than the rich marble holds,
Where from of old the mountain-throned Beauty frowned
On carven forms divine, and towers inlaid with gold.

The Austere Beauty with proud ætherial brows,
Moulds not the dusty clay, thinks scorn of the hard stone,
But, through her dreams, the shadow of forest boughs
Wave o'er the towers of the world, broken and
overthrown.

FROM THE WEST COAST

Here the Atlantic breakers shake the shore
And wild winds blast the life of grass and trees,
Brave rocks are broken in that endless war,
The very earth seems driven to her knees.

Fearless the sea-pink grows on the bare stone,
Her wan face lifted to the wind and wave,
Even as the Lonely turns to the Alone,
And the brave soul is rooted in the Brave.

'THE GREAT GOD HAS BEEN RELEASED FROM DARKNESS'

The sun that flames in the East, the Light-giver, Agni, Lord
of the House of Gold,
Rose radiant in Heaven and scattered afar the Gray
Maidens of the Dawn,
And men turned their eyes to the Light, and worshipped a
Majesty burning and old,
Till a fire sprang up in the soul of the wise, and delight,
and a new song was born.

But here under heavy boughs that droop over rain-
haunted pools in the West,
Whilst the daughters of Mannanan croon at sunset their
old and shadowy rune,
We, the children of dreams, who wander beside pale
waters where waves are at rest,
Have made a song for the white Life-giver, the Lonely –
the silver-souled Moon.

THE ANCIENT WISDOM

Time in dark underground dungeons brought the pale
seed to birth,
Whilst the slow array of the seasons shed sunshine, and
the centuries watered the sod,
Till the Tree of Knowledge grew silently towering out of
the darkness of earth,
And the sun's face was veiled in a mist of green boughs
like the face of an angry God.
But the broken dream that fell long ago from the far blue
deeps of the twilight skies,
Carved in the likeness of gods forgotten, great-browed
desolate Powers Divine,

Like a star that gleams in the blue abyss, or a moonlit wave in the soul of the Wise,
In the innermost chancel of dreams shall brood, o'er a secret and shadowy shrine.

THE CITY

On through the iron day each stone-bound square
The soul of the green grass entombèd hides,
The buried Spirit of the Wise and Fair
Imprisoned in the earth's heart still abides.

Then evening passes cool hands o'er the town,
Making a dream, against the conquering skies,
Of giant Labour-houses that crush down
The buried Spirit of the Fair and Wise.

As prisoners count the ray of sunshine dear
That filters dimly through their prison bars;
So my heart burns to feel the twilight near,
And the far presence of the inviolate stars.

Then does the Spirit of the Wise and Fair
Break from her sepulchre and walk the town,
The iron bonds are loosened everywhere –
No pavement gray can crush the green grass down.

A DREAM

Behind the scenes, before the play,
I watched the spirits dress their parts:
They decked themselves in robes of clay,
With patient skill and finished arts.

One moulds in beauty a white face,
One blurs the outline coarse and rough,
One wraps herself in furs and lace,
And one goes clad in tattered stuff.

One soul has got a golden crown,
Of strutting pride she takes her fill,
Another gambols as a clown
With all her limbs at her own will.

One paints a pale ancestral woe
On high cheek bones and pencilled brow,
One has a world to overthrow,
And one goes forth to drive the plough.

One fills with heavy words and long
The measure of man's patience up,
Whilst one pours out the shining song
Like wine into a golden cup.

ne dreams a joyous dream and dear,
And smiles on life with flashing eyes,
One carves on furrowed brows austere
The deep-set wrinkles of the wise.

One wraps herself in raiment fine
And poses as a warrior-lord,
One thinks the human form Divine,
And Life herself her own reward.

Content one gains her heart's desire
In carven beauty clear and trim,
Whilst one seeks for the Sacred Fire
To mould her rugged features dim.

But ever all the spirits said,
'We swathe our limbs in robes of clay

And veil our lightning from the dead,
And hide our secret selves away.

Behind the brows of king or slave
The selfsame secret lingers still,
The Rich, the Poor, the Base, the Brave
Can but in dreams our dream fulfil.'

INFLUENCE

Ye who would mould men's souls unto your tyrannous
will,
And soften the tiger's heart, and make the wild deer
brave,
Can ye then lower the crest of one most gentle wave?
Or shift the flowing lines of the dim absolute hill?

The soul stands like a mountain strong against cloud and
storm,
On the face of wave-built waters is the spirit shed,
And none are formless save the indifferent lost dead –
For the immortal carven spirit itself is form.

THERE IS NO AGE

There is no age, this darkness and decay
Is by a radiant spirit cast aside,
Young with the ageless youth that yesterday
Bent to the yoke of flesh immortal pride.

What though in time of thunder and black cloud
The Spirit of the Innermost recedes

Into the depths of Being, stormy browed,
Obscured by a long life of dreams and deeds –

There is no age – the swiftly passing hour
That measures out our days of pilgrimage
And breaks the heart of every summer flower,
Shall find again the child's soul in the sage.

There is no age, for youth is the divine;
And the white radiance of the timeless soul
Burns like a silver lamp in that dark shrine
That is the tired pilgrim's ultimate goal.

THE THISTLE

There's no shade in the woods, through the moveless fir
branches the sunlight streams down,
Lying thick on the roots and mosses, and delicate fronds of
wild fern,
And the gray hills stand carven about us like the cold dead
walls of a town,
And the pines are as pillars, the mountains like marble
towers at sunset burn,
Yet here on the sunburnt heights of the world the springs
of the cool rivers are,
Up here on the high mountain meadow, lost to the life of
the plain below,
The thistle has bloomed in a great white flower that
dreams on the grass like a star –
For out of sharp darkness and sword blades in silence the
light of the world must grow –
Whilst away on the distant mountain side the torrent
thunders afar,
And the thirsty valley stretches her lips to meet the cold
touch of the snow ...

Oh ye men who have built up the marble, and carved out
your hearts in the stone,
Behold, the white flower in the meadow was shaped by
the hands of a God,
By the storms of the world your high towers shall be
blasted and overthrown,
But the white thistle flower is rooted firm in the will of the
life-giving sod.

THE INNER LIGHT

Between the mountains and the sea
I trod last night on holy ground,
Standing beside the quicken tree,
I saw no sight, I heard no sound.

Between the darkness and the light
Vainly the haunted hour stood still,
Void of all vision came the night,
No magic fire burnt on the hill.

The mystic earth seemed but dull ground
And empty wastes of wood and sea,
Yet deep in my deep heart I found
The druid vision of the Sidhe.

I stand between the night and day
Once more in the dim world of dreams,
And over miles of glimmering gray
Far out at sea the sunset gleams.

Now between silence and a song
Once more the haunted hour stands still,
About my path the pale dreams throng,
And magic fires burn on the hill.

Through the greenlands a strange voice glides,
And lights flash near the quicken tree,
Yet deep in the deep soul abides
The druid vision of the Sidhe.

THE LADDERS OF LIFE

The heart of Life is lifted up with eager pride of birth.
The monkeys, throned among the beasts in almost human
shape,
Fling down their scorns on serpent forms left writhing on
the earth;
And snakes despise the helpless worm as men despise the
ape.

When sunshine and green shades serene the pleasant
hours divide,
The radiant lily holds her head high amongst dreams and
flowers,
No man may flout the crimson rout of the gay rose's
pride,
Who flaunts her royal flag above the garden's gracious
powers.

Oh silver lilies, rainbow lit, are ye the Fairest Fair,
Oh men who knit your brows in wrath are ye the Wisest
Wise?
Lo! moonlight gleams in silver dreams about a spirit's
hair,
And Wisdom dwells in the clear deeps of great untroubled
eyes.

Red rose, there is another rose that mocks your crimson
fine,
The rose that is the world's despair and wet with sacred

dew,
Though none ascend, all Ladders end in the one Dream
Divine,
Ye men who scorn the beasts, perchance calm eyes look
down on you.

The gods who dwell beyond our dreams have cast our
prayers away,
The angels leaning from their thrones have dealt us scorn
for scorn;
The monkey's pride that dares divide our brotherhood of
clay
Is hushed before the Life Unseen, Unknown, Undreamed,
Unborn.

Yet one fair truth amid the shades the troubled soul
discerns,
One ray of light Divine has pierced the world's
rainbattered roof,
In every shape of man or ape the sacred fire burns,
And God is buried in our clay though angels hold aloof.

ASPIRATION

Soul of the acorn buried in the sod,
Lord of high trees and sunset-haunted hills,
Planter of primroses and Very God
Of the bright daffodils,

Pity the weakness of the growing grain –
And drench our fields with rain.

Soul of the Light and Spirit of the Sword,
Flash one great thought through hosts of huddled years,
God of great deeds and dream-inspired Lord

Of pity and of tears,
Pity the weary ploughman's barren toil –
Cast sunshine on the soil.

Dream of dim lights and twilight-haunted wind,
Spirit that moves upon the waters' face,
Lighten the wave-washed caverns of the mind
With a pale starry grace:
Pity the midnight hours of Death and Birth,
Bring Hope back to the earth.

TIME

The soul would know the rhythm and sound of time
As men know music, cunning to divide
Into dull bars a melody sublime,
Breaking the song's wings, crushing down her pride,

They follow her swift steps among the flowers;
Thus do we break the radiance of the whole
Into this rainbow prism of days and hours,
Splitting the absolute glory of the soul.

Then like a milky way of many stars,
The manifold pale fires are brought to birth,
And men grope blindly against iron bars,
And pain and disappointment walk the earth.

THE TRUCE OF GOD

The wind has fallen at last, and the daylight has faded
away,
Peace lies on the hills and the sea, and peace on the rain-

drenched sod,
And the evening dreams in pity o'er the battlefields of the
day;
But those who shoot pigeons at twilight have broken the
Truce of God.

THE MERCIFUL KNIGHT
BURNE-JONES

In the dim twilight-haunted garden
Pardon has met with pardon,
And the proud flashing giant arms divine
That move the worlds, thus gently folded, rest
Long on the dreamer's breast,
Where Pity leans from that harsh cross of pain
That is the inmost and inviolate shrine
Of Him who is the Slayer and the Slain.

A SPIRIT IN PRISON

Oh pale discrownèd brow and quenchèd eyes,
And thick dull flesh, like heavy clods of clay,
Building a grave where some sad sleeper lies
Half drenched in dreams, half conscious of decay.

This is the mystery of prison bars
That guard the dusty windows of the mind,
Holding a long-lost glory from the stars,
And a free spirit from the roaming wind.

Yet shalt thou see beyond the nerveless brain
In the dark chambers of unknown desire,

A dim face pressed against the window pane –
Behind the quenchèd eyes immortal fire.

THE WEAVER

I was the child that passed long hours away
Chopping red beetroot in the hay-piled barn;
Now must I spend the wind-blown April day
Minding great looms and tying knots in yarn.

Once long ago I tramped through rain and slush
In brown waves breaking up the stubborn soil,
I wove and wove the twilight's purple hush
To fold about the furrowed heart of toil.

Strange fires and frosts burnt out the seasons' dross,
I watched slow Powers the woven cloth reveal,
While God stood counting out His gain and loss,
And Day and Night pushed on the heavy wheel.

Held close against the breast of living Powers
A little pulse, yet near the heart of strife,
I followed the slow plough for hours and hours
Minding through sun and shower the loom of life.

The big winds, harsh and clear and strong and salt,
Blew through my soul and all the world rang true,
In all things born I knew no stain or fault,
My heart was soft to every flower that grew.

The cabbages in my small garden patch
Were rooted in the earth's heart; wings unseen
Throbbed in the silence under the dark thatch,
And brave birds sang long ere the boughs were green.

Once did I labour at the living stuff
That holds the fire, the water and the wind;
Now do I weave the garments coarse and rough
That some vain men have made for vain mankind.

THE DESOLATE ARMY

In the world's wars we have no lot nor part,
No tattered flag, no sound of trampling feet
Thrills the dark caverns of a nation's heart
For us, no battle song makes danger sweet.

In the world's praise and love we have no place,
We have not turned the drunkard from his wine –
Nor toiled to build fine dwellings for the race –
Nor burnt new incense at an ancient shrine.

Yet have we seen a glimpse of radiant forms
Behind the blackness of these smoke-stained hours,
Where wisdom shines beyond all clouds and storms,
And pity dwells amongst the steadfast powers.

Then divine madness fills the heart and brain
Of the pale army passionately proud –
We toil on dimly through much strife and strain
To unveil those radiant brows unto the crowd.

THE LAND TO A LANDLORD

You hug to your soul a handful of dust,
And you think 'the round world your sacred trust –
But the sun shines, and the wind blows,
And nobody cares and nobody knows.

O the braken waves and the foxgloves flame,
And none of them ever has heard your name –
Near and dear is the curlew's cry,
You are merely a stranger passing by.

Sheer up through the shadows the mountain towers
And dreams wander free in this world of ours, –
Though you may 'turn the grass to gold,
The twilight has left you out in the cold.

Though you are king of the rose and the wheat,
Not for you, not for you is the bog-myrtle sweet,
Though you are lord of the long grass,
The hemlock bows not her head as you pass.

The poppies would flutter amongst the corn
Even if you had never been born,
With your will or without your will
The ragweed can wander over the hill.

Down there in the bog where the plovers call
You are but an outcast after all,
Over your head the sky gleams blue –
Not a cloud or a star belongs to you.

TO A FRIEND

Carve thou thy dream in marble, scrawl it clear
On the high walls of Art above the throng,
Shape it in towers that climb from sphere to sphere,
Fold it in music, mould it into song.

But live it not, nor let the wandering wind
Know of the gentle power in silence born,

For in the ways of men the dreamer's mind
Shall be by dogs devoured, by vultures torn.

Alas, dear heart, along the ways of sense
No glory save the light of gold can shine;
Men strive with angry deeds – ah! get thee hence,
Cast not thy star before these hungry swine.

The song would flood your soul in silver streams,
The tower holds on high the builder's trust,
The marble bends unto the sculptor's dreams,
But men tread out your fire in the dust.

FROM THE GARDEN OF PROSERPINE

I dare not bend the white rose to my will,
Nor break the lilies' stalk, nor idly part
The climbing sweetbriar from the green-clad hill,
Nor steal the emerald's fire from the earth's heart.

Yea, in the spring my fierce desires refrain
From the pale primroses, my hands are cold
To flaming poppies; through the woods in vain
My path is lit with the laburnum's gold.

No rose shall shed for me her delicate leaves,
No bluebell fade and die an hour too soon,
No poppy mourn the cornfield's golden sheaves,
No radiant lily pine for the hot noon.

Harmless I roam amongst the dreams that bloom
In the lost garden, passing them thus by,
Loath to pluck flowers too fair to deck a tomb,
Too bright to thrive under a cloudy sky.

Yet from the secret ways one dream I bring,
One vision braves the harsh unkindly air,
The blighting human touch, the world's cold spring,
The withering Autumn promise everywhere.

Fallen I found this broken branch of may
That once soared high above the bluebell towers,
Now in my soul it blooms from day to day,
White with the joy of lost immortal hours.

'THE SOUL ATTAINS'

Oh strife too short, oh victory too dear,
Deep in the artist's soul the flame burns cold,
Freed from the goad of dreams, the lash of fear,
He who attains, remembers, and grows old.

Oh youthfulness of failure, the long hours
Of uncrowned labour, unregarded toil,
Are as the wintry seed of the spring flowers,
The starry Hope that blossoms near the soil.

Is there not precious metal to be wrung
From the earth's heart and the streams' secret ways,
The stories not yet told, the songs unsung,
The dreams undreamed – oh, fair beyond all praise,

Like treasure buried underneath a hill,
In some sea-guarded isle, or barren land,
They wait the labour of the hero's will –
The magic touch of the adventurer's hand.

Joy dwells in austere deeds, the perilous climb
That leads tired footsteps to the mountain height,

And music trembles in the halting rhyme
That scales with lagging steps the hill of light.

Still are the world's unseen yet crownèd powers,
The courage and the ecstasy of toil,
And the sweet wind-blown breath of the wild flowers,
The starry Hope that blossoms near the soil.

LIS-AN-DOILL

Once in the year the ancient world grows young,
For me alone there is no dream of spring,
Alas there are many songs to be sung –
New songs and old – I am too old to sing,

Songs of the constant world that never grows
Tired of green boughs – impatient of the may –
That waits for the unfolding of the rose,
On fire with hope to-day as yesterday.

I am too old – I pass the daisies by,
And tread the grass down under tired feet,
Time washes all the blue out of the sky –
The very violets are no longer sweet.

Even the constant spring is false to me,
Not all the rosebuds ever yet unfurled,
Nor any dream of roses yet to be,
Can reconcile me to this evil world.

Once in the year the young spring's green and gold
Gleams in the sun and rustles in the wind;
Alas! there is neither light for the old,
Nor any dream of colour for the blind.

THE LITTLE WAVES OF BREFFNY

The grand road from the mountain goes shining to the
sea,
And there is traffic in it and many a horse and cart,
But the little roads of Cloonagh are dearer far to me,
And the little roads of Cloonagh go rambling through my
heart.

A great storm from the ocean goes shouting o'er the hill,
And there is glory in it and terror on the wind,
But the haunted air of twilight is very strange and still,
And the little winds of twilight are dearer to my mind.

The great waves of the Atlantic sweep storming on their
way,
Shining green and silver with the hidden herring shoal,
But the Little Waves of Breffny have drenched my heart in
spray,
And the Little Waves of Breffny go stumbling through my
soul.

MONNA LISA
LEONARDO DA VINCI

Her narrow eyelids radiantly obscure,
Veiling the profound smile of her strange eyes,
Trouble the Well where the world's secret lies
Lost in blue grottos icy cold and pure,
Deep in the buried spirit of the Wise.

LA PENSÉE
RODIN

Hiding in mazes of marble her chin sunk deep in the
stone,
She breaks away from the senses five, the warders of the
soul,
Alone in the wind-swept deeps of Being she seeks the
Alone,
The adventurer's innermost light, the dreamer's perilous
goal.

THE LOST STREAM

Down this dry watercourse once long ago
The Living Waters strong and clear and cold,
Fresh from the mountain summit and the snow,
Shining with dreams, into the valley rolled.

Now the green valley mourns, the rock-hewn bed
Of the loud torrent lies sunstruck and still,
The wild flowers droop, the very grass is dead,
And the tired traveller faints on the parched hill.

THE PLACE OF PEACE

The Fear that lurks in the crowded street
And hides in the market-place,
And follows the stranger with unseen feet
And a half-averted face,
Shall fly from the silence that sanctifies
The lonely wood and the wind's held breath,

From the sorrows of fools, and the dreams of the wise,
And the shadows that darken the gates of death.

CLAIRVOYANTE
'Nothing that is vast enters into the life of mortals
without a curse.'
– Antigone.

Long ago a spirit was torn from the fire of the opal
spheres,
To light the lamp of the world with a spark from the
infinite,
Though dull is the lamp and stained with the smoke of the
dusty years,
Behind the dark glass burns ever a magic circle of light.

Comrade, your soul goes crowned with an aura of
gracious rays,
Burning brighter about your brow as the sunbeams fade
and cease –
For passion and pity and love are the moonlight of your
days,
But in my soul is a flame of the pitiless astral peace.

Wings that are pale with dreaming or folded in flaming
wrath,
Crowd round us rainbow-hued through the shadows of
dread and desire;
But in the mirror my soul has the shrivelled wings of a
moth,
Blackened and blistered and scorched by the magic circle
of fire.

THE TRAVELLERS
(TO E.G.R.)

Was it not strange that by the tideless sea
The jar and hurry of our lives should cease?
That under olive boughs we found our peace,
And all the world's great song in Italy?

Is it not strange though Peace herself has wings
And long ago has gone her separate ways,
On through the tumult of our fretful days
From Life to Death the great song chimes and rings?

In that sad day shall then the singing fail,
Shall Life go down in silence at the end,
And in the darkness friend be lost to friend,
And all our love and dreams of no avail?

You whose Love's melody makes glad the gloom
Of a long labour and a patient strife,
Is not that music greater than our life?
Shall not a little song outlast that doom?

THE PROUD PHILOSOPHER

Plotinus , like a proud and idle boy
Ashamed to study in the lowest class,
Himself the comrade of the sons of joy,
Disdained the secrets of the earthbound grass.

He sought not beauty in the dawn's pale fire,
Nor sorrow in the stream of human tears,
But mourned the broken wings of his desire,
And loved the songs of far ancestral spheres.

He knew whence he had come, there was no bar
Between his spirit, into darkness hurled,
And the blue deeps that mocked him from afar,
Dreaming in sorrow over a lost world –

Shrinking before his mighty comrade's scorn,
He hid from men the country of his birth,
For shame and grief to think he had been born
Far from the spheres of light on this dull earth.

Unmoved he passed through mystic twilight hours,
Flouted the very sunset on the hill,
Brother of shadowy, proud, immortal powers,
Child of the spirit's iridescent will.

He who thus claimed high lineage rent the vail
Between the worlds, and tore away the cloud
That hides the snowclad summit from the dale –
The world is fairer for the Pure and Proud.

THE INCARNATE

Deep in the soul there throbs the secret pain
Of one homesick for dear familiar things,
When Spring winds rock the waves of sunlit rain
And on the grass there falls the shadow of wings.

How should one bend one's dreams to the dark clay
Where carven beauty mixed with madness dwells?
And men who fear to die fear not to slay,
And Life has built herself ten thousand hells.

No wave that breaks in music on the shore
Can purify the tiger's bloodstained den,

The worms that crawl about the dark world's core
Cry out aloud against the deeds of men.

Alas, the peace of these still hours and deep
Is but a dream that wanders from afar,
And the great Dreamer, turning in His sleep,
Smothers in darkness all our little star.

Yet in the gentle spirit of the wise
Light flashes out through many a simple thing,
The tired ploughman, with impassive eyes,
Knows in his heart that he was once a king.

He sees in dreams the crown long lost and dear,
That glittered on a fallen spirit's brow,
A shattered gleam from some far shining sphere
Has dazed the eyes of him who drives the plough.

The long brown furrows of the broken soil
Lead in straight lines unto the sunset's gates;
On high green hills, beyond the reach of toil,
The vision of the twilight broods and waits.

The silence folded in about the heart
Whispers strange longings to the broken soul,
That lingers in a lonely place apart,
Stretching vain hands to clasp the secret whole.

PROSERPINE IN HADES

Prosèrpina , who sought for poppies, fell
Beyond the reach of summer and sweet flowers,
Content to reign amongst the Lords of Hell,
Queen of gray shades and dreams and outcast Powers.

Was she content? – nay, Charon saw her weep,
When Orpheus came from the bright world above,
And sang his way across the twilight deep,
And found and lost his unforgotten love.

Was she not dreaming of fair meadow lands,
And sunlit rivers, when that Other came,
And the spheres broke like glass beneath His hands,
And souls rushed forth in spires of wandering flame?

The Light beyond all dreams of hours and days,
The Songs that break their way from sphere to sphere,
In broken gleams they pierced the sunless ways,
And bound her soul to hopes that once were dear.

PROSERPINE ENTHRONED

All day she reigns in dreams amongst the dead,
At night, strong-winged, she flames across the skies,
O'er the dark world her floods of light are shed,
The silver goddess of the pure and wise.

Oh soul that gropes on through the drowsy day
Amongst dead thoughts and deeds and fading flowers,
Dost thou not leave at night the foolish clay,
To join the starry throng of radiant Powers?

Rising amongst the gods on moonlit wings,
Dost thou not drive thy fiery wingèd steeds
Right through the sheer abyss and soul of things,
Forgetting the dull round of dreams and deeds?

Incarnate Spirit fallen from great light,
Doomed many days in darkness to endure,

Thou art yet Proserpine – the Queen of Night –
The Silver Goddess of the Wise and Pure.

THE BODY TO THE SOUL

You have dragged me on through the wild wood ways,
You have given me toil and scanty rest,
I have seen the light of ten thousand days
Grow dim and sink and fade in the West.

Once you bore me forth from the dusty gloom,
Weeping and helpless and naked and blind,
Now you would hide me deep down in the tomb,
And wander away on the moonlit wind.

You would bury me like a thing of shame,
Silently into the darkness thrust,
You would mix my heart that was once a flame
With the mouldering clay and the wandering dust.

The eyes that wept for your sorrowful will
Shall be laid among evil and unclean things,
The heart that was faithful through good and ill
You scorn for a flutter of tawdry wings.

You were the moonlight, I lived in the sun;
Could there ever be peace between us twain?
I sought the Many, you seek the One,
You are the slayer, I am the slain.

Oh soul, when you mount to your flame-built throne
Will you dream no dream of the broken clay?
Will you breathe o'er the stars in your pathway strown,
No sigh for the daisies of yesterday?

As you wander the shining corridors,
A lonely wave in the ocean of light,
Have you never a thought of the lake's lost shores,
Or the fire-lit cottage dim and white?

Shall not the dear smell of the rain-wet soil
Through the windless spheres and the silence float?
Shall not my hands that are brown with toil
Take your dreams and high desires by the throat?

Behold, I reach forth from beyond the years,
I will cry to you from beneath the sod,
I will drag you back from the starry spheres,
Yea, down from the very bosom of God.

You cannot hide from the sun and the wind,
Or the whispered song of the April rain,
The proud earth that moulds all things to her mind,
Shall gather you out of the deeps again.

You shall follow once more a wandering fire,
You shall gaze again on the starlit sea,
You shall gather roses out of the mire:
Alas, but you shall not remember me.

RE-INCARNATION

The darkness draws me, kindly angels weep
Forlorn beyond receding rings of light,
The torrents of the earth's desires sweep
My soul through twilight downward into night.

Once more the light grows dim, the vision fades,
Myself seems to myself a distant goal,

I grope among the bodies' drowsy shades,
Once more the Old Illusion rocks my soul.

Once more the Manifold in shadowy streams
Of falling waters murmurs in my ears,
The One Voice drowns amid the roar of dreams
That crowd the narrow pathway of the years.

I go to seek the starshine on the waves,
To count the dewdrops on the grassy hill,
I go to gather flowers that grow on graves,
The world's wall closes round my prisoned will.

Yea, for the sake of the wild western wind
The spherèd spirit scorns her flame-built throne,
Because of primroses, time out of mind,
The Lonely turns away from the Alone.

Who once has loved the cornfield's rustling sheaves,
Who once has heard the gentle Irish rain
Murmur low music in the growing leaves,
Though he were god, comes back to earth again.

Oh Earth! green wind-swept Eirinn, I would break
The tower of my soul's initiate pride
For a gray field and a star-haunted lake,
And those wet winds that roam the country side.

I who have seen am glad to close my eyes,
I who have soared am weary of my wings,
I seek no more the secret of the wise,
Safe among shadowy, unreal human things.

Blind to the gleam of those wild violet rays
That burn beyond the rainbow's circle dim,
Bound by dark nights and driven by pale days,
The sightless slave of Time's imperious whim;

Deaf to the flowing tide of dreams divine
That surge outside the closèd gates of birth,
The rhythms of eternity, too fine
To touch with music the dull ears of earth –

I go to seek with humble care and toil
The dreams I left undreamed, the deeds undone,
To sow the seed and break the stubborn soil,
Knowing no brightness whiter than the sun.

Content in winter if the fire burns clear
And cottage walls keep out the creeping damp,
Hugging the Old Illusion warm and dear,
The Silence and the Wise Book and the Lamp.

THE SOUL TO THE BODY

The lamp has gone out in your eyes,
The ashes are cold in your heart,
Yet you smile indifferent-wise,
Though I depart – though I depart.

I was the Joy that made you young,
The Light on the moon-haunted sea,
The Soul of each song that was sung,
And the Heart of Mystery.

I was the Harper old and blind,
The Breaker of Waves on the shore,
The Sorrow that cries on the wind –
I weep no more – I weep no more.

I was the Cloud that made your grief
In the gray twilight of the year,

Now you fall like a fallen leaf,
Without a tear – without a tear.

I was the Force that made you strong
From your brain to your finger tips,
And lifted your heart in a song,
And fashioned the words on your lips:

I was the Hour that made you great,
I was the Deed you left undone,
The soul of love – the heart of hate,
I was the Cloud that hid the sun.

I was the Light that made you wise,
I was the Dream that broke your heart –
Now the tears are dry in your eyes
Though I depart – though I depart.

THE THREE RESURRECTIONS
(1905)

THE THREE RESURRECTIONS

I

LAZARUS

Like driven cattle groping in blind herds
The hours passed me by, I stood alone,
And human dreams and light-winged prayers and words
Singed their frail wings about a flame-built throne.

Lost among outward things the poor limbs lay,
Holding no hint of the fled fire divine,
Like painted towers that crumble and decay,
When the God vanishes from some fair shrine.

Then from the broken edge and granite sheer
Of this harsh world, unto her heart of flame
A cry rang inwards, through the secret sphere,
Till the soul trembled at the body's name.

A wild wind sweeping through the fortressed gate
Of fire precipitous, in storms of will,
Did through the fibres of my sould vibrate,
And shook the Lilies on the Holy Hill.

Down in the deep abyss the deep voice sighed;
The pitiless voice that rhythmic tides obey,
Did through the inner courts in whispers glide,
And thrust my soul forth on her lonely way –

Yea, with strange fires down to the crumbling soil,
Amid the shambling herd of days and hours,
Drove the poor soul back to her patient toil,
And bid the slave rebuild her broken towers.

Oh Mary, dreamer without ruth or fear,
Brave through the radiant aether to descend
Into the holiest inner deeps austere,
Was this well done of Him who was thy friend?
Lo, when amid past homely hours serene,
One called to thee for service, thou didst stand
Silent, thine eyes fixed on the Light Unseen,
And the bread broken in thine idle hand.

Did then His voice call back to outward things
The radiant spirit wandering afar?
He bade us not to break the wild bird's wings
With heavy loads, nor wreck our sister's star.

Now does He break Himself the wing that flies
Too far, and quench the starlight on the wind,
Yea, the lost light still dazzles my sad eyes,
And the lost silence haunts my fevered mind.

How shall I thank Him? With but little zest
I grind the corn of Life in His dark mill,
Close to the hard heart of the Manifest,
I grope through days and hours that are His Will.

Ah, Love can drag the soul down from the spheres,
And bind her to the heart of human things,
And turn her high resolves to sighs and tears,
And break her wings, alas, and break her wings.

Still it may be hid treasure on the earth
Shall make this life of shadows worth its cost
Of dust and dreariness and death and birth
And broken wings and blue-lit radiance lost.

And though my soul athwart the great white way
Uncrowned, mysterious, weeping, starry-eyed,

Flared down into her humble house of clay,
Lonely amongst dim meadows to abide,

Yet strange it is that He whose voice rang through
The austere deeps found fire in clay concealed,
Found in the false the likeness of the true,
And His own inner will in each green field.

This thought of all the thoughts that flash and blaze,
Lightens the kingdom of my shadowy trust,
He knew the wisdom of the secret rays
Who drew my soul back to the alien dust.

This is the fixed heart of each changing dream,
The inner light that burns but for the blind –
The gold that lies beneath the flowing stream –
The buried treasure of a lonely mind.

Now He is dead, and no man understands
The mystery folded round each living heart,
What gulfs of mystic seas and unknown lands
Hold every man from his own soul apart.

But He dwelt ever on that desolate verge,
Amid the roar of winds and whirling tides,
And in His soul the moaning of the surge
And broken waters of the world abides.

His hidden thought was veiled by too much light;
Yet even when He wept I understood
That the stars shine on many a moonless night,
And bright streams glitter through the pathless wood.

Each crazy hut, all walls of mud or clay
Can hold the Eternal Beauty's light Divine.

This kingdom fails not, passes not away ...
He said so, who was Mary's friend and mine.

II

THE RETURN OF ALCESTIS

When wise Alcestis, risen from the grave,
Stood by Admetos for whose sake she died,
Her eyes were fierce that once were only brave
And her heart hard with an unearthly pride.

Admetos, the pale King who feared to die,
Feared the dead risen, shrank from the proud Queen,
Her white cheeks flushed with fading ecstasy,
Bright with the radiant breath of the Unseen.

He Knew she saw straight through the kingly guise,
Into his soul's poor garret starved and grim,
Behind the threatening brow and flashing eyes,
Discerned the secret coward soul of him.

'Fear not, Admetos, the long road' – she said –
'Led me through wind and fire, made pure by these,
I bring no deadly vapours from the dead,
No dreadful grave dust clings about my knees.

How shouldst thou, hearing but the last harsh sigh
Of the poor noisy flesh, dream of the smile,
Of the unheard, invisible ecstasy,
Lo, I have lived in light a little while!'

Then did Admetos praise her with soft phrase
And Love's dear silences, but she stood cold,
And slowly the fire died from her white gaze,
And her pale lips, once sweet, grew stern and old.

The King raved, 'Thou whose stony eyes austere,
Lay humbled in the dust that I might live,
Hast thou no love for him once held so dear?'
And naught she answered save 'O King, forgive!'

Men brought her children to her, with cold hands
She touched their hair and left them, murmuring
'No prince or priest or peasant understands
That this our life is but a shadowy thing.'

At last Admetos tired of his dull bride
And went back to his comrades and his wine,
Whilst the cold silent Queen throned at his side,
Dreamed of the Vision and the light divine.

The coward King had but another dread,
A white-faced phantom stood beside his throne;
But sad Alcestis, risen from the dead,
Faced this dark world and her own soul alone.

And Heracles, whose death-defeating sword
Had saved her, looking in her starving eyes,
Knew he had robbed her of that just reward
That crowns the desolate courage of the Wise.

The freed bird comes not for her own delight
Back to the narrow cage and prison bars,
Lo, the wide air scarce held her far-flung flight
What time her will was throned beyond the stars.

III

PSYCHE IN HADES

When Psyche staggered through the darkness dense,
And stood in Hades, still she feared to taste

The feast of the dark gods of clay and sense,
But ate dry bread with tears and fled in haste.

Yet did she bear a gift from Proserpine
To Aphrodite in the spheres of light,
A casket holding the lost dream divine,
The perilous beauty of the Infinite.

As forth she journeyed on her homeward way
The Unseen Light lay clasped against her breast,
And through the darkness piercing ray on ray
Troubled the deeps of the Unmanifest.

Yea, down among the earth's uncared-for things
Rushed forth a sense of greatness unfulfilled,
Till in the darkness secret faëry wings
Deep in the grub's dim being stirred and thrilled.

And daffodils, whose petals of pale gold
Lie folded round the bulb's heart, buried deep,
Seemed in the darkness softly to unfold
As if the sun were shining through their sleep.

Then Psyche journeyed o'er the dangerous hills
And read the secret of forbidden streams,
And gazed into the hearts of daffodils,
And knew life's treasure-house of buried dreams.

Yet some men say the casket of white brass
She brought from Hades with such loving care
Held only the long sleep of flowers and grass,
And silences of dumb things everywhere.

She heeds them not, who knows the hidden worth
Of day and night and twilight, flower and weed,
The strong white roots that shake the crumbling earth
And frail wings of the sycamore seed.

Again she wanders through this world not ours,
Far from the unseen beauty, prison bound,
She seeks to steal the radiance of the flowers,
To ravish the ground's secret from the ground.

She knows no idle dream of fair and foul,
With the same rapturous breath she tells the tale
Of the high soaring lark or the brown owl,
The corncrake or the urgent nightingale.

For her the sea-thrift from her rocky ledge
Blazons the secret of the passing storm,
And briony leaves carve out in the green hedge
The decorate delight of sculptured form.

Her will the universal will allows,
The snake's dark poison, yea, and the wasp's sting,
She has no special favour for May boughs,
Nor craves long life for the frail painted wing.

And we in this dull house of tears and clay
Seek but her treasure, labouring everyone
To take the starlight with us on our way
Or steal some fire of beauty from the sun,

Till, in the darkness, banished Proserpine
Flashes her fierce torch in our shrinking eyes,
And thrusts into our hands the gift divine,
The magic treasure casket of the Wise.

Thus, when we pass again the long-closed door
That leads unto the Real, we bear afar
The will of seaweed on the barren shore,
The thought that holds in heaven star on star.

The riches of new powers accumulate
Have made of dying herdsmen gods and kings,

Life takes with both hands all the gifts of fate,
Till each poor soul grows worthy of her wings.

Oh, whiteness of the dawn and sacred fire,
The folded strength of the light sycamore seed,
And the hid rose's heart in the wild brier,
Are all the incarnate spirit's utter need.

THE UNKNOWN GOOD

All dreams seem but a bunch of withered flowers
Beside the living joy from anguish rent;
We wrestle with the world's embattled powers
To mould the outline of the fair event.

With labour each great deed is hammered out,
On every battle-field the dead are strown,
Fair truth is carven out of anguished doubt,
The builder's heart lies crushed beneath the stone.

The price of every joy the soul may gain
Is paid in blood and sighing and sharp tears,
Who is a miser of the hoard of pain,
Shall win no great good from the crafty years.

Because the Ferry-man still takes his toll
Of fear and agony and sobbing breath,
Because of the torn fibres of the soul,
I know there is a great good gained by death.

POVERTY

One swallow dared not trust the idle dream
That called her South through fading skies and gray,
One spirit feared to follow the wild gleam
That drives the soul forth on her starlit way.

As the starved swallow on the frozen wold
Lies dying, with her swift wings stiff and furled,
So does the soul grow colder and more cold,
In the dark winter of this starless world.

Poorer than slaves of any vain ideal,
These are the saddest of all living things –
Souls that have dreamed the Unseen Light unreal,
And birds without the courage of their wings.

THE PERILOUS LIGHT

The Eternal Beauty smiled at me
From the long lily's curvèd form,
She laughed in a wave of the sea,
She flashed on white wings through the storm.

In the bulb of a daffodil
She made a little joyful stir,
And the white cabin on the hill
Was my heart's home because of her.

Her laughter fled the eyes of pride,
Barefoot she went o'er stony land,
And ragged children hungry-eyed
Clung to her skirts and held her hand.

When storm winds shook the cabin door
And red the Atlantic sunset blazed,
The fisher folk of Mullaghmore
Into her eyes indifferent gazed.

By lonely waves she dwells apart,
And seagulls circling on white wings
Crowd round the windows of her heart,
Most dear to her of starving things.

The ploughman down by Knocknarea
Was free of her twilight abode;
In shining sea winds salt with spray,
She haunted every gray cross-road.

Some peasants with a creel of turf
Along the wind-swept boreen came,
Her feet went flashing through the surf,
Her wings were in the sunset's flame.

Beyond the rocks of Classiebawn
The mackerel fishers sailing far
Out in the vast Atlantic dawn
Found, tangled in their nets, a star.

In every spent and broken wave
The Eternal Beauty takes her rest,
She is the Lover of the Brave,
The comrade of the perilous quest.

The Eternal Beauty wrung my heart,
Faithful is she, and true to shed
The austere glory of Art
On the scarceness of daily bread.

Men follow her with toil and thought
Over the heavens' starry pride,

The Eternal Beauty comes unsought
To the child by the roadside.

NARCISSUS

I gaze at my own form from morn till night,
Reflected in the stream, thus do I find
Great wisdom in flung curves of windblown light,
And am the jest and scorn of all mankind.

The ploughman bending over the dark soil
Dreams himself free and every flower his slave,
Well may he, pausing in his useful toil,
Frown at the thought of such an idle knave.

The shepherd labouring o'er the cloudy height,
The warrior storming the high fortressed hill,
Dream not at all of the Diviner Light,
Or the clear waters of the lonely Will.

The King who rules our lives with flame and sword
Sees not his own face mirrored in the tide,
He knows that every warrior calls him Lord,
And scorns to linger at the river-side.

All these have many deeds: here the dark firs
Dream on the edge of silence, mirrored green;
Deep in the river's magic crystal stirs
The image of the Seen and the Unseen.

Down in the river's heart strange broken dreams
Float luminous and tremble and recede,
And the lost torch of vanished wisdom gleams,
Caught in the green net of the water weed.

I gaze into my own eyes, finding there
The silver flame of Beauty's austere powers,
The sunlight dazzles me from my own hair,
My face is but a flower among the flowers.

Behold each shining curl, in watery curves,
Presses the circle of all living things
To my dull heart; the current breaks and swerves,
And back to heaven the drowning starlight flings.

THE HARVEST OF SILENCE

Gay is the call of the Sower going forth in the morning
refreshed from sleep,
Glad is the song of the Reaper coming home in the evening
laden with sheaves,
But in silence the lonely plough the fields, and sow, and
the patient labourers reap,
And in silence the Reaper comes home empty-handed on
desolate rain-soaked eves.

Beyond the clang of immortal verse, and the prayers of
men and whispers divine,
In the Holy of Holies, where lights burned dim, and only
the Wise Ones might go,
Corn reaped in silence by silent Reapers lay shrined in the
innermost shrine,
Whilst outside in the darkness the priestess fell tranced,
and the god paced to and fro.

ECSTASY
'God holds the soul attracted to Him by its roots.'
– Plato

He who seeks God has yet no need of wings,
Down in the deeps of being a dim road
Leads through the soul unto the roots of things,
And that abyss that is the gods' abode.

There in the elemental caves of night,
And dim recesses of unconscious mind,
The Wise Men's star burns with a steady light,
And a faint whisper lingers on the wind.

THE HUMAN ADVENTURE

On these wave-haunted sands the children play,
And silver twilight, clad in radiant gleams,
Comes laughing down the hill from Knocknarea,
With a gay company of wandering dreams.

The while a dog in careless ecstasy,
Trusting the guidance of a human hand,
Plunges forth headlong into the wild sea,
Brings but a stick and courage back to land.

So in the incarnation of the Wise
At times it seems a light and foolish whim
To brave the abyss for such a doubtful prize,
Plunged in wild waters of the twilight dim.

Yea, the tired spirit struggling with the tide
Of flowing life and monstrous waves of time,
Clutches but feebly her immortal pride,
And clings unto a broken bough of rhyme.

When the strong swimmer rescued from the wave,
Deep in the sunlit grass enraptured lies,
May she hold fast the secret of the grave,
The light of Peril in her dauntless eyes.

TRAGEDY

'The radiance of heaven diffused all about me lifted up
my soul to its own contemplation.'
– The Emperor Julian.

The soul dwells in the body as sunshine
Dwells in the air, wide, radiant, intense,
Drowned in untroubled blue the Light Divine
Would make transparent all the walls of sense.

Across the blue a ragged cloudlet sails,
A little wandering shadow delicate
Vails the sun's face, the supreme glory vails,
So small a cloud can hide a light so great.

A DWELLER BY THE OCEAN

Oh very near the wide Atlantic shore
Is my white cottage homestead dark and low,
No idle neighbours stand about the door,
But great waves storming past the window go.

At times I dream the Atlantic infinite
Watching the sun rise over fields of foam,
And smile to think those floods of gracious light
Flow round the darkness of my narrow home.

When light fades from the green-lit fields of surf,
Wave shadows flicker on the white-washed wall,
I stir to flame the smouldering heap of turf,
And dream of greatness in my cottage small.
Then the wind moans athwart the unquiet sea,
Thin streaks of white across the ocean creep,
And, in my soul, forgotten ecstasy
Stirs restlessly and shudders in her sleep.

But when the bitter storm wind lifts and shakes
My little cottage, least of fragile things,
Out of the deeps of memory awakes
The soul's voice weeping o'er her broken wings.

Again the lost divine procession fair
Crosses the humble threshold of my mind;
A rush of wings makes pure the evening air,
And the dark hour gives sight unto the blind.

Then is the vail of woven fancy rent,
Into the eyes of truth again I gaze,
And read the doom of the long banishment,
My soul shrinks backward from the lightning's blaze.

Not pure enough for vision, and not just
Enough for justice, yet too pure and wise
To be thus lightly mingled with the dust,
And look at earth and sea with clay-built eyes.

Yea, the poor soul, the sorry charioteer,
By wings uplifted, by desire undone,
Seems to my heart that God dethroned and dear
Who yet was Lord of the far-shining sun.

Oh, fallen majesty, austere, unseen,
So weak and captive, easy to forget,

My heart gives homage to the Vailèd Queen,
Phoebus among the herds is Phoebus yet.

I who eat porridge from a wooden bowl,
Whilst one dim candle gutters in the gloom,
Do wonder at the greatness of the soul,
And narrow windows of the little room.

THE FALL

Alas , the twisted evil word.
Under the olives yesterday,
I heard a passing satyr say
Unto the small brown singing bird:
'Oh, fly from these dull garden thieves;
She who plucks daisies in the wood
Will surely come to nothing good.
There is but greenness in green leaves,
Who seeketh beauty findeth woe,
Down where the fairest flowers are,
Though light on light and star on star
The silver shrinèd lilies grow,
Though still the ancient Pan abides
And wild winds to the olives tell
The secrets of the oracle,
Whilst through dim glades the moonlight glides,
Till wood nymphs dream themselves divine,
Behind the twisted boughs and gray
The dark god lies in wait alway,
And the earth gapes for Proserpine ...'
Oh, they are wise, these woodland things,
Yet 'this is but a satyr's tale,
Told unto the nightingale,
And birds are conscious of their wings.

THE GODDESS OF THIS WORLD

'Matter exists for the sake of the Form which it
contains.'
– Proclus

Queen Proserpine , from yonder shining star,
Came long ago to our brown world of clay;
Because of her I keep my door ajar
For every thought or dream that comes my way,
Since to our world of brown
Prosèrpina came down.

Unto her will, men say, the giant toil
And little flowers of earth were over dear,
Now does she mix the sunlight with the soil,
And with the dusty clay a shining tear,
Prosèrpina the Queen
Has made the whole world green.

Queen Aphrodite, rising from the waves,
Finds rose and honeysuckle scents too sweet,
Finds the green grass of earth too full of graves
For the delicate white splendour of her feet –
The skies sprang blue and wide
For Aphrodite's pride.

Once long ago, lost amid dreams and lies,
Queen Pallas wandering held her dreadful shield
Between her and the Wisdom of the Wise,
And thus she lived a few short hours concealed,
Till at the end of day
From earth she fled away.

May Aphrodite reign in light afar
Where flowers are fairer and the skies more blue,
And Pallas find a perilous white star
Where all her dreams are true,

But Princess Prosperine
Has made our life divine.

And the green earth is hers, is hers,
The primrose springing from the sod,
Anemones beneath the firs
And laurels know no other god,
Day meekly follows night
For Proserpine's delight.

ANDROMEDA

Chained to the rock of this sheer world, the Will
Endures the slow wash of the rising tide,
And the cold stars above her far and still
Through the dark secret spheres in silence glide.

Who steals the sacred fire shall be the prey
Of elemental forces; think not thou
To cheat the gods who art not strong as they,
To crown with starry light a mortal brow.

Yet doth Andromeda, her labour past,
Stand among stars, herself a shining star,
So shall my will burn through the dust at last,
To that far sphere where truth and wisdom are.

Yea, by the magic force miscallèd death,
The vibrant drawing of the inmost light,
The hidden rapture of the failing breath,
The Blessed Vision of the fading sight.

Shall not one storm the gateway of that sphere
Where dwells the soul of our pale twilight skies,

And every austere beauty shines as clear
As winter starlight on the True and Wise?

THE ELM BOUGHS

The Elm boughs shudder in the sooty wind,
From their bright leaves the City children know
That somewhere the black world is glad and kind,
And through green woods the sunlit breezes blow.

All starved and stunted from the poisoned sod,
They shiver upwards through the stainèd air;
These are the battered pioneers of God,
Waving His green flag in the city square.

Thus in the gray-built city of the mind
Wave the green boughs of a few hostage powers,
Their secret whispered to the soilèd wind
Holds all our faith in Beauty's austere flowers.

Somewhere the fair and secret troops of Spring
Shine in strange colours icy clear and cold,
But I pass on through dark streets wandering,
Or dream a dream beneath the elm boughs old.

THE ARTIST

The spirit lonely in the spheres of night
Would draw down fire from other worlds and far,
And with a flash of the Diviner Light
Trouble the darkness of this narrow star.

As the young dreaming Christ, with power at play,
Moving among the earth's unsculptured things,
Moulded the crumbling balls of dust and clay
Into the swift delight of swallows' wings,

So do we gather up the stubborn soil,
Carving weak forms to hold the primal spark,
O God, have mercy on the artist's toil,
Lest the swift flame slip back into the dark,

Unfold the wisdom of those secret rays
That break in violet waves from sphere to sphere,
Piercing our starry nights and sunny days
With the strong rhythm of perilous fires and dear.

THE SECRET SPRING
'All our fathers were under the cloud.'

A tale that Maximus the Tyrian tells
How Alexander, flushed with warfare, came
To ask a question of the oracles
That speak to dreaming souls in Wisdom's name.

He asked not for the conquest of the world,
Nor craved to know the fortunes of his sword,
Should Victory's flaming wings be soon unfurled
Above the rout of the wild Persian horde.

As one deep sunk in an abyss of thought,
The warrior smiled a dim and gentle smile,
And prayed for wisdom long and vainly sought,
The secret of the sources of the Nile.

Thronèd above the high Egyptian gate
Still doth the unknown goddess radiant pale,

Queen over many waters, brood and wait,
No mortal hand can lift her shining vail.

And no man knows whence comes the magic tide
Of moving water that makes fair our dreams,
Though where hard soil once crumbled, scorched and
dried,
The roses nod their heads, the lily gleams.

Where once the land was waste, the harvest yields
Full measure down of corn and wine and oil,
The Mighty River floods our thirsty fields,
The waves of life soak through the barren soil.

The sacred stream o'erflows her banks of clay,
And who can tell where those great floods arise
That wash the barriers of the soul away
And purify the wisdom of the wise?

Still we, like that great king of long ago,
Must question idly 'twixt a sigh and smile,
From what deep spring do the bright waters flow –
Where are the hidden sources of the Nile?

REALITY
'Beloved Pan, and all ye other gods who haunt this
place, give me beauty in the inward soul; and may the
outward and inward be at one.'
– Socrates.

You think the joy and sorrow passionate
Of human life should be the singer's theme,
And man's old idle dream of love and hate
More real than the proud, fierce, immortal dream.

Not mine the hot desires and scornings proud
That shake the strings of a rose-crownèd lyre,
And all the blood-red passions of the crowd
Setting the singer's heart and brain on fire.

The secrets of the soul, have they no place
In the earth's heart, and should her children then
Despise the hand that moulds all beauty's grace,
And carves a dream out of the lives of men?

Shall, then, a song of this fair world hold all
The force of life out of the silence grown?
Nay, Helen held the sons of men in thrall,
But Psyche built among the gods her throne.

Though Helen's beauty ravaged a fair town,
And drenched the songs of men in blood and tears,
Yet before Psyche did that god bow down
Whose dreams are all the light of flaming spheres.

FOREBODINGS

Whate'er I touch to-night I spoil,
No rhythm sings, no light burns clear,
My weary fingers blur and soil
The glory of each crystal sphere.

The twilight lingers in the West
And light fades into burning flame,
Yet deep in the Unmanifest
Burns my soul's secret, why she came.

What pale hands, beckoning from afar,
Could bind her delicate fibres white

Round the earth's heart, whilst every star
In heaven shines with a purer light?

The secret of the sensible world
Smiles out of blue transparent skies,
Deep in the bulb's deep heart lies furled,
Mocks at the wise and the unwise.

This living will of thine and mine
Is stranger and more secret yet
To catch a glimpse of light divine,
And go away and straight forget.

Has, then, the spirit no bright goal
Beyond the radiant opal waves,
That one should mix with dust one's soul
And wander amongst dreams and graves?

To-night my spirit vails her face
And weeps beyond me lonely tears;
My heart shrinks back from her embrace
And all the dust within me fears.

THE DREAMER

All night I stumble through the fields of light,
And chase in dreams the starry rays divine
That shine through soft folds of the robe of night,
Hung like a curtain round a sacred shrine.

When daylight dawns I leave the meadows sweet
And come back to the dark house built of clay,
Over the threshold pass with lagging feet,
Open the shutters and let in the day.

The gray lit day heavy with griefs and cares,
And many a dull desire and foolish whim,
Leans o'er my shoulder as I spread my wares
On dusty counters and at windows dim.

She gazes at me with her sunken eyes,
That never yet have looked on moonlit flowers,
And amid glaring deeds and noisy cries
Counts out her golden tale of lagging hours.

Over the shrine of life no curtain falls,
All men may enter at the open gate,
The very rats find refuge in her walls –
Her tedious prison walls of love and hate.

Yet when the twilight vails that dim abode
I bar the door and make the shutters fast,
And hurry down the shadowy western road,
To seek in dreams my starlit home and vast.

THE SACRED FIRE

Folded about my soul is deep content,
For well I know that every wild deed done
Is shaped by the strong hand that moulds the event,
The hand that broke the stars and lit the sun.

I weep not for false hopes and baffling foes,
Our lives are metal welded in the fire,
The earth's cold iron in the furnace glows,
The Forger bends hard facts to his desire.

The Sacred Fire that is the Forger's will
Flashes in speed about the wings of birds,

And lights the lonely sunset on the hill,
And flames across the world in human words.

That passionate fire and fierce has burnt its way
Down to the innermost abyss of sense,
And shakes the spheres and breaks our towers of clay,
And moulds the struggling shapes that issue thence.

DEATH
'I thought in going to the other world he could not be
without a divine call.'
– Plato.

Amongst the daisies on the dewy lawn
The melody, with delicate steps and slow,
Comes radiant forth, from vibrant wood withdrawn
By the strong fibres of the patient bow.

About my heart a broken music clings,
Shut in this prison of senses five, I pray
That the tense fibres of the sobbing strings
May draw my soul from her close cell of clay.

No fumbling hands can loose the nerves that bind
That music folded in about my heart,
Thrilling with every breath of haunted wind,
In the far silent deep she dwells apart.

Patient she waits the Player's rhythmic touch,
The skill that draws her from her dark abode,
In austere joy not fearing overmuch
The lonely starlight or the open road.

POWER

The soul who knows herself dreams not of rest,
Brooding in secret o'er her new-found wings,
Having no fear of the Unmanifest,
Safe from the primal nothingness of things.

She breaks her way athwart the inmost fires
And moulds the force of life unto her mind,
Shaping the lightning to her fierce desires,
Shifting the currents of the unseen wind.

The world's six crownèd powers are but her slaves,
Unto the end of time, for good or ill,
Her rainbow wings beat out in rhythmic waves
Of fiery aether all her vibrant will.

And men who strive, and cry, and dream they rule
Are but in very truth the instrument
Of the wise soul, who carves with a sharp tool,
Sculptor of life and god of the event.

HEREDITY

There is one thing I know
About life, and thought, and art –
That my soul did not grow
Out of my mother's heart.

To the Wise and the Unwise
Life is a secret still,
But my spirit did not arise
Out of my mother's will.

Our dreams are weak and wild,
And nothing is made plain,
But my soul is not the child
Of my mother's brain.

Behold this muddy star
Knows the laws of mine and thine,
But the soul dwells afar
Child of the Light Divine.

These things I know because
In Life, and Thought, and Art,
The soul obeys strange laws
That break the heart.

THE CADUCEUS

Though I lie all day on the green hillside, where the
bracken waves and sighs,
And my soul is too happy for dreams, and my heart too
heavy for deeds,
And the song of my rhythmic and idle hours is a scorn to
the wise,
And my hopes float winged in the sunshine like the fragile
sycamore seeds.

As I lie all day where the bracken sighs, frond upon
whispering frond,
Watching the way of the wind in the grass and the blue
sky overhead,
Know this, I am forging out of my will a strong and
delicate wand,
To guide the footsteps that falter and swerve in the ways
of the newly dead.

MAGNETISM

'Matter, at any rate in its relations to other matter at a
distance, is an electrical manifestation ... and electricity
is a state of intrinsic strain in a universal medium.'
– Whetham

The mountains tower in snow-built curves austere,
White and eternal peaks of carven mind,
Rather to me are the green grass blades dear,
That wave their delicate curves in the soft wind.

The mountain torrents down their rocky course
Rush with a rainbow riot of foam and strife,
Nearer to God is the dumb silent force
That burns behind the atoms' whirling life.

The hills are as the Earth's aspiring brow,
Covered with snowy peace and eagles' wings,
Yet do the green fields yield unto the plough
The secret of the buried life of things.

Deep down amid the forces of the soil
Lies hid the path of that electric spark
That rushes forth in flowers to crown our toil,
Yet holds the world together in the dark.

BEYOND

Because the world's soul looks me through and through
From every breaking wave and wild bird's wing,
I trust my own soul, knowing to be true,
Full many a worn-out old discrownèd thing.

Because of those unearthly fires that shine
Beyond Duneira of the sunset waves,

I know that life is deathless and divine,
And dead men's souls rest never in their graves.

Because of twilight over miles of green
And one small fishing vessel sailing far,
On through the torment of wild winds unseen
I steer my little boat by a great star.

Because the rose is sweeter after rain,
Because fierce lightning strengthens the weak sod,
I know life flares behind the golden grain,
And ecstasy beyond the thought of God.

THE NEW RAINBOW
'Obscurity being perhaps the matter of every invisible
colour.' – Plotinus.

Of old the rainbow on the water's face
Showed forth to men the divine promise fair,
That no dark flood should quench the golden air,
Nor great wave rob the daisy of her grace.

Now in our souls mysterious rays are shed,
And stranger lightning of the later years
Uplifts our hearts unto the fortressed spheres
Beyond the violet, beyond the red.

This is the secret of the spirit's wings,
The strong mysterious promises of pain,
The shining of the rainbow after rain,
The strength and surety of eternal things.

Beyond all fires that wither in the west,
Immortal rays of the aethereal arc

Blaze the world's rapture out across the dark,
The rainbow of the will is manifest.

We that are sense encompassed, put our trust
In light that shines in darkness, the lost will
That hides in dim bulbs of the daffodil,
And raises radiant lilies from the dust.

No man can dream of beauty without light,
The blue lit Adriatic to the blind
Is but thick darkness and a wandering wind,
And cold death creeping through the shades of night.

We, worshipping the sunlight, have not found
The limits of desire in summer's green;
We pass from lovely forms to light unseen,
That draws forth beauty out of broken ground.

And find the winds and waves we dreamed exist
Are but pale pictures on the walls of sense
Of that far throbbing inner life intense –
The Life and Light of the Evangelist.

Eternal light beyond the rainbow's scope
Of coloured fire unseen about us gleams,
And no dark flood shall quench our golden dreams,
Nor death's deep waters rob our souls of hope.

RADIUM

The secret of this sensible world of ours
Blazed out for centuries close to human eyes,
Yet hidden from the wise and the unwise,
Folded in twilight, flaming forth in flowers.

For years the labourer drove his heavy cart
O'er treasure buried under the white road,
And amid unseen armies reaped and sowed,
And no man knew the flame in his own heart.

Till the wise dreamer with unflinching toil,
Brake through the narrow walls of sense and sight,
And to the dimness of the outer light
Dragged forth the ultimate secret of the soil.

Who thought to find this radiance in the sun,
This hidden glory in the heart of earth,
Deep in the shadow beyond death or birth
Lay hid the treasure of the All-seeing One.

And darkness seemed the end, now mystic light
Enfolds all shadows, surely each wild gleam
That once seemed but the radiance of a dream
Shines from some true star in the spirit's night.

Thus should one find at last the god who hides
In every wood, by whose lost light divine
The gods are beautiful and the stars shine,
And the white moon through clouds and darkness glides.

UNDINE
'The sun draws up all things out of the earth.'
– The Emperor Julian.

The one light throned beyond the starry spheres
Draws forth the Wise, the True, the Pure, the Just,
From the earth's heart beneath the mounded years
As sunshine draws the flowers from the dust.

Each primal force strives upward to the light,
Among the lily roots there is no rest,
And every delicate fibre frail and white
Would be in higher beauty manifest.

Down in the earth's heart the deep mining gnome
Seeks buried treasure under each green hill,
The river nymph is weary of her home,
The sylph would bend the wild winds to her will.
Who knows the fire spirit's hidden goal,
Or tracks the sylph through thunder-haunted skies –
But the nymphs toil for an immortal soul,
And men would toil for love if they were wise.

SURVIVAL

In the darkness I planted a rose
And it withered and died,
Now a poisonous fungus lives and grows
By the dead rose's side.

Full many an ill weed evil and old
In caves and dungeons thrives,
'Mid poisonous forces manifold
The bitterest life survives.

Out in the fields there's rain and sun
And a rustle of wind-blown wheat,
There's nought to shrink from and nought to shun,
The fittest is honey-sweet.

Honey-sweet from the heart of toil
The inner life of flowers,
The scorching sun and the rain-drenched soil,
The war of living powers.

There is nothing good, there is nothing fair,
Grows in the darkness thick and blind –
Pull down your high walls everywhere,
Let in the sun, let in the wind.

PEACE

I am sad with the city's sadness, sick of toil,
Choked with smoke and tumult, weary of noisy mills,
Weaver of twilight hold me close to the brown soil,
Fold round my soul the lofty peace of thy green hills.

The lonely winds of twilight o'er gentle waters glide,
Grown secret with the magic thrill of unseen wings,
Here doth the soul of the wild land in peace abide,
And tired hearts find rest from world-old wanderings.

The great white daisies toss at ease in the long grass,
I will fling down my soul to rest in this green glade,
Where amongst waving fronds the silent angels pass,
And brown hares fawn about their knees noiseless and
unafraid.

THE WORLD'S THIEF

The light shines on the rich man's feast
From many a flickering brazen lamp,
God set that great star in the East
To guide the footsteps of a tramp.

Each long moon shadow shakes my soul,
And every gust of harsh wind flings

Rich treasure in my wooden bowl,
Beyond the dreams of the three kings.

The dark night is my coverlid,
I steal from God my grassy bed,
And in this beggar's bowl lies hid
The ravished secret of the dead.

The wind of God I make my own,
My soul was once His starry will,
Flesh of my flesh, bone of my bone,
His world is mine for good or ill.

Here on this wide star-haunted waste
I trespass on His lonely grief,
I have no need for fear or haste,
No prison waits for the world's thief.

His rainbow lights to me are dear,
And stolen moonlit forms divine
Shine in my soul's deep waters clear –
With God there is no mine nor thine.

THE MYSTIC
'Your soul has set sail like the returning Odysseus for
its native land.' – Plotinus.

Nay , though green fields are fair
And the fiords are blue,
I need a clearer air,
I need a region new,

Out beyond the Northern Lights
Where the white Polar Day
To herself in silence sings,

Without thought of words or wings
The secret of a hundred nights.

I shall find there I know
The lost city of my birth,
Innocent white wastes of snow,
A new heaven and a new earth.
Neither lamb, nor calf, nor kid,
In those lonely meadows play,
All things calm and silent are
Underneath the Polar star,
Where all my dreams are hid.

I am sick of wind and tide –
Tired of this rocking boat
Creaking ever as we glide
Into the white waste remote,
Out there no sound is heard
Save the icebergs' crash and grind,
No human voice e'er shuddered through
The realms of white, the realms of blue,
Nor cry of a sea-bird.

Lying at ease in the dark ship
I watched the last pale night depart,
I dreamt I saw blue shadows slip
O'er the white snowfields in my heart;
And the world had grown so wide
There was room for all mankind –
The icebergs round about the Pole
Crashed in the silence of my soul,
And hemmed me in on every side.

In that crowded world of white
There are many joys unknown,
Without colour there is light,
Loneliness for the alone,

Heedless stars that blaze and shine,
O'er the world's untrodden edge,
You come with me, you who dare
Leave the cart and the plough-share,
For the white horizon line.

Over many seas we sail
Passing many peopled shores,
Like the Greek in the old tale
Homeward sailing from the wars.
Gentle voices bid us rest
From green isle or barren sedge,
'In our world all things are new,
We have passed away from you,
You must seek another guest.'

Voices of enchanted time
Call to us to leave our ships,
Hyacinths of honeyed rhyme
Float from Aphrodite's lips,
We for Circe born unkind,
All the songs the sirens sing
Seem but idly to oppress
Hearts in love with loneliness,
Sails that flutter in the wind.

O'er the wide cold wastes serene
Rise the walls of wandering white,
Circles of strange gods unseen
In the electric arc unite.
Arctic faces flash and glide,
Glimmers many a flaming wing,
Where the aether strains to hold
The hard heart of the Manifold
All the greater gods abide.

IMMORTALITIES
'Again a voiceless statue is Apollo, and Daphne a
shrub bewailed in fable.'
– Gregory Nazianzen.

Now do men say that though the gods be fair
Phoebus who moulded beauty into rhyme
And Irish Niamh of the wind-blown hair
Are but the children not the lords of time.

It is not true, still does Apollo hide
In little songs the world's great mysteries,
And the white beckoning hands of Niamh guide
The hero-hearted over pathless seas.

My secret treasure-house beyond the grave
Holds but the stars of heaven, the gods of Greece,
And some faint echo of the voice of Maeve,
And the One Voice that is the Eternal Peace.

THE EGYPTIAN PILLAR
(1907)

ROSES

When her twigs are bare
In the grim air,
And her leaves are shed,
Is the Rose dead?

Does she dream, does she sleep,
In her roots buried deep?
Does she lie at rest
With the earth on her breast?

Ah no, the Rose goes –
The spirit of the Rose
Blooms, and is fair
Elsewhere.

Behold, there is no birth
From the earth to the earth,
But the Roses, wise and dear,
Live in heaven half the year.

THE DARK VALLEY

No honey for the busy artist throng,
No glittering texture dear unto the mind;
No shining web of many-coloured song
Shalt thou here find.

In this dark valley shadows everywhere
Whisper and mock at life's so radiant will;
Thus do I know the golden sun shines fair
Behind the hill.

I bring you but a little magic shade ...
A dream found true when one awakeneth ...
A shadow that the sun's dear light has made
In the Valley of Death.

FREEDOM

We who are mourners make no moan
For the Body lost in the grave,
For the Soul is a shining wave
And the Body is but a stone
Dragged out in the under tow
And tossed by the waves to and fro,
And worn and tormented and cast
Back again on the rocks at last.

Ah, the body lost in the grave
Is freed from the tyrant soul,
Delivered from wind and wave,
Current and quicksand and shoal,
Freed from the cruel sea ...
But the spirit is never free ...
There is no truce in that war
Of the tides that clash near the shore.

Quietly under the green roof
Does the worn-out body lie,
With a shadow of strange reproof
The soul wonders it could die –
Wonders that her slave is dead,
Has no need of daily bread,
Free as dust and free as air,
With nothing in the world to bear ...

IMMORTALITY

Is there nothing you care for or dream to remember
When the earth crumbles off from your sharp-edgèd will?
Now through your life's last tormented December
Howls the ravenous wind round the desolate hill.

When you pass in great joy the storm-shaken portal,
Shall the welcoming Angels in unison cry:
'What flower have you brought of the spirit immortal
  From the tenebrous earth to the æther-lit sky?'

Lo! this will I tell them, to their shining bowers
I bring but a light from the House of the Blind,
For earth hath great need of each one of her flowers,
Whilst last Summer's last roses have failed from my mind.

Yea, the dreams and the deeds and the sorrows of night
In the opal-cut splendour forgotten shall be,
Yet clear in my mind burns a ray of starlight,
In my soul flows immortal a wave of the sea.

My life, with its burden of toil and derision,
Is lost as the leaves of the sycamore shed.
Yet the verses' dark waters reflecting the Vision
Roll on evermore through the soul of the dead.

THE WELL AT THE WORLD'S END

Here on dark waters falls the yellow leaf,
Here many broken days and stormy hours intense,
And moments of deep passion buried gleam;
This is the Pool of Patience, Toil, and Grief,
Ah, Life, the river of song doth issue thence ...
These things are but the waters of the stream.

THE THRONE OF OSIRIS

In the roof the swallow has built her nest,
And the martins under the eaves,
And all wingèd things have a chamber of rest
In the shadow of swaying leaves.

The rabbit has dug for himself a hole,
The green worm lies at the heart of the rose,
And there is rest for the vagrant soul
Wherever the shallowest river flows.

THE STREET ORATOR

At Clitheroe from the Market Square
I saw rose-lit the mountain's gleam,
I stood before the people there
And spake as in a dream.

At Oldham of the many mills
The weavers are of gentle mind;
At Haslingden one flouted me,
At Burnley all the folk were kind,

At Ashton town the rain came down,
The east wind pierced us through and through,
But over little Clitheroe
The sky was bright and blue.

At Clitheroe through the sunset hour
My soul was very far away:
I saw Ben Bulben's rose and fire
Shining afar o'er Sligo Bay.

At Clitheroe round the Market Square
The hills go up, the hills go down,
Just as they used to go about
A mountain-guarded Irish town.

Oh, I have friends in Haslingden,
And many a friend in Hyde,
But 'tis at little Clitheroe
That I would fain abide.

WOMEN'S TRADES ON THE EMBANKMENT
'Have Patience!'
– The Prime Minister to the Women's Franchise
Deputation, 19th May 1906.

Where the Egyptian pillar – old, so old –
With mystery fronts the open English sky,
Bearing the yoke of those who heap up gold,
The sad-eyed workers pass in silence by.

Heavily hewing wood and drawing water,
These have been patient since the world began –
Patient through centuries of toil and slaughter,
For Patience is the ultimate soul of man.

Patient with endless lords and overseers,
Since long-dead Israelites made bricks to please
A King whose heart was hardened to their tears,
What time they still besought him on their knees.

Their patience was the King's confederate,
Their weakness helped his power unaware;
In vain men pray unto the rich and great,
For only God-like spirits answer prayer.

Long has submission played a traitor's part –
Oh human soul, no patience any more
Shall break your wings and harden Pharaoh's heart,
And keep you lingering on the Red Sea shore.

THE GOOD SAMARITAN

Robbed and wounded, all the day
The great cause by the roadside lay.
The Rich and Mighty in their Pride
Passed by on the other side.
With smiling lips indifferent
On their way the statesmen went.
At evening in the sunset flame
Out of the mill the winders came;
She who with four great looms weaves
Found Justice fallen amongst thieves,
Stone-breakers resting from their toil
Have poured out wine and oil.
The miner hurrying from the mine
Has seen a flash of light divine,
And every tired labourer
Has given a helping hand to her.
The workman leaning on his spade,
Or the tramp resting in the shade,
The navvy who the roadway mends,
These are our comrades, these our friends –
Beggars, never yet in vain
Have we stood in wind and rain
For hours at the Factory Gate;
Never idly do we wait
In the dark and empty street,
Till the thronging shadows fleet
Gather round us; grief, despair,
Is no idle story there:

Patient faces from the loom,
Eyes dark with the whole world's gloom,
Haunted faces, sorrowful eyes,
Read the secret of the Wise,
Look the round world through and through,
Seeing naught but false or true,
Seeing in the whole world wide
But one side or the other side.
Want and hunger linger near
The Divine Fire burning clear.
The cold sleet and the bitter wind
Open the eyes of the blind.
Gracious deeds are dreamed and done
By those who seldom see the sun.
Lips grow pitiful, drawn, and pale
Where the darkness does not fail;
But one dim street lamp braves the night ...
Yet in these souls burns a great light.
Thus from the poor we beg our bread ...
And Justice rises from the dead ...

VAGRANTS

Oh , Little Human Words and delicate,
You wander through the great world up and down;
Though rich men heed fine phrases of the great,
Poor Words and wingless tramp from town to town.

He who loves Wisdom for her rich attire
Will turn her ragged children from his door,
And yet an empty chair beside the fire
Kind hearts keep for these Vagrants evermore.

A LOST OPPORTUNITY

Others there were who spake with fire and art;
I stammered, breaking down beneath the weight
Of that great stone that lies upon my heart
When with one passion all my nerves vibrate.

Little I said, who had so much to say –
This is the memory that sears and stings,
My soul was fire, my thoughts were clear as day,
Yet had my soul no wings.

No matter, when that force beyond control
Sweeps on one side the cobwebs of the brain,
In broken stammers speaks the inmost soul ...
Nor shall her passion smite the air in vain.

THE THRIFTLESS DREAMER

Psyche , the Queen, says truly the old tale,
Into the heart of life's thick darkness fell,
And she dwelt lonely in an obscure vale,
Yet waited on by Powers Invisible.

Thus Ireland many blame and many praise,
And she the while, radiant in meadows green,
And following silently her ancient ways,
Is served by hosts of delicate hands unseen.

You whom the bitter hour maketh wise,
In vain you urge on her your prosperous goal,
She has her visions in her own eyes,
She has her destinies in her own soul.

Down from her mountains still the old cart crawls
As it crawled long ago laden with turf;
There are still gaps, thank God, in all our walls,
On lonely shores still breaks the Atlantic surf.

Ye who would measure all things by a rule
And cut the holy day in busy hours,
There is one land you cannot put to school,
And therefore shall she be one of the world's powers.
On through your anxious voices' fret and jar,
The soul pursues unmoved her silent course,
You shall not shake her trust in her own star,
Her unseen legions and embattled force.

For round her, driven from this dark world, wait
Mysterious powers and unseen ministers,
And all the vailèd Angels at the Gate
Guard with their swords this thriftless dream of hers.

ON THE EMBANKMENT

The Rich, the Great, the Wise are here, the Living and the
Dead,
Where the Great Towers of Westminister hold the high
heavens at bay,
And the poor souls who have no hope take fame or power
instead,
Whilst many an obscure wingèd one goes smiling on her
way.

This I know of the poor, 'tis when the Great Hopes fail
That men have gained possession of material things;
But all the praise of all the crowds shall not prevail
To make good to a human soul the loss of her wild wings.

WOMEN'S RIGHTS

Down by Glencar Waterfall
There's no winter left at all.

Every little flower that blows
Cold and darkness overthrows.

Every little thrush that sings
Quells the wild air with brave wings.

Every little stream that runs
Holds the light of brighter suns.

But where men in office sit
Winter holds the human wit.

In the dark and dreary town
Summer's green is trampled down.
Frozen, frozen everywhere
Are the springs of thought and prayer.

Rise with us and let us go
To where the living waters flow.

Oh, whatever men may say
Ours is the wide and open way.

Oh, whatever men may dream
We have the blue air and the stream.

Men have got their towers and walls,
We have cliffs and waterfalls.

Oh, whatever men may do
Ours is the gold air and the blue.

Men have got their pomp and pride –
All the green world is on our side.

HAVE PITY

Because some seed, no man knows why,
Has not got the heart to grow,
I think the fountains have run dry,
The Living Water ceased to flow.

Because that such a little Tower
Is built with so much strain and toil,
I think there's but a feeble power
Hiding behind the broken soil.

Under the blue and beaming sky
I watched a white bud fading brown,
The lost and folded mystery
Unborn unto the dust go down.

Unto the weak all weak things cried,
And pity in the human breast –
Ah, break not the hedge-sparrow's pride
Nor rob the blue eggs from her nest.

All the world's weak and shackled will
    Would fain bring every seed to bear –
Spare thou the Primrose on the Hill,
    The frail wind-shaken Tower spare.

COMRADES

Men who are born to die, whose dreams are soiled by the dust,
Are yet most dear to their friends, and gentle lovers and kind;
But only the gods in heaven are true enough to be just.
Alas that Justice dwells not in any human mind.

That star that fell from heaven, dethroned and lost long ago,
Thou shalt not find it hidden in the wisdom of the wise,
Thou shalt not see it glimmer in the deep heart of a foe,
And hardly shall it shine on thee from any comrade's eyes.

We who have followed the same star and fought for the same dream,
Are bound together for ever by the wild deed's bond and power.
Behold we have cast our nets into the same dark stream,
We have climbed the same sheer cliff to seek the same blue flower.

ON THE CLIFF
(AT DUNRAVEN)

Where the waves in a moaning throng
From darkness to darkness glide,
And the everlasting song
Is chanted by wind and tide,

In the wood on the cliff's face
The gentle primroses flower,

And by the sun and the wind's grace
The daffodils have their hour ...

All round me the tides moan –
And my soul, to battle hurled,
Is wounded and overthrown
In the wars of the dark world.

But ever at evening,
Through the great tide's ebb and flow,
And the waves' moan and the spray's sting,
Out of the world I go.

To the soul's secret place,
Where in the golden air,
By the sun and the wind's grace,
The primroses grow fair,

There to that flower-lit hill,
Whither all joy has fled,
By the sun and the wind's will,
Come the holy dead.

Broken beauty, quenchèd light,
Soul of truth, out-faced, denied,
Violets blue and snowdrops white
Grow on that lost hill-side.

THE FLAMING SWORD

Oh , softly falls the shining leaf,
There is no beauty without grief,
And all our loving is one long regret,
Seeing in the pageant of the sunset

But shadows of those pure mysterious skies
That hid the secret of the white sunrise.

Harsh streams of cold forgetfulness,
Far from the great tide's strain and stress,
Silver at dawn, and when the day is done
Gliding through the fires of the red sun –
Shadows are these of that sharp flaming sword
That hides from us the garden of the Lord.

The Hidden Eden in our dreams
Beyond the shining barrier gleams,
Thither it is that all our loves do go,
There between the tide's ebb and the tide's flow
With silent footsteps doth the spirit glide,
Amongst her secret comrades to abide.

Alas, the great sword flaming red
Between the living and the dead;
Those who yet sojourn from eve till morn
With the newly dead and the pale unborn,
At noon with dazzled eyes disconsolate
Stand weeping by the barred and dreadful gate.

For all our heavy sorrows sink
Deep down beneath the thoughts we think;
Thus can no comfortable sayings cure
Grief for the separate, dead, obscure.
One flash of secret Light may the gods give
To all who in the wilderness must live.

Lord of the sunset's flash and shine,
Lord of the hard dividing line
Between thy stars and our so barren heath,
Till thou has thrust thy sword back in its sheath,

Till we can wholly know, or quite forget,
Still all our love must be one long regret.

THE VISIONARY
'Constant use of will power extends the sphere of its
action.' – Eliphas Levi.

Dear life has cast me forth from her gay throng;
Unto her pipings I could never dance,
Nor learn the music of her simplest song –
I was a traitor to her brave romance.

A traitor to her flag of gold and blue
I sought for wisdom silently apart,
What was there left for such an one to do,
But trust the stranger voices in her heart?

He who would search the silence dwells alone.
From far-off towers in the inner air
Floats down the sudden cry of the Unknown,
The lonely Eastern Voice that calls to prayer.

I dream a dream of comrades, but not here –
Of fellowship, not now, that life denies.
These songs that I in truth alone hold dear
When I am dead shall fall under strange eyes.

And some brave spirit, smiling and serene,
Where I trod blindly, choked with dust, shall say:
'She sought her whole life through the Light Unseen;
    Stumbling and lost she still held on her way.'

Ah, gentle comrade of the coming time,
For you there is no danger in that road;

Casting aside the broken staffs of rhyme,
You enter easily the gods' abode.

From that rash mountainous and sheer ascent
You gaze down on the weakness of the will,
The darkness of the feeble lost intent,
The blind soul groping on the perilous hill.

You shall not scorn dark seas or wind-swept caves,
You Dweller on the Rainbow Towers of Light,
While through your being thrills in stormy waves
The call of the Abyss unto the Height.

Few flowers but fair on the high mountains grow –
Whilst to the Rich belongs the sunny day,
And Wise men walk where living waters flow,
The Poor are the best comrades either way.

You shall not scorn the feeble voice that cries
In the world's wilderness ... for his reward
The rough-voiced pioneer whom men despise
Doth yet prepare the way for a new Lord.

With toil one groped along the path you tread,
Your gay robe shining in the sun and wind,
Yet shall the Living join hands with the Dead,
The Seer find a Comrade in the Blind.

So might one boast: 'Lo, I have climbed the crest
Of the high hill and stood on that sheer peak
Whereon the golden eagle builds her nest' –
This is the giant labour of the weak.

The Mighty Spirit of the secret place,
The little coward soul afraid to climb,
Shall meet upon the mountains face to face,
As Moses met with God in the old time.

In Light you pass unto your star-lit goal,
Yet my harsh purposes and baffled feet
And little foolish songs cry to your soul,
And surely in the end we two shall meet.

MAN AND WOMAN

When Solomon of old
Shewed all his stuffs of silver sheen
And walls inlaid with gold
To Sheba's Queen,
Her very spirit sank in her,
Such treasure of white ivory
And crystal bowls and scented fir
And marble did she see.
And loud she praised the great King's store
Of carven wood and flashing stone,
Where cedar was as sycamore
Before the lion-guarded throne.
And all his words were very wise,
And his great temple passing fair,
And humble were her soft replies,
Treading his ivory stair.
But when she came to her own place
She smiled to think of him,
And all the glory and the grace
Of his wise words grew dim.
Behold she sent a slave
With gifts unto the King.
She bade her goldsmiths cut and grave
For him an agate ring.
'This too will pass' – the Queen's reply
From her dark jewel shone.
Thus did she answer with a sigh
The wise King Solomon.

RETROSPECT

When I was young the world looked old
And all the mountains hard and gray,
I shivered in the winter's cold;
The very sunshine was not gay
When I was young.

When I was old the world seemed young;
On primroses the sphered dew
Shone with a sudden radiance flung
From miles of gold and miles of blue
When I was old.

I feared the world when I was young,
I loved the world when I was old;
But now in vain her songs are sung,
Her strangest stories leave me cold
As tales twice told.

Now I am dead the vernal earth
Seems very small and very far,
And every soul in death or birth
Too great for such a narrow star
Now I am dead.

For broken is the golden bowl,
And old and young are reconciled,
All things are frailer than the soul,
And life seems but a faery child
Now I am dead.

THE AGATE LAMP (1912)

THE AGATE LAMP

How is it doomed to end?
Shall I, when I come again,
Watch the old sun in a new eclipse,
Breathe the same air with different lips,
Think the same thoughts with a different brain,
With a new heart love the same old friend?

How shall I hold the thread? –
The brittle thread of the past,
On through the terrible maze –
The labyrinth of lost days –
A pilgrim through tireless centuries vast,
Where one dreams with the living and sleeps with the
dead?

What is there that will not change
That I can recognize?
The sun, and the wind, and the April rain,
And the wild sea's shining plain –
The ancient joy in the world's young eyes –
The blue hills' dim eternal range?

Ah! there are other things
That shall not fade –
The painter's dream, the poet's thought,
The calm-browed Muse in marble wrought –
Pan's pipes out of dry reeds at twilight made –
And Orpheus' lute, and Niké's wind-blown wings.

LEONARDO DA VINCI

He in his deepest mind
That inner harmony divined

That lit the soul of John,
And in the glad eyes shone
Of Dionysos, and dwelt
Where Angel Gabriel knelt
Under the dark cypress spires;
And thrilled with flameless fires
Of Secret Wisdom's rays
The Giaconda's smiling gaze;
Curving with delicate care
The pearls in Beatrice d'Esté's hair;
Hiding behind the veil
Of eyelids long and pale,
In the strange gentle vision dim
Of the unknown Christ who smiled on him.
His was no vain dream
Of the things that seem,
Of date and name.
He overcame
The Outer False with the Inner True,
And overthrew
The empty show and thin deceits of sex,
Pale nightmares of this barren world that vex
The soul of man, shaken by every breeze
Too faint to stir the silver olive trees
Or lift the Dryad's smallest straying tress
Frozen in her clear marble loveliness.
He, in curved lips and smiling eyes,
Hid the last secret's faint surprise
Of one who dies in fear and pain
And lives and knows herself again.
He, in his dreaming under the sun,
Saw change and the Unchanging One,
And built in grottos blue a shrine
To hold Reality Divine.

SANO DI PIETRO
(SIENA)

Floating in pale rose waves the sun has set,
Slowly on silver feet doth twilight glide
Among the hills, flooding with violet
Those marble mountains where the gods abide.
Here Sano's lingering dim Madonnas hold
The sky and all its stars and mysteries,
In their strange robes of shadowy blue and gold.
Here voices haunt the twisted olive trees
With magic whispers of a far-off goal,
Where fortune finds, beyond her turning wheel,
All light and colour in the radiant soul.
Here with the sunset's all-enfolding dream
Harsh lines and broken curves do blend and cease.
Lo the hoar olives on the mountains gleam –
The hills grow pale with that white dream of peace.
Ah, let no sob of pain, nor bitter cry,
The fragile robe of beauty rend or soil!
Slay not the smallest creature doomed to die,
The fruit of million weary years of toil.
Here, in this little city on the height,
Hatred and sorrow into shadow blend,
Deep in rose marble sinks the evening light,
And all things come to beauty at the end.
Of days to come, here might one dream awhile –
How men were gentle and had ceased to kill,
How Sano dead such years ago would smile,
To find the world grown lovely with good-will.

RODIN'S CARYATIDES

Poor weary mortal crushed beneath the weight
Of the harsh stone, with muscles strained and tense,
And limbs all wrenched and torn and dislocate,
Writhing beneath the stony load immense.

Thine is the strife and struggle of our age,
On heavy labour and hard toil intent,
The fury of fierce dreams and blinding rage,
Thou art of all weak souls the monument.

Ah, let us go to where glad peace divine,
On many an ancient sun-warmed marble gleams,
The sorrow of all pitiful deeds is thine –
Our deeds that are not sisters to our dreams.

From thee we turn to those divinely fair
And marble-soulèd Caryatides,
Who bore great walls like garlands in their hair,
And smiled beneath the carven temple-frieze.

Oh, long ago, in lost Hellenic hours,
That heavy burden did but lightly press
On the calm patient brows of austere powers,
Terrible in their unmoved loveliness.

ADORATION OF THE SHEPHERDS
(BY DOMENICO GHIRLANDAJO)

The pale Madonna, radiant and serene,
Smiles the long summer hours in peace away,
Where the child lies on the bird-haunted green,
Nor heeds the patient folk who come to pray.

So this was Ghirlandajo, eager-eyed,
Who had not seen the hidden light in vain,
With those sad shepherds from the far hillside
He, sleepless, under the white stars had lain.

And he who smiles as he gives thanks to God,
With humble gaze serene and kindly just,
He then was that Magnificent who trod
The liberties of Florence in the dust.

Nay, no dark soul of proud and evil mind
Was he who round the stiff lamb folds his arm,
A gentle labourer, most wise and kind,
No tyrant ever knew his gracious calm.

And he had listened to the Thracian's song,
And seen the gray light of Athene's eyes;
And for his joy the gracious white-limbed throng
Of laughing nymphs did from the marble rise.

The little golden daisies, silver-rayed,
Were dear to him as the great golden sun,
And he who bent before the Holy Maid
Saw in the Many glimpses of the One.

Thus be it said of him: Here was a man
Whose faith in God was very deep and wide,
Yet did he keep a little shrine for Pan
And wise Athene by his heart's wayside.

The friend of all things lovely and sincere,
This pale Madonna kneeling on her knees
Dwelt in his heart's deep twilight silver-clear,
Where white gods gleamed among the olive trees.

And all the shining forms of joy and grief,
And every broken dream of truth divine,

Were to his soul the reapèd golden sheaf
And garnered treasure of the Eternal Shrine.

Yea, this was rather one who comraded
With Plato, one who loved all visions fair;
The shepherd who the angels' warning read –
Peace upon earth and beauty everywhere.

The pale Madonna, lost to mortal things,
Still through the long-drawn silence kneels to pray,
Meanwhile the grand procession of the Kings
Comes glittering down the winding mountain way.

DAVID
(BY MICHELANGELO: IN THE BARGELLO)

This was the shepherd boy who slung the stone
And killed the giant; sunshine and the wind
Had given his harp so clear and strange a tone
That all the world forgave him when he sinned.

The gently formed and stately Greek who stood
On the Piazza, throned in classic pride,
Was not the boy who roamed through field and wood,
Fighting and singing on the bright hillside.

Swift on the mountains, swift to save or slay;
Eager and passionate, and lithe of form;
Fighting and singing, pausing but to pray
Unto his God of music and of storm.

The bare hillside and sharp rocks castellate
Rang with the clanging of his restless bow,
Where, in the dawn of the world's love and hate,
He found and would not slay his sleeping foe.

No sorrowful shadow of the evil years
Falls on this boy's face of the wood and wild;
Vanished are rage and lust and passionate tears;
The king is dead, immortal stands the child.

THE DAWN
(MICHELANGELO)

Not as Aurora of the smiling eyes
And rosy fingers doth this dawn awake;
Neither, like Aphrodite, doth she rise
From the bright waves, all silver for her sake.
Rather is she the Image in the Soul,
The beautiful young dawn of all things fair,
Who wakes in a dark world of gloom and dole,
Wrapped in the marble coldness of despair.
Thou sorrowful Dawn invincible, alone,
Pale sleeper, from thy long rest turn aside;
Four hundred years of slumber hast thou known;
Long broken is that Florentine's fierce pride
That held thee tranced through years of storm and stress;
Oh, buried in the marble calm and cold,
Wake thou, the world is full of heaviness,
And men have need of beauty, as of old.

ANGELS OF THE INCARNATION
(BOTTICELLI)

These are those brows no life or death has marred –
The wistful eyes and wingèd forms that guard
The fortress of our thoughts, too dim and frail
To hide from us the shadowy faces pale
Mourning outside the cloudy-pillared gate,

To some mysterious sorrow consecrate.
Sad angel faces that the Florentine
Made wistful with strange longing more divine
Than any ghastly arrow-ridden saint,
Or God Himself (whom Angelo did paint
High in the Sistine, which may God forgive)
Who shews Himself in swift gleams fugitive,
And dwelling in the world's deep heart unseen,
Shines through the thin veil of the spring's young green,
And the breaking wave, and the shadowy wind,
And the opal dream in the painter's mind.
These Angels in their pale arrested flight,
Flooding with rays of a mysterious light
The lilies in the twilight garden cool
And great stars shining in a little pool, –
Ah, shadowy angels, ye are they that weep
Beside the waters flowing still and deep
Above our dreams, hiding, since time began,
God's sunken image in the soul of man.

ATHENE
(RESTORED)

Hers is the patient waiting of the wise
Who beareth all things, e'en the clownish fist
Of lumpy restorations that disguise
The delicate clear carving of the wrist.

Yet o'er her form that vacuous face, intent
Its ancient holiness to desecrate,
Casts not a shadow of disfigurement;
For beauty is no passive toy of fate.

The tireless light of her undaunted dreams,
Above all littleness of heart and brain,

Through simple curves and patient carving gleams
In a white mystery of peace and strain.

Athene triumphs, deathless and divine:
She waits her wisdom's hour, the end of all.
The eternal glory of the gracious line
Flows through the heavens, though the great stars fall.

SILENZIA
(BERNARDINO LUINI)

Deep buried dreams dwell in her laughing eyes;
She holds one finger on her lips close pressed;
Hers are no solemn phrases of the wise;
Smiling, she hides a secret in her breast.

Treasure is hers; she has great joy of it,
Nor cares that men should count her vain and gay,
No thought has power her gentle brow to knit
Or turn her red-gold hair to anxious gray.

Hers is no frown on the world's outer things
Who in the deeps of silent wisdom knows
The meaning folded in the wild bird's wings,
Wrapped in the curvèd petals of the rose.

The love of all things, in that peace unknown,
Has wrapped her round through centuries of strife;
And wisdom slowly into joy has grown,
An oft-returning guest, she smiles on life.

Faithful to earth through crowding ages past,
Her eyes, grown gentle to the things she sees,

Shrink not from the deep Quiet and the Vast:
Her lips are shut on many memories.

THE ANNUNCIATION
(LEONARDO DA VINCI)

Through silver twilight, lily-laden, came
The Angel unto Mary. Everywhere
Small flowers lit the grass with gleams of flame,
Between those two, in the pale evening air.

It was the gentle hour of violet light,
The Angel smiled and sank upon his knees;
Darkly athwart the marble terrace white
Fell the chill shadow of the cypress trees.

ANGELS OF THE PASSION
(BOTTICELLI)

Are not these they who, since the world uprose
Out of the darkness, haunt man's desolate fate,
Who knows not whence he comes or where he goes,
Or if he is the child of love or hate?

Their tirèd eyes and pitiful faces pale,
With wistful passion and long weeping spent,
Keep watch about our sorrows, and avail
To throng with mysteries the steep ascent.

The riddle of the ancient world looks out
Of their strange faces; sighing do they spoil
Man's triumphs with the shadow of their doubt,
And gently bring to nought his passionate toil.

Ah, pitiful angels, since the world began,
And from the rock flowed forth time's bitter stream,
You have brought sorrow to the soul of man,
Knowing his purpose other than his dream.

You hold the harsh nails and the crown of thorns
In trembling hands waiting with patient eyes,
Through the long waste of many-coloured morns,
The white dawn of the eternal truth's sunrise.

THE EVERLASTING HERETIC
(A WOUNDED AMAZON; IN ROME)

In age-long silence patiently she stands,
Hiding deep in her wounded breast of stone
The secret of her lifted arms and hands
Raised by a lost dream to a deed unknown.

The world's first heretic and questioner
Of the dark instincts, this was her reward –
Red fire that burned the very heart of her –
She took the sword and perished by the sword.

The wild world went its way, since her harsh breath
Failed on the air, the wandering soul of man
Has passed from faith to faith, from death to death,
Seeking through centuries the ultimate pan.

She, through the storm of breaking dreams, wind-built,
Has seen religions fail and empires fall,
Whilst through the ages blood in torrents spilt
Has blurred the secret writing on the wall.
She has seen temples burned and faiths recede,
Catching swift gleams athwart the glare of strife,

Through the torn rift in every world-worn creed,
Of that brave purpose buried under life.

The centuries passing on their way, consigned
The world that conquered her to dust and fire,
They are but shadows shut out of her mind:
Eternal doubter of the world's desire.

Again and yet again, through the long years,
She hears the confident clear voice of youth
Unfold the secret of all joys and fears,
Claiming a captive in the chainless Truth,

Who silently eludes the feverish grasp
And desperate glamour of that fierce embrace;
For the sad soul of man outgrows his grasp,
And dreams but soothe him for a little space.

Oh, secret of the world and far-off goal
Of that long road that life's first pilgrim trod,
Most dear art thou unto the rebel soul,
Herself grown lovelier than her dream-built God.

Surely we dream; this calm-browed Amazon,
Whose will was like a great stream at the flood,
In whose fierce eyes the light of battle shone –
Shaker of iron laws, shedder of blood –

She whose hard deeds and gentle thoughts once braved
The swords of men, and all the world's dark powers –
Now on her marble brow holds deep engraved
The secret of a nobler will than ours.

Her soul aloof from our wild wayfaring,
No more the bitter pilgrim of a day,
Has found the goal of every swallow's wing,
Her marble peace smiles on our broken clay.

Thus doth the harsh defeated beauty, spent
In the lost battle, all sweet dreams outshine –
Soul of the white force and the sheer ascent,
Wounded, implacably at peace, divine.

THE FISHERMEN
(BY HOLMAN HUNT)

Though they live in a faery land
Homely people are they,
Dragging their nets o'er the sand
Of the opal and luminous bay.
There are prizes and honours to win
In the world as of old,
And they watch for a silver fin
In a sea of gold.
Those who read the signs of the skies
Make haste to crowd on sail,
And all men born who are wise
Get home before the gale.
This is the world's desire –
This is the fisherman's goal –
The lamp and the cottage fire,
And shelter and ease of soul.
Ah, but the voice in the wind
The call of the glittering wave?
Better an easy mind,
Long life, and a grassy grave!
Thus the sunset glory in vain
Rose flashes over the bay:
To the village safe in the plain
Unmoved they take their way.
Alas these fishermen so blind
May that wise God forgive,

Who hides in dreams from all mankind
The light by which they live.

DIVINA COMMEDIA
'In la sua volontade è nostra pace.' – Dante

These things have passed; no more through twilight
hours,
In that dark Eden of the coloured May,
On the brown river's bank among the flowers,
Countess Mathilda takes her painted way.

And little red anemones, and white
Narcissus seem to dream in vain
Of the blue sky and the sun's gentle light,
And the lost streams of the far Tuscan plain.
Now long forgotten is that wood serene
Where Lethe's moonless waters onward glide,
Bending the ragged blades of grass that lean
Forth from the green bank underneath the tide.

Noble Piccarda's pearly brows divine
Holding the secret of the world-old rune,
Like a fair jewel in a carven shrine
Trouble no more the white ways of the moon.

Long mute is Cavalcanti's broken prayer;
The smile of Beatrice, to earth denied,
Shines now no more on Saturn's golden stair;
Through no sad town shall Virgil be our guide.

Along the dark ravine, in single file,
Monks of Bologna now no longer tread
The weary mazes of the dismal aisle,
Beneath the torment of the cowls of lead.

No flaming tomb can smother down the chords
Of the new music delicately harsh,
Beyond the glint of crowns, the clash of swords,
And the lost horror of the bloodstained marsh.

For we, men say, have lost our heaven and go
Along dim valleys shadowed everywhere,
Far from the hills where, glittering, the white snow
Yet stabs with cruel knives the sunny air.

As Dante's fierce God, throned in love and light
Yet pierced the hearts of gentle folk and kind,
And drove out gracious Virgil from his sight,
And turned to bitterness the sunny wind.

We sigh where Dante sang, our hungry eyes
Grown weary of the angels' flaming wings,
Have made a rainbow heaven of tears and sighs,
And the sea's voice, and pale and sorrowful things.

We sigh where Dante sang – thus have we found
His poor lost people on that open road,
That leads through marsh and fire and broken ground
Unto the ultimate divine abode.

Piccarda triumphs in that dream of hers
That bitter grief and outrage had not slain,
The secret that the world's soul shakes and stirs,
That Dante sought through conquered stars in vain.

And Beatrice, – vanished is the shining sphere
And saints' high throne above the world apart,
Yet with us dwells the dream divine and dear
That folds in beauty every living heart.

The heaven time brings us shall not be too strait
For pale Francesca; only broken bars

Lie prone where once was hid, by the sad gate,
'The love that moved the sun and the other stars.'

A love grown wide enough for Plato's dream
And Homer's story; not too cramped to hold
Those pilgrim souls, by Acheron's sad stream,
For ever shut out of the barrèd fold.

Death without glory, heaven without wings
On angels, bright hopes overthrown,
We sigh where Dante sang, our wanderings
Have brought us to the gate of life unknown.

No heaven is ours of lights and whirling flame –
For dying warriors a starlit goal –
But a lost country called by a new name,
Deep buried in dim valleys of the soul.

A gentle land where the white singing waves
Move softly under silver twilight skies,
And life with her fierce wars and dreadful graves
Seems but a little wind that falling sighs.

No painful voice makes pitiful that wind,
All bitter dreams sleep in the quiet vale
Where, out of clashing darkness fierce and blind,
A new dawn glimmers gently, olive-pale.

The poet's laurel and the martyr's palm
Wither, the old enchantments fade and cease;
Yet still the vision of the ancient calm
Folds, round this weary world, wide wings of peace.

And all men passing down beneath the boughs
Of the dim forest to the magic sea
Mysterious, have felt against their brows
The buffet of the ancient mystery.

A drift of scattered spray, a fallen leaf,
Bear witness to that strange and unseen wind
That drives the high tide over shoal and reef
And lonely beaches of moon-haunted mind.

The light that passes, with a sudden thrill,
The moonlight's glamour and the twilight's gleam –
Waking beyond our world of good and ill
The sleeping purpose underneath the dream.

The ray of cold reality austere,
Shining beyond the gates of joy or dole,
That to the eyes of sorrow shall make clear
The hidden dweller in the darkened soul.

For whose sake Dante by the convent door,
Sure of his golden heaven at close of day,
When the monk asked what he was seeking for,
Answered but 'Peace' and went upon his way.

Shrinking from dreadful creeds of storm and stress
And dreams of passionate wrath, bitter and blind,
To seek in his own soul for gentleness
And find the Divine in a comrade's mind.

As one who knew the inner unseen tide
Of beauty beating up against the walls
At evening, breaking down their coloured pride
When all things are as one, and twilight falls.

This was his grief, shut behind iron bars,
Roaming through darkened rooms in sunless towers –
His soul yet caught a glamour from the stars,
And knew the dauntless will of the wild flowers.

The captive soul of gentleness in him
Looked out through narrowed windows, passion-blurred;

Yet through the darkness of his prison dim
The far faint voices of the rain were heard.

With them he trysted outside heaven's gate
Who mould the gracious word and carve the stone,
To thrust aside one moment love and hate
And gaze into the eyes of the Unknown.

For he was one of those sad souls who wrought
Life into glory, marble into form,
And carved across the brows of human thought
The Eternal Beauty's pale and frozen storm.

Now that the sunshine has quenched all his fire
And time has swept his narrow gates apart,
We lean across the sundering ages dire
To greet the dreamer of the pitiless heart,

Knowing the Infinite Quiet, pale and vast,
Floats round his dreams, as the dark tide floats round
The loud green waves that rise and thunder past,
And sink to rest in silent seas profound.

LUCIFERA

Oh, tired of many lives and many dooms,
Breaker of waves and shedder of all tears,
Staggering beneath the weight of the world's years,
Builder of cities, hewer out of tombs,
What though thy torch, amid these ancient glooms,
Burns dimly in a flicker of hopes and fears,
Casting pale shadows on the shining spheres
From that lost verge where giant darkness looms –
Yet is the secret of all beauty thine,
Oh, mother of many sorrows! Thou art still

Witness of peace and the one light divine,
Shedder of rays, yet the dark secret will
Of troubled waters in this soul of mine,
And bright cloud shadows on the blue-lit hill.

FORM

The buried statue through the marble gleams,
Praying for freedom, an unwilling guest,
Yet flooding with the light of her strange dreams
The hard stone folded round her uncarved breast.

Founded in granite, wrapped in serpentine,
Light of all life and heart of every storm,
Doth the uncarven image, the Divine,
Deep in the heart of each man, wait for form.

THE INNER EGERIA

Once long ago in this dim wood
The Wise Nymph of the shining stream
Before the dreaming Numa stood,
Her clear voice mingled with his dream.

At Rome amongst the ilex glooms
When all the world waits for the spring,
And while the early crocus blooms,
She whispered wise words to the King.

Though Rome be far as Nineveh
From the dark road my feet must tread,
Yet do I meet her every day –
Salt on my cheek her tears are shed.

Nymph of the stream of life, she hides
In that small sacred wood apart,
Where the enchanted king abides,
And the first flowers bloom in my heart.

THE DEATH OF ORPHEUS

One was the undivided Holy Light
When those wild wills found Orpheus on the plain,
And tore apart the rhythmic limbs and white:
Thus was the music of the whole world slain,
Thus was the deed of devastation done,
And broken rays split from the wingèd sun.

Soft music lingers through sea-scented days,
And songs can harden coward hearts to war,
And streams with sweet sounds fill the wild wood ways,
And the waves chant on every broken shore;
But the lost music's secret strain and thrill
Shall break no more the heart of each green hill.

The west wind rustles through green leaves and brown,
The white clouds sail along the chanting breeze,
On the glad grass the rain comes singing down,
Piercing through green boughs of unbending trees;
And all these singers mourn the great dream fled,
The music of the world broken and dead.

Now do swift gleams and shining circles float
In each bright stream that glitters on the wind;
And ever and anon a sudden note,
Harsh in the singing, brings the dead to mind.
Lost rhythms sigh in every wind that blows,
And sleep in the curved petals of the rose.

Yea, at the twilight hour when white waves break
On silver shores under the rose-lit blue,
The world is hushed awhile for Orpheus' sake,
And the lost music of the Wise and True
Her rainbow arch across the silence flings,
And to the sun gives pale translucent wings.

Faithful are all things to that Holy One,
There is no traitor under the blue skies.
Beyond all golden dreams and deeds once done
The memory of the Eternal Beauty lies,
And buried deep beneath the grass and fern
The fires of the Eternal Beauty burn.

Thou who didst lift the mountain from the vale
With song, and drag the red rose from her root,
And o'er the secret herbs and stones prevail,
Amongst the hemlock lies thy broken lute;
Nor shall the echoes of that singing cease,
Nor any tree, nor wind, nor wave, have peace.

Children of Dionysos, ye were strong
To shatter all the tense strings of the lyre,
To break the fierce line of the embattled song,
To wreck the boat that held the Eternal Fire:
For the one Light ye gave us many gleams,
For the one Dream a host of shining dreams.

THE IMMORTAL SOUL

Pure gold did Nero's palace shine,
O'er mighty ships the Eagles soared,
Lord of the world was Constantine,
Of a lost dream was Julian lord.

The eagles passed on bloodstained wings,
Blurred is the broken marble's pride,
Yet fair amongst immortal things
Did that rejected dream abide.

The golden house has passed away,
And sunk is every fierce trireme;
The conquered dreamer men could slay,
No man could conquer the proud dream.

The trumpets, mute for many days,
Call forth no more the embattled host;
And Cæsar, in his crown of bays,
Is but a weak and wandering ghost.

Yet amongst columns overthrown
Of the white vestal temple fair,
A Pilgrim from the far unknown
Breathes here once more the golden air.

Once more in Rome she takes her rest,
Holding from the great life outcast,
Safe in a little human breast,
The august secret of the past.

Into her hands in ages gone
The great dreams of the spirit fell –
From life to life she hands them on
Inviolate, invincible.

No great thought crumbles with the hours,
No dreams decay, no gods grow old.
Though broken are the temple towers,
Shall not our hearts those shrines enfold?

We look at life with our new eyes,
The ancient spirit in us stirs,

Piercing the flimsy fresh disguise
Wrapped round that secret past of hers.

Each Soul holds all the oracles –
In a few years, to every man
Who hears her gentle voice, she tells
Life's mysteries since time began.

Like a child playing in the grass
On through the wind-blown sunny hours,
The patient ages as they pass
But fill her lap with fallen flowers.

The golden asphodel that shone
Beyond dim Hades' gate of glooms;
Great dreams of Tyre and Babylon,
And pale Egyptian lotus blooms;

Green laurels from the victor's car;
Deep Syrian roses, white and red;
And that pale scented Eastern star,
The jasmine flower that crowns the dead.

All these are hers, who, weeping strange,
Deep in the heart of hearts abides,
And all the woes of time and change
Beneath our joys and sorrows hides.

Glad is she through the centuries
With each new morning's golden air,
Beneath all beauty she is wise,
Beyond all wisdom she is fair.

Once in the brave lost dawn of time
She watched, with an exultant thrill,
The crownèd victor's chariot climb
In triumph the steep sacred hill.

Now the low wail of death and grief
She hears in every trumpet call;
She shudders, at the falling leaf,
Who saw Troy burn and Carthage fall.

To her the conqueror's battle-cry
Is as a doomèd army's moan,
She has seen thousands fail and die –
Alas, the soul grows wise alone.

Veiled watcher in the deeps unseen,
Thou ancient childlike soul of mine,
Life after life hast thou not been
The priestess of a crumbling shrine?

As vestals in a city marred
By war and famine, change and fate,
Through the long centuries could guard
The dreams of Rome inviolate:

So has she held in her long trust
The wisdom and the fire of earth;
She stands between us and the dust,
From death to death, from birth to birth.

And ever, through sunshine and cloud,
She guards the ancient holy flame,
And shares with all things fair and proud
Her radiant secret whence she came.

Hers are the dreams that once were Rome's,
No light nor flame shall she forget,
Deep in her secret catacombs
The Lord Christ's footsteps linger yet.

Older than Rome, through ages dark
She knew swift smiles and bitter tears,

And heard the singing of the lark,
Self-conscious through ten thousand years.

Strong with a strange transfigured youth
The ages cannot break her wings,
She is the witness of the truth,
The guardian of immortal things.

Scant new light on her path is shed,
She follows where the dreamers trod,
Behind the banners of the dead
Unto the temple of the God.

THE MAN WHO WOULD REMEMBER

'All of them marched into the plain of Lethe amidst
dreadful heat and scorching ... When night came on
they encamped beside the river Amalete whose waters
no vessel contains. Of this water all of them must drink
... and he who from time to time drinks forgets
everything.' – Plato.

Parchèd and thirsty on the river bank,
In that pale meadow of the long since dead,
Amongst the waving poppy blooms he sank,
Deep in long grasses laid his weary head.

Here the dead passed, a pale and changing throng,
The king, the priest, the fighter and the knave,
The wronger and the sufferer of wrong,
The true, the false, the coward and the brave.

And many lingered by the sighing stream
And wept a little while ere they could part
With the sharp sword of wrath, or the bright dream,
Or the king's mantle folded round the heart.

Yea, even those whose sorrows craved an end
Shrank from the verge of that so dark relief,
And mourned the sad face of a dying friend
In the dim features of their fading grief.

The coward and the false, the foully slain,
The poor, forlorn, despised, shed bitter tears,
Clung to the memory of their withered pain
And folded round them all their heavy years.

As Hector parted weeping from his bride
On that dark morn when Ilium's towers fell,
So did each mourner by sad Lethe's side
Unto his own soul say a long farewell.

Though many a one in that dim resting-place
Did from a heavy burden find release,
Yet all men wept over the river's grace
Of fair oblivion and most blessèd peace.

And he who would remember with sad eyes
Watched the white stars burn forth his horoscope,
And saw his soul, in many a strange disguise,
Build up the baffled walls of light and hope.
Soft winds swayed rustling in the fringèd reeds,
And gentle voices cried 'Drink, dreamer, drink,
Go forth unhindered to the life of deeds,
Deep in the stream thy heavy burden sink.'

A poet passed him singing in great praise
Of fair oblivion, the Eternal's grace
To those who toil along the rough earth ways,
From life to life, finding no resting-place.

He sang of moon-lit waters rippling cool,
And how one might forget this life of pain

And drown one's burden in deep Lethe's pool,
And be a little laughing child again.

'I will lay down,' he said, 'Remembrance cold,
And all the store of dreams that once were mine,
And thoughts and lives and wisdoms manifold,
For the restored light of my lost youth divine.

'A child among the children of the earth,
I will go forth and laugh and weep once more,
Remembering not the woes of death and birth,
But a new soul with new worlds to explore.'

Then, at his word, the ever-mourning host
Saw the white fearlessness of life-to-be
Safe in the arms of every pallid ghost,
The promise of a new youth shadow-free.

And each one, clasping close the radiant dream,
No more from the pale river's margin shrank.
Like ghostly willows bending o'er the stream
The silver shadows swayed and stooped and drank.

Then did a voice speak in the dreamer's soul:
'Drink not, behold, the tears of all men flow.
Better set out for thine appointed goal
Dry-eyed and watchful, with thy haunting woe.

'Lest thou once more should be as thou hast been,
Hold closely thy dead selves to be thy guides
To that lost treasure of the Light Unseen
That in the soul of every man abides.

'Who drinks of this dull tide must thirst again,
For him are strife and peace and death and birth,
The long monotonies of joy and pain
That bind men to the circle of the earth.

'But he who seeks beyond the waves of sleep
The star that shines above the shadow-strife,
Finds the lost stream, the well of waters deep,
That springeth upward to Eternal Life.

'His soul, deep set in the eternal mind,
A broken light in Saturn's star-strewn ring,
In blue transparent deeps of life shall find
The gulf of ages but a little thing.

'He shall be one with all men's striving, one
With every passing hour and sorrowful fate,
Whose heart through centuries of wind and sun
Is still a beggar at the ivory gate.'

Then he who would remember, undismayed,
Laid down the lovely form of shining youth,
To the Eternal in the twilight prayed:
'I give my childhood for thine ageless Truth.'

SONNETS

I. SUNSET NEAR THE ROSSES

Mysteriously the last hour's opal light
Doth on the glamoured sea in peace descend,
The great winds fail, and gently comes the night,
The wild swans float on sunset waters bright.
All coloured tides and fire-born rhythms blend,
Intent the veil of mystery to rend
Where secret things glide upward into sight.
Poseidon tending his white flock of sheep
Has driven them downward to the twilight fold
And lulled each restless breaking wave to sleep;
A thin cloud, wrapped about the sunset's gold,

O'er fallen waves a little rain doth weep;
Surely the secret Lazarus never told
Lies buried somewhere in the silent deep.

II. THE HIDDEN PURPOSE

Silver the river flows out of the West –
Into the deeps of the ocean she flings
Her singing streams and her radiant springs –
Serenley she flows to her age-long rest.
Child of the hills and the green meadows' guest,
Here under the flash of the sea-bird's wings
She learns the wild song that the free wind sings,
Great waves and new wonders surge in her breast.
Blue sweep her tides o'er the opaline shells,
For her joy no longer the primrose blows,
She scorns the high hills and the shadowy dells,
Forgetting the lily and false to the rose,
She is faithful unto her hidden wells
And straight to the heart of the deep she goes.

III. 'WHERE GREAT WAVES BREAK'

Far from the downs and the safe farm lands
And the quiet meadows and comforting trees,
And the gladness of men who take their ease,
Where the tide flows over treacherous sands,
Earth fenced about with her sharp rocks stands,
With her waters gathered about her knees,
Where the breaking waves of impossible seas
Build up dream houses not made with hands –
The soil is scant and stubborn and bare,
There is light and to spare and yet not a sound

Save the surge of the wild sea everywhere;
But the grimmest of rocks are folded round
By the glory of moving waters fair,
And where great waves break there is holy ground.

IV. THE LOST COLOUR

The small blue waves in the great flood of light
Break on sunk rocks and shiver and are still,
Whilst seas of gold flow onward with a will –
Great waves that break on the far mountain height,
Or foam away through yellow cornfields bright,
Where to the sunlight strains each wind-swept hill,
And earth holds up her cup for heaven to fill
With the clear glory of the gold and white.
Outcast from earth the ripples scattered lie,
Reflected, tossed back like a baffled prayer,
Gliding through silent pools of shining air,
Far from the broken sunbeams, high and dry
Above the green world, flooding everywhere
In deep lost lakes of blueness, the vast sky.

V. SHELLS

Cowries among the rocks the children find,
Sharp cut and shining in the sunset glow,
Eternal victims of the ebb and flow,
Moulded by rhythms of the mournful wind
In those deep waters, terrible and blind,
Where mighty waves draw out the under-tow,
And the sea's precious things drift to and fro,
And God moulds all things mortal to His mind.
Breaker of Waves, and Lord of the High Tide,

Has the long pilgrimage no end nor goal?
Is there no peace here under the blue sky?
Nothing but sand and storm and rock and shoal,
And the dark water's sullen heave and sigh,
The eternal tumult of the baffled soul?

VI. WAVES

Surely this life is as a flowing wave,
Foaming itself away on rock and shoal
And thundering into many a dark sea-cave,
And finding many a dim mysterious goal
Where on black rocks the Atlantic breakers rave,
Shattering in wrath the sea's untroubled whole –
Or near the blue hill and white cairn of Maeve
Flinging on grey sands down a silver soul,
Waves of the world and children of the tide,
Broken and battered on earth's sharp-set shore.
Were it not then much better to abide
Far from the endless elemental war,
In the sea's deep and silent heart to hide,
And break on the world's jaggèd edge no more?

VII. TRAGEDY

Dark earth of fading leaves and dying flowers
Behold, the blue and golden summer air,
And mighty waters moving everywhere,
And all the joy of sunshine and swift showers,
Are but the gentleness of kindly powers
That help us with cold strengthening hands to bear
Our restless doom and agonising share
Of the great sorrow of this birth of ours.

Yet in this world of waves and flashing wings
We dream awhile of lost and broken spheres,
And learn among life's deep mysterious springs
That pain is all the wisdom of our years,
And sorrow, deepest of life's hidden things,
From all men's eyes at last shall dry the tears.

VIII. KNOCKNAREA

Where silver lights and twilight shadows glide,
And the last coloured air grows tense and keen,
Floating aloft in the pale water's sheen
The mountains seem to rise out of the tide,
So blue it looks and near the other side
Of that great stretch of sea that lies between,
Though many meadows gold and white and green,
And grassy lawns, do on that far shore hide.
For all men's ways, trodden of weary feet
By many pilgrims, up the mountain wind,
Past fields of barley and deep golden wheat:
Some on the haunted cairn still hope to find
The light of dreams, and some but dig for peat
Where the high hills hold fire for all mankind.

IX. BY THE SEA

The people who live in the Midlands know
How to build cities and temples and towers,
And live fair lives in gardens of flowers
Where round their windows the roses blow.
But we, who can neither reap nor sow,
Find little enough in the land that is ours;
We have lost touch of the green earth's powers;

The tides of our being ebb and flow
With those lonely waters that all men shun.
We seek the swift current's secret goal:
Ours are the dreams that are many and one,
The waves that shatter the sea that is whole,
The spirit's rhythm of wind and sun,
And eternal broken waves of the soul.

X. WALLS

Free to all souls the hidden beauty calls,
The sea-thrift dwelling on her spray-swept height,
The lofty rose, the low-grown aconite,
The gliding river and the stream that brawls
Down the sharp cliffs with constant breaks and falls –
All these are equal in the equal light –
All waters mirror the one Infinite.
God made a garden, it was men built walls;
But the wide sea from men is wholly freed:
Freely the great waves rise and storm and break,
Nor softlier go for any land-lord's need,
Where rhythmic tides flow for no miser's sake
And none hath profit of the brown sea-weed,
But all things give themselves, yet none may take.

THE VAGRANT'S ROMANCE
(A REINCARNATION PHANTASY)

This was the story never told
By one who cared not for the world's gold.

One of the idle and unwise,
A beggar with unfathomable eyes.

One who had nothing but dreams to give
To men who are eager to labour and live.

For the world in its wisdom deep and dim
Had taken all pleasure and treasure from him.

This was the story his soul could tell,
Immortal and unfathomable.

There was no record in his brain,
He did not know he should live again.

But there was one who read the whole,
Buried deep in a dead man's soul.

'In the days of Atlantis, under the wave,
I was a slave, the child of a slave.

When the towers of Atlantis fell,
I died and was born again in hell.

From that sorrowful prison I did escape
And hid myself in a hero's shape.

But few years had I of love or joy,
A Trojan I fell at the Siege of Troy.

I came again in a little while,
An Israelite slave on the banks of the Nile.

Then did I comfort my grief-laden heart
With the magic lore and Egyptian art.

Fain was I to become Osiris then,
But soon I came back to the world of men.

By the Ganges I was an outcast born,
A wanderer and a child of scorn.

By the waters of Babylon I wept,
My harp amongst the willows slept.

In the land of Greece I opened my eyes,
To reap the fields of Plotinus the Wise.

When the great light shattered the world's closed bars,
I was a shepherd who gazed at the stars.

For lives that were lonely, obscure, apart,
I thank the Hidden One, in my heart,

That always and always under the sun
I went forth to battle and never won.

A slayer of men, I was doomed to abide,
For ever and aye, on the losing side.

Whenever I dream of the wonderful goal,
I thank the hidden God in my soul

That though I have always been meanly born,
A tiller of earth and a reaper of corn,

Whenever through ages past and gone
The light divine for a moment shone,

Whenever piercing laborious night
A ray fell straight from the Light of Light,

Whenever amid fierce lightning and storm
The divine moved in a human form,

Whenever the earth in her cyclic course
Shook at the touch of an unknown force,

Whenever the cloud of dull years grew thin
And a great star called to the light within,

I have braved storm and labour and sun
To stand at the side of that Holy One.

No matter how humble my birth has been,
There are few who have seen what I have seen.

Mine the shepherd's star and the reaper's reward,
And the dream of him who fell by the sword.

One thing I have learned the long years through,
To know the false words from the true.

The slave who toiled on the banks of the Nile
With wisdom gladdened his long exile.

From Buddha at eve by the Ganges' side
An outcast learnt the worth of the world's pride.

To the tired reaper, when day was done,
Did Plotinus unveil the hidden sun.

Amongst the stars, on a Syrian night,
A ragged shepherd found the Light of Light.

From dream to dream, o'er valley and hill,
I followed the Lord Christ's wandering will.

Kings there are who would barter a throne
For the long day's toil and the light unknown,

The deed of the strong and the word of the wise,
And the night under cold and starry skies –

The white light of dawn on the hillside shed
On Him who had nowhere to lay His head.

Behold there are kings who would change with me,
For the love of the ancient mystery.

Shepherd and reaper and slave I have been,
There are few who have seen what I have seen.

I have been a gipsy since those days,
And lived again in the wild wood ways.

Wise with the lore of those hidden things,
Learnt from Lord Christ in His wanderings,

Beggar and reaper and shepherd and slave,
I am one who rests not in any grave;

I will follow each stormy light divine,
And the secret of all things shall be mine.

These things have I seen, would you bid me mourn
That I was never an Emperor born?'

HARVEST

Though the long seasons seem to separate
Sower and reaper or deeds dreamed and done,
Yet when a man reaches the Ivory Gate
Labour and life and seed and corn are one.

Because thou art the doer and the deed,
Because thou art the thinker and the thought,
Because thou art the helper and the need,
And the cold doubt that brings all things to nought,

Therefore in every gracious form and shape
The world's dear open secret shalt thou find,
From the One Beauty there is no escape
Nor from the sunshine of the Eternal mind.

The patient labourer, with guesses dim,
Follows this wisdom to its secret goal.
He knows all deeds and dreams exist in him,
And all men's God in every human soul.

THE ANTI-SUFFRAGIST

The princess in her world-old tower pined
A prisoner, brazen-caged, without a gleam
Of sunlight, or a windowful of wind;
She lived but in a long lamp-lighted dream.

They brought her forth at last when she was old;
The sunlight on her blanchèd hair was shed
Too late to turn its silver into gold.
'Ah, shield me from this brazen glare!' she said.

THE VISION OF NIAMH
Niamh was perhaps the Uranian Aphrodite of Irish
legend – the goddess of remote and spiritual beauty.

Life grows so clear, beneath the dreaming lamp,
I can see through the darkness of the grave,

How, long ago in her high mountain camp
The stars shone on the stormy soul of Maeve.

And leaning from the shadow of a star
With hands outstretched to hold the hands of clay,
One looked into her spirit fairer far
Than sun or moon of any mortal day.

Oh Niamh, thou art child of the dim hours
Between the day and night, when Summer flings
A little flashing dew on the wild flowers,
And all the starlight glimmers in thy wings.

Thou sorrow of lost beauty, thou strange queen
Who calls to men's soul out of twilight seas,
Whose white hands break the stars in silver sheen,
Whose voice is as the wind in the fir trees.

For thee Maeve left her kingdom and her throne,
And all the gilded wisdom of the wise,
And dwelt among the hazel trees alone
So that she might look into Niamh's eyes.

No sorrow of lost battles any more
In her enchanted spirit could abide;
Straight she forgot the long and desolate war,
And how Fionavar for pity died.

Ah, Niamh, still the starry lamp burns bright,
I can see through the darkness of the grave,
How long ago thy soul of starry light
Was very dear to the brave soul of Maeve.

THE PROMISE OF SPEED

Drive faster, the spirit out of the vast
Stands in the storm knocking at the heart's door,
There's truce, there's a truce in the ancient war,
And my heart and my soul are at peace at last.

Fast follow the clouds on their wind-driven wings,
The white road writhes under our rushing wheels,
And rent with fierce rapture the air reveals
The innermost truth at the heart of things.

Now, through the torn sunlight and shaken blue air,
Waves of the fury and storm of our speed
Thrill to the heart of the hard world's need,
Break on the stones of the earth's despair.

Light shines in the body's innermost glooms,
The senses thrill, with mysterious power,
The deeps of the heart where a magic flower
In a rapture of life and laughter blooms.

Dark element rushing forth into light
In the crumbling brain and the vanishing fire,
She shall not die with the dead desire;
She shall not abide in the shades of night.

Blue sky, the immortal design of her!
In thy gleam is her dream-power manifest,
To build up a palace fit for her guest,
A prison fit for her prisoner.

Therefore, long after the last disgrace
Of ashes to ashes and earth to earth,
She stands at the gate of the second birth,
She too is of proud eternal race.

She who was one with the grass and the weed
Shall be one with the sunshine, one with the soul,
One with the restless illuminate Whole,
One with the flower who was one with the seed.

She who was one with the wind and the storm,
One with the whirling and glittering stars,
Shall break through the elemental bars
And fold her white dreams in the Ultimate Form.

She who swayed in the shadows and flashed in the sun,
And danced with the hail on the desolate plain,
And rose in the rainbow and fell in the rain,
Shall be gathered at last to the deeps of the One.

She who lay dark at the roots of the flowers
Shall soar with the White May and shine with the Rose,
And gleam in the River of Life that flows
Deep under the Spirit's embattled towers.

She who was one with the broken sod,
One with the worm and one with the dust,
One with the terror, one with the trust,
Shall be one with the radiant and lightning-winged god.

Oh, dim burns the lamp of the Infinite!
In the unknown Spirit's innermost shrine
Does the little candle of this world shine;
No shadowy power can quench the frailest light.

No man shall sever the part from the whole,
Nought shall be refuse or thrown away,
The sculptor shall never forget the clay,
The Body knocks at the door of the Soul.

THE ROMANCE OF MAEVE

The harvest is scant, and the labourer,
Returning at sunset with so few sheaves,
Has gathered gold bracken and silver fir
And boughs of the elm and the brown beech leaves.

Fuel enough for the evening blaze,
When the blue of the sky grows wintry and pale,
And the pilgrim home from the wild wood ways
Can read by the fire an ancient tale:

How a great Queen could cast away her crown,
The tumult of her high victorious pride,
To rest among the scattered fir-cones brown
And watch deep waters through the moonlight glide.

'I'
'All this is threaded on Me as jewels on a string.'
Bhagavad Gita.

If I could be one with the waves of grief
That break on the earth's unquiet shores,
One with belief and unbelief,
The digger of graves and the maker of wars,

One with the passionate dreams of the brave,
One with the changing and idle throng,
One with the tyrant, one with the slave,
I should be one with the whole world's song,

One with the rising and falling tides,
The guiding stars and the perilous deep
One with the opal shadow that glides
Over the blue-lit mountain steep,

One with the flash of storm-driven wings,
One with the river of light that flows
Over the meanest of trivial things
Into the heart of the wild rose.

My heart would be as the moonlight still,
The silver light on the cold night wind,
The soul of good in the evil will,
The dream of peace in the painful mind.

If I could lose myself in the whole,
My soul in the sunshine, my heart in the storm
I should find peace in the human soul,
And the spirit of God in a human form.

CLEOPATRA'S PEARL

In the deep world unseen,
Under the wash of the tide,
On bright sands coraline
Did the pearl of pearls abide
Till the Queen's valiant slave,
He who had eaten her bread,
Sank down through the blue wave
To the land of the white and red,
The land where no man embalm or bury the wandering
dead.

The evil sharks in the bay
Waited in vain to kill.
More swift and subtle than they,
The fisherman had his will.
The pearl that shone in the Queen's hair
Brought light from the shades profound.

The fisher had night for his share:
Yea, the pearl fisher was drowned,
And clasped in his rigid hand was the glory of Egypt
found.

Ah, the Queen had a crown of gold!
Such a pearl for her crown!
With a bitter acid and cold,
She has melted it down.
Hers was the precious draft,
White from the shades of night;
And the fisherman's broken raft
Lies buried and out of sight.
But deep in the diver's soul burns clear the lost pearl's
hidden light.

BROKEN GLORY
(1918)

THE AGE OF GOLD

When Jacob's Ladder reached the skies,
And the earth shone like other stars,
And men were not called great and wise,
Nor had they fashioned prison bars,
And tigers had not learned to slay –
I slept alone in the dark wood,
And when the sun rose every day
I saw why God called his work good.

GOVERNMENT

The rulers of the earth, savage and blind,
Have dug Gethsemane for all mankind.
For their honour and their glory and their pride,
In every age the heroes of all nations died.
Thus Joan of Arc and Socrates were slain
By the world's bane,
Jesus Christ a thousand years ago,
They servèd so,
And Roger Casement, just the other day,
Went the same way.
Now is their hour of power and life's despair
From blasted earth and desecrated air
The universal death that is their dream
Flows o'er the earth in a great lava stream,
Whelming men's thoughts in floods of liquid fire,
To light the old world's funeral pyre.

Shall then our hearts in hell-fire burn
To serve their turn?
God's splendid rebels, and men's stupid slaves
Earn the same graves.
Oh! rather let us scorn life's baser gains,

The joyless spoils of death-strewn battle plains,
Where for our rulers' glory and their lust
Some million human brains are bloodstained dust.
Far better labour for that purpose known
Unto the gods alone,
That hides behind the darkness and the storm
In every human form,
If but to die on God's dear battle plain,
Where daisies mount to life through sun and rain,
Whilst the wild winds their rapturous tumults rouse,
And the trees fight for beauty in green boughs.
Peace be to those who rule and hate and kill –
The world's true will
Has brought, in this dark hour of pain and strife,
A violet to life.

EASTER WEEK

Grief for the noble dead
Of one who did not share their strife,
And mourned that any blood was shed,
Yet felt the broken glory of their state,
Their strange heroic questioning of Fate
Ribbon with gold the rags of this our life.

HEROIC DEATH, 1916

No man shall deck their resting-place with flowers;
Behind a prison wall they stood to die,
Yet in those flowerless tragic graves of ours
Buried, the broken dreams of Ireland lie.

No cairn-heaped mound on a high windy hill
With Irish earth the hero's heart enfolds,
But a burning grave at Pentonville,
The broken heart of Ireland holds.

Ah! ye who slay the body, how man's soul
Rises above your hatred and your scorns –
All flowers fade as the years onward roll,
Theirs is the deathless wreath – a crown of thorns.

TO CONSTANCE – IN PRISON

Outcast from joy and beauty, child of broken hopes
forlorn,
Lost to the magic mountains and parted from all flowers,
Robbed of the harvest moon that shines on far-off fields of
corn,
Bereft of raindrops on green leaves, bright wrecks of fallen
showers.

Nay, not outcast, whilst through your soul a sudden
rapture thrills,
And all your dreams are shaken by the salt Atlantic wind,
The gods descend at twilight from the magic-hearted hills,
And there are woods and primroses in the country of your
mind.

Yours is that inner Ireland beyond green fields and
brown,
Where waves break dawn-enchanted on the haunted
Rosses shore,
And clouds above Ben Bulben fling their coloured
shadows down,
Whilst little rivers shine and sink in wet sands at
Crushmor.

CHRISTMAS EVE IN PRISON

Do not be lonely, dear, nor grieve
This Christmas Eve.
Is it so vain a thing
That your heart's harper, Dark Roseen,
A wandering singer, yet a queen,
Crownèd with all her seventeen stars,
Outside your prison bars
Stands carolling?

TO C. M. ON HER PRISON BIRTHDAY
FEBRUARY 1917

What has time to do with thee,
Who hast found the victor's way
To be rich in poverty,
Without sunshine to be gay,
To be free in a prison cell?
Nay on that undreamed judgment day,
When on the old world's scrap-heap flung,
Powers and empires pass away,
Radiant and unconquerable
Thou shalt be young.

ROGER CASEMENT

I dream of one who is dead,
As the forms of green trees float and fall in the water,
The dreams float and fall in my mind.

I dream of him wandering in a far land,
I dream of him bringing hope to the hopeless,
I dream of him bringing light to the blind.

I dream of him hearing the voice,
The bitter cry of Kathleen ni Houlighaun
On the salt Atlantic wind.

I dream of the hatred of men,
Their lies against him who knew nothing of lying,
Nor was there fear in his mind.

I dream of our hopes and fears,
The long bitter struggle of the broken-hearted,
With hearts that were poisoned and hard.

I dream of the peace in his soul,
And the early morning hush on the grave of a hero
In the desolate prison yard.

I dream of the death that he died,
For the sake of God and Kathleen ni Houlighaun,
Yea, for Love and the Voice on the Wind.

I dream of one who is dead.
Above dreams that float and fall in the water
A new star shines in my mind.

COMRADES

The peaceful night that round me flows,
Breaks through your iron prison doors,
Free through the world your spirit goes,
Forbidden hands are clasping yours.

The wind is our confederate,
The night has left her doors ajar,
We meet beyond earth's barrèd gate,
Where all the world's wild Rebels are.

FRANCIS SHEEHY-SKEFFINGTON
DUBLIN, APRIL 26, 1916

No green and poisonous laurel wreath shall shade
His brow, who dealt no death in any strife,
Crown him with olive who was not afraid
To join the desolate unarmed ranks of life.

Who did not fear to die, yet feared to slay,
A leader in the war that shall end war,
Unarmed he stood in ruthless Empire's way,
Unarmed he stands on Acheron's lost shore.

Yet not alone, nor all unrecognized,
For at his side does that scorned Dreamer stand,
Who in the Olive Garden agonized,
Whose Kingdom yet shall come in every land,

When driven men, who fight and hate and kill
To order, shall let all their weapons fall,
And know that kindly freedom of the will
That holds no other human will in thrall.

UTOPIA

Cruelty, bloodshed and hate
Rule the night and the day,
The whole earth is desolate,
To what God shall one pray?

Is there a force that can end
The woe of the world's war?
Yea, when a friend meets a friend
There shall be peace once more.

For love at the heart of the storm
Breaks the waves of wild air,
And God in our human form
Is life's answer to prayer.

THE ARTIST IN WAR TIME

Oh, shining splendour of the human form
That takes my heart by storm,
Strong as a river, subtle as a prayer,
Or the first moon ray in the twilight air,
Line upon line of moving silver light,
Building our dreams up to the spirit's height,

Enfolding the grey dust and the earth's green
In coloured ecstasies of light unseen!
The Spirit that moves among the forest trees
Has doubtless built this shrine,
That erring men may fall upon their knees
And worship God and man, one soul divine –
Yea, and the little children of the earth
That make the world sweet with their wanderings,
And wild-willed pilgrims of mysterious birth
Gliding across the sky on silent wings.
Ah, surely no man born dare rise and slay
Eternal Beauty wrapped in robes of clay,
Or break and blast and utterly destroy
Life's little ivory tower of fragile joy!
Loud answerèd the black and stupid guns,
'We are the darlings of man's heart, the wise
Call us the world's Redeemers, mighty ones
Have bid us clear for them the troubled skies,
And holy souls have blessed us, for we stand
For God Almighty in a godless land.
God, Who art feeble grown and blind and dumb,

Take heart, through us Thy Kingdom yet shall come.'
Labourers in mad mechanic purpose bound,
They dig in vain Immortal Beauty's grave,
And bury the very starlight underground,
And crash above the song of wind and wave
Their monstrous rhythms of fire and steel and lead.
On some red field or battle-blasted hill
Men dream the Eternal Beauty lieth dead,
And all our souls are subject to their will.
Most ancient Beauty, scorned and thrust aside,
Who doth yet in white peace and silence dwell,
Pity us tortured slaves of bloodstained pride,
Lean out once more from the invisible,
Let fall from thy dream-haunted obscure throne
One ray of moonlight in earth's broken brain.
Our souls are thine, Belovèd, thine alone,
Behold thy lost world at thy feet again.

THE LOST TRAVELLER'S DREAM

Men say amid the hosts of hidden morrows hides
A real day lit with sunshine, wind-blown and dewdrop-
pearled,
A day of gentle dreams and magic flowing tides,
When dead shall lie the hates and sorrows of the world.

Alas! 'tis but a flame that falters on the wind,
A little spark of hope quenched in the world's dark wars,
A phantom light that haunts the sleep of men born blind,
A shipwrecked sailor's dream of lost and perilous shores.

Yet ever in the twilight our hearts throw off their load,
And fearless dreams with coloured wings in rapture shine,
Yea, you may meet the gods on any mountain road,
And every labourer knows the heart of earth divine.

Shall not the starlit Beauty, leaning from the hills,
Come down at last with her great winds for our release,
And lay cold hands of quiet on hot human wills,
And move the souls of men to Mercy and to Peace?

THE ETERNAL REBEL
1914

The phantoms flit before our dazzled eyes,
Glory and honour, wrath and righteousness,
The agèd phantoms in their bloodstained dress,
Vultures that fill the world with ravenous cries,
Swarming about the rock where, chained apart,
In age-long pain Prometheus finds no rest
From the divine flame burning in his breast,
And vultures tearing at a human heart.

Not yet the blessed hours on golden wings
Bring to the crucified their sure relief,
Deeper and deeper grows the ancient grief,
Blackest of all intolerable things.

Eternal Rebel, sad, and old, and blind,
Bound with a chain, enslaved by every one
Of the dark gods who hide the summer sun,
Yet art thou still the saviour of mankind.

Free soul of fire, break down their chains and bars,
Drive out those unclean phantoms of the brain,
Till every living thing be friends again,
And our lost earth true comrade to the stars.

THE WORLD'S GRIEF

'In all earthly happenings
Claws are better far than wings –
Force has dug the grave of Love,'
Said the Tiger to the Dove.

'A little venom on the tongue
Beats any song that e'er was sung –
Great are lies and shall prevail,'
Said the Snake to the Nightingale.

'Always with the great pack fight,
For the pack is always right –
Oh, be loyal if you can,'
Said the Wolf unto the Man.

'For every good under the sun
Man must fight with sword or gun –
Woe to the gentle and the mild,'
Said Man to the human Child.

'In the war of right and wrong
The victory is to the strong –
Great guns must clear your darkened sky,'
Said Man to the Lord Most High.

The moon turned pale, the stars stood still.
'Peace upon earth, to men good will,'
The Angel to the Shephered cried.
Christ turned in His sleep and sighed.

DREAMS

The swallows flit through twisted branches fine
And silver arches of the bare plane trees,
Where scant stiff leaves sway in the passing breeze,
Clinging to dreams of May, green robed, divine.

Alas! our dreams are only of the dread
Red fields of France where unreaped harvests rot,
And the One Soul by all the world forgot
Moves silently amid the hosts of dead.

German or French or English, words most vain
To that which knows not any nation's pride,
Whose pity is as all men's sorrow wide,
Folded about our broken world of pain.

Knowing no foe in any death or life,
Moving in dreams in every darkened mind,
Whilst still to death the blind lead on the blind,
That comradeship is deeper than our strife.

Men drench the green earth and defile her streams
With blood, and blast her very fields and hills
With the mechanic iron of their wills,
Yet in her sad heart still the spirit dreams.

True to all life, war-worn and battle-tossed
Doth the One Spirit, faithful to the end,
Live in that peace that shall be the world's friend,
The dream of God by men so lightly lost.

TO C. A.

You seem to be a woman of the world,
Gorgeous in silky robes of blue and green,
Hair in soft shining coils, white throat bepearled.
It is not true, you are what you have been.

I know you for the Umbrian monk you are,
Brother of Francis and the sun and rain,
Brother of every silver pilgrim star,
And the white oxen on the golden plain.

Where one bird's song the evening silence thrills
To beauty, white your mountain convent gleams,
Brown-robed, barefoot, across the Tuscan hills
I see you wander, smiling at your dreams,

Stopping to help a peasant at his toil,
Gathering the olives, watering the vine,
Guiding the plough, turning the red-brown soil,
Sharing the evening meal of bread and wine,

And passing on your way at the day's end
To sleep on the pine-shadowed, leaf-strewn sod,
Fearlessly finding all the world your friend,
And living in the Beauty that is God.

PINEHURST
1916

Dew-pearlèd cobwebs glitter on green boughs,
Beneath our feet the grass is wet with dew,
It seems as if this clear dawn must arouse
Our broken world to something strange and new.

Deep in the high-built fortress of the pines,
Lost to her stars dark night imprisoned lies,
Near my hushed soul in peace a white rose shines,
Like a new dream down flung from ancient skies.

Alas, the bugles on the distant plain –
The guns break forth with their insistent din,
The dews of noon-day leave a crimson stain
On grass, that all men's feet must wander in.

Oh, singing splendour of the morning furled
About the souls of trees, the hearts of flowers,
Have you no dream of beauty for the world –
This bitter bloodstained world we men call ours?

THE LITTLE GIRL'S RIDDLE

A jelly-fish afloat on the bright wave –
A white seagull – a great blue butterfly –
A hunted hare – a wolf in a dark cave;
All these I was; which one of these was I?

A gold-maned lion, mad with rage and fear,
A white bear ranging over trackless snow,
A savage living by my bow and spear,
A mighty fighter giving blow for blow,
A student gazing at the starry skies,
A Rebel planning the downfall of Kings,
A searcher of the wisdom of the wise,
A questioner of all mysterious things,

A priestess singing hymns to Proserpine,
An old king weary on a golden throne,
A marble-carver freeing limbs divine
From their cold bondage of enfolding stone,

A hot-head poet by the world reviled,
A heretic of desolate dreams and dire,
And now a little silent long-legged child
Weeping alone beside the nursery fire.

Ye who have guessed the hidden lights that burn
Behind the blue wings of the butterfly,
In a child's grief the riddle's answer learn –
'I was all these – yet none of these was I.'

AN EXPERIENCE

I laboured and studied and toiled and thought,
And it all came to nought –
My thoughts and my mind and my soul seemed dead
As the books that I read –
When suddenly a little door,
Hidden far down in the deeps of consciousness,
Swung open, and a ray of light
Flooded each dim recess.
I left myself's safe shore
And swam across the night.
Deep down beyond life's overthrow
Where only the reckless care to go,
I caught a glimpse of a star divine,
That changed the lights and shadows of all things
With rays as swift as a seagull's wings.
And for a moment brief
As the flash and fall of a leaf,
A yellow leaf on a hurrying stream,
I saw strange meanings shift and change and gleam,
As if some new enraptured hope
Had shaken life's kaleidoscope
To patterns little understood,
Beyond the evil and the good –

It may have been a dream
But it was not dead
Like the books I read,
And the labour and the toil and the pain
Seemed suddenly worth while,
If I might see and understand again
Life's strange and secret smile.
Shall my sad heart be prisoned evermore
In a dark cave behind a barrèd door?

TO J. W. IN WINCHESTER PRISON

Yet once again the barred and bolted gate,
The smiling face seen through a wire cage,
The foolish tools of state-entrenchèd hate,
The prisoner's dream beyond all fear and rage.

Outside men's maniac fury shrieks and raves,
And dark submission chained in sunlight dwells,
The only free souls in a race of slaves
Live in strange solitudes and prison cells.

THE WOOD

Turning in blind distress
From war's dark ugliness,
O'er the wide common heather-spread
Through rain-soaked grass I fled,
And crooked ways half understood –
Gorse needles tore my ankles bare,
And wiry brambles clutched my hair;
Thus came I to the haunted wood,
And there where carven fronds of gentle ferns

Wave o'er the brown leaf-strewn and mystic ground,
And the world's starry light still burns,
Beyond all hate and fear I found
What once men found in marble-hearted Greece,
Beauty, the world's lost peace.

SACRIFICE

'If Jesus Christ had not been crucified,
God's mercy would have passed this sad world by.' –
'Our deed is then most greatly justified,'
Pilate and Caiaphas might well reply.
'If love and mercy had been scattered wide
In all men's hearts, so that no judge would try
Or slay his brother, then were God's will denied,
And His high purpose broken utterly.'

'If Christ had never died, this world of ours
Would have been lost and damned'? – Nay, rather say:
'If Christ had not been foully slain, the flowers
Would fairer bloom in fairer fields to-day,
The world would have been saved by sun and showers,
Mercy and Truth in the old glorious way.'

THE POET'S GOD

'What is God?' men said in the West,
The Lord of Good and Ill,
Rewarder of the blest,
Judge of the evil will.

'What is God?' men said in the East,
The universal soul

In man, and bird, and beast,
The self of the great whole.

I saw the primrose flower
Rise out of the green sod,
In majesty and power,
And I said 'There is Love, there is God.'

THE SUBMERGED APOLLO

The Vision fair has failed and passed away,
And down beneath deep waters drownèd lies,
As under the brown stream for centuries
The fairest of the gods forgotten lay.

The barnacles made rough his carven breast,
His patient brow through years of ooze and slime
Bore the hard muddy dull embrace of time,
The burden of a light unmanifest.

What of the secret beyond good or ill?
Have not men quenched the fair light of the mind
Beneath a flood of mud-stained waters blind
The black ungentle tides of angry will,

The rushing river of our passionate woes,
The flowing joys and fears, the pious dream?
Deep down beneath the waters of that stream,
The lost God dwelleth in the heart's repose.

Who has not seen the flash of white limbs shine
Out of the deep, through sand-strewn twilight dim
And darkened waters, in the mind of him
Who in his soul of souls is yet divine?

Yea, in the deeps of each obscurèd mind
The drownèd god in broken beauty lies.
When shall Apollo from the Tiber rise,
And a new music cry along the wind?

Joy, that the dweller under the dark wave
Is still a secret power, a living part
Of the eternal granite-folded heart,
The deep and patient life that knows no grave.

THESE THREE ...

Glory of heart and brain,
All that has made me man –
Where the forest waves and swings,
Out in the wind and rain,
Flies together and sings ...
All of us children of Pan ...

Soul driven by grief and desire
Onward to some lost goal,
Fierce with the rhythm and storm
Of the subterranean fire,
Dream of the Ultimate Form,
Child of the Infinite Soul.

Mind that is fairer than these,
Stronger than fire or wind,
Gazing where thou has trod
Pan must fall on his knees,
Thou art child of the Innermost God,
The Universal Mind.

TO DORA SIGERSON SHORTER
'THE SAD YEARS'

You whom I never knew,
Who lived remote, afar,
Yet died of the grief that tore my heart,
Shall we live through the ages alone, apart,
Or meet where the souls of the sorrowful are
Telling the tale on some secret star,
How your death from the root of my sorrow grew –
You whom I never knew?

Nay, perhaps in the coming years
Down here on our earth again,
We shall meet as strangers on some strange shore,
And dream we have known one another before,
In a past life, weeping over the slain –
Because of a thrill and a throb of pain,
And eyes grown suddenly salt with tears ...
Perhaps ... in the coming years ...

THE SHEPHERD OF ETERNITY
(1925)

THE SHEPHERD OF ETERNITY

Statues of 'the Shepherd, the Beautiful One,' were carved by
early Greek Christians to decorate the fountains of
Constantinople.

Joyful and swift, who led
The souls of the dead
In a shadowy band
To the Twilight land,
Surely deaf wert thou to our crying,
In silence conceivèd, in darkness dying,
And we wept as we went
Down the dark descent.
Hermes, thou Beautiful One, thy smile did but mock our
despair,
Who wept for the light of the sun and the shining and
silvery air.

Glad shepherd of joyless sheep,
We, children of those who weep,
We who have lost all things
Shudder at thy swift wings,
For thou wert deaf to our crying,
In silence conceivèd, in darkness dying,
And thy smile so fair
Knew not woe or despair
As thou leddest thy people to Hades, with sorrow and
sighing and tears;
Small profit had they in their dying, of thee and thy
radiant years.

Through the grave and the gloom
And the Gateway of Doom,
Through Hades' dim pain,
Back to hard earth again,
With bitterness striving, reviling
The grace of thy passionless smiling,

Dull and helpless and blind
Did we drift with the wind;
Now shall you seek us in vain, where no sun of the world
ever shone,
But the shadows flit by the gloomy waves of tideless
Acheron.

Now do we kneel at ease
Under the cypress trees,
For the new God who leads the dead
His own tears has shed; –
We have carved on all the fountains
A young shepherd from the mountains,
Being the image of Him
Whose Sorrow made the sunlight dim,
A shepherd of strange melodies, playing the pipes of goat-
foot Pan
To call out of her sepulchre the earth's dim soul, the soul
of man.

Somewhere beyond the earth
There is respite from birth
For the mourners who stray
Down the Desolate Way.
He who lives in Life, Life-bringing,
Gives a new song for our singing;
And we, who are doomed to go
In darkness to and fro,
Like the wind in the trees, or the driven clouds, or the
wandering tide,
Have found at last the place of that peace where our weary
souls may abide.

Every fountain to the skies
Clear and foamless shall arise;
There are bright wings for all things,
Even the worms shall have wings;

The Living Waters, ascending,
Rainbow-coloured, shining, blending
With the everlasting Light,
Transfigure the world's night:
This is the Song the Shepherd sang, with many runs and
shakes and trills,
The Shepherd of Eternity, piping o'er cypress-shaded hills.

THE CHILD OF PROPHECY

Virgil said, 'O child, for you
Of itself the plain turns gold with waving corn,
Purple clusters of grapes hang down from the wild thorn,
On the oak's hard trunk lies the honey-dew, ...'
Mysterious child, for you.

'The gold age returns, the wild
Flames with foxgloves and Egyptian lilies rare,'
Bright acanthus fit for the Emperor's heir,
Or a crown of thorns for another child, ...
Who knows the will of the wild?

'A new Achilles shall be sent
To a new Troy, crowded with heroes once more,
Another *Argo* shall sail, bound for a far shore,
With a new pilot on a strange quest bent ...'
Who knows what Virgil meant?

AT THE WATERFALL

As the water fell sheer,
I shuddered to know

Whence it came here
And where it must go.

A child's thoughts at play
Whispered, 'Each little stream
Did but yesterday
In the rainbow gleam.'

And a thought like a friend
In the midst of foes
Said, 'Each stream in the end
Into Heaven flows.'

THE MIRACLE AT CANA

As the rain soaking down to the vine's root
Is caught up in the wild ways of change,
Where sunlight from the tree's soul draws the fruit,
And water becomes the world's wine, sweet and strange;

Turn Thou the waters of my life to wine,
O Love Eternal, O far-shining Sun,
Who sayest to each man, 'What is Mine is thine,'
At the Feast where Spirit and Soul are made one.

THE QUEST

Deep in that world where pale tides ebb and flow,
And wild shapes wander under the vast blue,
A man once sought, beneath the shadow show,
To find himself, the living one, the true.

And first he met a gentle silver shade,
And held it as it would have floated by.
He cried to it. 'Art thou my self?' he said.
'Nay, but the form of all thy dreams am I.'

'Not thou, but thine,' thin voices and swift gleams
Mocked at the darkness of the lonely quest,
For though he found his soul, his burning dreams,
Himself seemed always an unbidden guest.

He laboured on through sorrow, toil, and strife,
Till in the labyrinth a strange voice said,
'I am the Resurrection and the Life.'
He woke at last – himself – transfigurèd.

THE CHAPEL IN THE FOREST

With sculptured form the porch is decorate,
The holy Shepherd carved in wood stands there
Where the dark branches of the pines grow thin,
And sunlight blesses the freed forest air,
That they who wander shadowed aisles of fate
May enter softly by the lowly Door,
And find the Hidden Christ who dwells therein,
And know themselves, and go out nevermore.

THE WELL WHERE THE WORLD ENDS

On the King's robe the Mother of Emerald shivered and
shone,
Flashing green in the sullen glow of the sacrificial flame,
Whilst, wrapped in a vision ecstatic, the wizard Solomon
Breathed from the height of his glorious hour the

Everlasting Name.
The people fell prostrate, the trumpets shrilled, the priests
cried aloud;
In vain, in vain, for the Face of the Lord was hidden
behind a cloud.

When the Pilgrim spoke to the woman, tired by the sun's
hot glare,
As seeking the well at noonday o'er burnt-up grass she
trod,
Love sang through the rustling corn in a little wind of
prayer,
And Truth came gently into her soul, radiant, the Son of
God.
Reflected in quiet waters, strange coloured and clear
outlined,
She found the Face of the Lord in the deeps of her inner
mind.

As she drew water from the well, the Living Water ran
Shining among her thoughts, singing the heart-breaking
song divine
Of the Spirit that seeks the hidden desolate soul in man
As a miner seeks for a sapphire deep in a perilous mine,
And she fled away triumphant, to bring the news to her
friends
That Spirit and Soul should meet at last at the Well where
the World ends.

REVELATION

I ASKED for news of God from the shining sea,
Flowing in streams of sapphire, tides of chalcedony,
And the little waves were seven, but the great waves were
three.

I asked for news of God from the blue of the air,
For joy and wonder and peace were singing and soaring
there,
And a dream of the Ultimate Beauty answered my prayer.

I asked for news of God from the starlight on the wind:
'We are the children of Heaven, we lighten the dreams of
the blind,
We are the Logos shining under your shadowy mind.'

A man stole my coat from me, I asked him for news of
God,
Flinging my cloak before him down on the rain-drenched
sod;
Yea, this was the messenger whose feet with the Truth
were shod.

Out of his mouth there came the Wisdom of the Wise,
And the Life and the Truth and the Love of God shone
from his startled eyes:
My soul rose up to greet him in a great and strange
surprise.

LIFE

For God's sake, kill not: Spirit that is breath
With Life the earth's gray dust irradiates;
That which has neither part nor lot with death
Deep in the smallest rabbit's heart vibrates.
Of God we know naught, save three acts of will:
Life that vibrates in every breathing form,
Truth that looks out over the window sill,
And Love that is calling us home out of the storm.

THE DESCENT FROM THE CROSS

He had made of his soul a Temple to hold the Glory of
God,
Now his heart is cold, his breath has died into silence, his
eyes are dim,
The house that held his radiant desires lies lifeless and rent
on the sod,
But his soul arises to splendour eternal out of the wreckage
grim,
For to him shall be given a house more fair than the
Temple he built for God,
The Glory of God itself is the Temple that manifests him.

THE ACORN

The Acorn is a common thing and small,
Child of the sun and plaything of the wind,
You think it is of no account at all,
Yet at its heart great forces crash and grind.

The Acorn's jade-wrought chalice holds concealed
The Eternal Host, with dreams and death at strife,
Great are the issues, small the battle-field,
Where infinite will drags beauty into life.

The Acorn is a holy thing and dear,
The green leaves shudder out to meet the Light,
The great Tree rushes upward, tier on tier,
Stretching wild boughs towards the Infinite.

IN PRAISE OF LIFE

Sappho said long ago,
'If Death be good,
Why do the Gods not die?'
Sappho was wise;
She said, 'If Life be ill,
Why do the Gods live still?'
O beautiful Life, in this grim age of ours
Still art thou crowned with flowers,
Still, like a torrent down a mountain glen,
Thou comest Beloved of men;
Out of the acorn's cup thou dost arise,
And shinest in the squirrel's eyes,
Moulding to grapes the strong soul of the vine.
As Sappho saw thee, thou art yet Divine,
High on the pine-tree's topmost wind-swayed bough,
Deep in the ox's heart that drags the plough,
Guiding the hand of him who sows the grain,
Buried in seed, rising in wheat again;
Where death is under the sun,
Mercy and Life are one.
Oh, leave to all poor creatures made of clay
The shortness of their little shining day;
Take not from the swift nations of the air
Their wide blue house, their radiant stair,
Kill not the smallest thing,
Nor break the frailest wing,
For, buried in Life's stream,
God's purpose and His dream
Gleam gold beneath the tide.
Time is not long, space is not wide,
And every little river is the sea Potentially;
Transfigured by strange waves and waters wild,
Time will not know his child.
    Sappho was right:
Life that is Love is God, and Mercy wise

Is that which never dies –
Life, Love and Light.

TIME

In time the whole of things shall alter,
And the earth shine as shines the sun,
In time the hangman's hands shall falter,
In time the gunner shall leave the gun.

In time the hater shall cease from hating,
In time the judge shall judge no more,
For time the wave of Life is waiting
To thunder on the Eternal Shore.
In time no man shall kill his brother;
Of every living thing the friends,
We shall all see God in one another
Before the day when Time ends.

THE LOGOS OF LIFE
'Said I not unto thee, that, if thou wouldest believe,
thou shouldest see the glory of God?' – *Christ to Martha*

There was silence for a space,
The sun had ceased to shine,
The ground was wet with tears,
The strange deep flowing tears divine,
Where the sisters knelt on the sod
At the rock-hewn burial place,
Shrinking with indrawn breath
From the hideous sight of death.
Three words shook the spheres ...
No deathly damp shall mar

The face of the Morning Star;
There, beyond sight or sound,
Those who sought death found Life, they found
The Beautiful Glory of God.

SANTA MARIA MAGGIORE

A little way beyond the village street
The whole wide earth becomes articulate;
You hear no more the sound of hurrying feet,
And clamorous human breath of love and hate,
But the green silence of impenetrable firs
Cries to the Light of mountains white with snow;
A little wind the jewelled grasses stirs
And sings unto the unborn columbine,
Till even the river dying on the plain
Doth with that hidden melody vibrate,
And all life shivers with the same refrain,
Crying, like Psyche, outside Heaven's gate.
So near, so far the Living Waters flow,
So far, so near the Eternal Life Divine.

Just a few steps beyond our noisy dreams,
Outside our gloomy caves of fear and care,
Over our heads the shaken sunlight gleams
In waves of luminous blue cerulean air.
A little space under our grinding wills,
And lo, all heaven in peace before us lies,
Ours are the white clouds shining o'er the hills,
And delicate blueness of all-folding skies;
Here, on the storm-swept slope of the hillside,
Where the pines soar above the populous clay
In high eternal beauty, without pride
To drag them downward from their golden day,
Shall our dreams reach the mountains white with snow,

And Psyche find at last her ancient shrine.
So near, so far the Living Waters flow,
So far, so near the Eternal Life Divine.

THE LIVING AND THE DEAD

A dewdrop in the sun, her radiant mind
Climbed the high wall of the Divine Desire,
As amongst falling stars the night fell dead,
Lo, she was born again of the Dawn Wind,
Lo, she was born again of Spirit and Fire.

Waves of her joy poured backward from the height,
Into a child's soul falling, unwithstood,
Wild dreams by God's great mercy shepherded;
They flooded all the snowdrops with new light
On a spring morning in a little wood.

Here once a garden was, now wintry trees
Pierced the blue sky with long boughs silver-bare.
The child saw earth by heaven transfigurèd;
Wild with strange joy she fell upon her knees,
Her soul rose up in shining waves of prayer.

THE MYSTERY OF PAIN

Fair is the Garden, you say,
Full of scents and colours and beautiful things –
The daisies' eyes and the sweet-peas' wings,
Cherubim of the Grass,
And Seraphim of the Flowers;
But the thorns, the thorns that tear
Your face and your hands as you pass

The ivy-wreathèd door –
Nay, though you strive and pray,
You shall not tear the brambles down,
Because, some day,
All these must be woven into a crown
For the Son of Man to wear,
Rose-radiant evermore
In green immortal bowers.

THE HIDDEN BEAUTY

I have sought the Hidden Beauty in all things,
In love, and courage, and a high heart, and a hero's grave,
In the hope of a dreaming soul, and a seagull's wings,
In twilight over the sea, and a broken Atlantic wave,
I have sought the Hidden Beauty in all things.

I have found the Hidden Beauty where the river finds the
sea,
Or the dark cloud finds the rainbow, or the desert finds the
rain,
Where the night sails out on the Dawn Wind and the
darkness ceases to be,
Or the Spirit builds a rainbow from whirling rings of pain,
I have found the Hidden Beauty where the river finds the
sea.

A BUILDER OF RAINBOWS

As it was willed and done in the secret councils of
yesterday,
Out of my dreams and desires was built this fragile body
of clay,

And now in the deeps of the air, in a sinister place apart,
The form of my dreams and desires lies curled like a snake
round my heart.

Yet is it not greatly decreed, in the innermost council of
things,
That every man on the earth becomes what he loves and
sings?

Then who can tell the day and the hour when the Son of
Man shall arise,
With a cry in his heart that shudders beyond the ultimate
skies?

No longer the slave of the storm-wind tossed between fear
and faith,
No longer a clay-built body, no longer an earth-bound
wraith,

A sinking ship with a broken rudder, lost in the whirlpool
of years,
But a passionate mortal invader of far immortal spheres,

A builder of rainbow arches, a sculptor of Light and Fire,
Moulding, out of the Spirit of Love, the Body of Love's
Desire.

COMETS

Nay, not the Great Lights of the Firmament,
Calm centres of all whirling things,
Bring my soul balance and content ...
    A sense of wings,

But those that pass in a flash and a glow
With a vanishing wake of flame,
And we know not whither they go,
   Nor whence they came.

These are the Virgins who run with their lamps
When at midnight there is a cry,
And word goes out among the tramps,
   'The Lord is passing by.'

'WE SHALL BE CHANGED'

The snake-weed and geranium flower
Nod in the scented sunshine blithe,
Soon finished is their little hour,
They fall beneath the scythe.

The purple monkshood fine and tall,
The white and golden daisies gay,
Down amongst broken grasses fall,
And wither into hay.

Blue gentian and frail columbine
No man shall ever mow;
Their delicate bright dreams divine
God gathered long ago.

God of the Gentian's Blue
And the Columbine's Desire,
Who callest all things true
To come up higher,

Thou Lord of Light and Tears,
Leave Thou me not, I pray,

After such years and years,
To wither with the hay.

MARY

She who broke the precious jar,
And through the house new fragrance shed,
Mournful and glad as prophets are,
Saw sunrise on the newly dead.

She saw the broken golden bowl,
And the Divine Light, strong and free,
Whispering within each living soul
The wild song of Eternity.

She felt the House of Life grow sweet
With a strange presence everywhere,
Earth's corn change to immortal wheat,
As a dream changes to a prayer.

YESTERDAY AND TO-MORROW

How all the stars did glitter and gleam
Through the gate of ivory, open wide,
    Last time I died,
Cradled in the soft arms of a dream.
Through the gate of horn in mercy and ruth,
May the One Light shine from a blue sky
    Next time I die,
Clasping the feet of the Beautiful Truth.

Love, all our little lives forgive,
On pain and failure be Thy radiance shed,

Raise Thou the Dead,
Give Truth to all the world, that all may live.

A PRAYER FOR DONKEYS

The Wise Ass turnèd from the hay
Where the Child in the manger lay.
Lord, pity the poor Ass, we pray.

Lo, with Joseph old and bent,
And Mary, on the Child intent,
The Wise Ass into Egypt went.

Yet once again, with God his Guide,
And blessèd Mary at his side,
The Lord did to his Passion ride.

Thrice did the patient beast and wise
Gaze into those strange secret eyes
That hid Life's uttermost surprise.

Lord, whom the stars and suns obey,
Remember the poor Ass, we pray,
In thy Resurrection Day.

THE DIVINE MESSENGER

Immortal, to whose heavy eyes of old
Fell open the Light's everlasting Doors,
Forgive me counting faults that once were yours,
As a dull miser might count out his gold.

Now thine is all the promise of all things,
And thou a Light, a Messenger, a Flame,
Thy name the Eternal Universal Name
That is the world's desire and the angel's wings.

But once thy mortal eyes shed bitter tears,
Foolish as men are foolish, false and vain,
And in thy soul a ceaseless throb of pain,
Crushed with the burden of a thousand fears.

Thus when my heart sinks down beneath the weight
Of an age-long despair, knowing my soul
Too lame and blind to reach the spirit's goal,
Bound to the dizzy wheel of the earth's fate,

I count my gold, seeing what chains and bars
Held back thy flight, and dream of One who came
And freed thee in the might of that mysterious Name
That echoes from far suns and lonelier stars.

THE DELIVERANCE

In vain, in vain the wild Atlantic dreams
Shine, and shudder, and break on my heart of stone,
And the sea-birds cry, and the rainbow gleams,
O'er my low-roofed cabin frail and lone.

In vain, in vain great green waves storm
My soul in a tumult of yea and nay,
My dreams have cast off the colour and form
Of many a sorrowful yesterday.

Lo, I have had enough of this earth,
I would climb the high walls of life and death.

Why should one crawl through the gates of birth
To weep in this whirlpool of bitterest breath?

I would build a form of my fierce desire,
My feet shall be free of the grass and its graves,
Strong with the secret of Love and Fire,
Standing with Christ on the glimmering waves.

For the rainbow's light, and the wild birds' wings
And the waves have pierced through an age-long sleep,
With a broken song at the heart of things ...
No more shall I wander, and wonder, and weep.

'A BROKEN STAMMER OF THE SKIES'

Christ said to God,
When his sweat ran blood-red
On the olive-shaded sod,
'Thy Truth and Love I hold
In my cup of gold';
And God answerèd,
'When the vessel breaks, the Light is shed,
Love on the dark earth deathly cold,
But to thee I will give more than a golden bowl,
My Life to hold thy soul.'

THE INNER TRINITY

As the tide rising fills with light the dank sea-caves,
Vast Spirit, deep and valiant tide of Love, arise,
Fill every cavern of my spirit with wild waves
Of Mercy, the One Beautiful, the Only Wise;

Till the clear water deepens, luminous and still,
Be thou the Surge of Love tremendous in my will.

Wrapped in a human cloud, Thou brighter than the sun,
Shepherd and Door and Vine, who giv'st all men the key
To the Kingdom of Truth, where Light and Love are one,
Thy great eyes looking everywhere call men to Thee ;
Thou inner voice of courage crying on the wind,
Be Thou the living Truth dynamic in my mind.

Father of all Life, when the Sun's trumpet calls,
May perfect primroses glide silent into flower,
From the sharp cliffs may rainbow-prismèd waterfalls
Soak all the humblest grass in an emerald shower,
May the sap rise in the oak-tree's gnarlèd bole,
Be Thou the Life Eternal rising in my soul.

THE TWO SECRETS

What was the secret Pan to Psyche told?
He showed her silent pools of mirrored things,
And down among his dreams of blue and gold,
The image of her own translucent wings.

Now has she flamed forth on her way alone,
Her sad voice cries no more in every storm,
Her wild wings waft her unto heights unknown,
And vibrant rhythms of Eternal Form.

Yet still life holds that dream-enthrallèd hour,
When a white hush empties the earth of pain,
Split sunlight slants athwart a gleaming shower,
And wingèd Psyche walks the world again.

Then sudden sapphires from the rainbow's arch
Fall flashing down amid wind-shaken reeds,
Faint laughter sways the new green of the larch,
And ripples whisper in the water-weeds.

What is the secret Psyche told to Pan
Among the dark-boughed pine trees green and tall?
'Brother art thou,' she said, 'not slave of man':
You could have heard the smallest fir-cone fall.

As Pan stood gasping at the river's edge,
All things seemed but to mock him, and her words
Strange as the wind that rustles in the sedge,
And idle as the empty songs of birds.

That night at midnight thus it came to pass,
As the moon rose white and the earth slept,
When Christ went sighing over the wet grass,
Pan cried out in his dream, and waked, and wept.

IN THE TEMPLE
'I came to put an end to sacrifices.'
– Trad. Saying of Christ

Mary, young but very wise,
Pondered many mysteries.

Likely to her Son she told
How she went in days of old

To the Temple with a song,
Praising God the whole day long,

(Soul that prays and heart that loves),
In her hand a cage of Doves!

Two live pigeons prisoned there,
(Heart of Love and soul of prayer!)

How the old indifferent priest
Sacrificed them at the Feast ...

Did she pray in broken words
For the fluttering dying birds?

Soilèd silver, lifeless wings –
God's pity on all helpless things!

Did she stand and weep alone
By the bloodstained altar stone?

Haply even then the Child
Out of his deep wisdom smiled,

Knowing that from God he came,
To lighten every dying flame;

Knowing he himself would pay
Her debt to the wild birds one day.

II

When Christ, in the Father's Name,
Into the bloodstained Temple came,

All the Doves began to sing,
Stretching every prisoned wing.

And he said, 'The Spirit of Love
Is as a living, flying Dove.'

As once in his babyhood,
Sheep and oxen round him stood.

'God made them living souls,' he said ...
(Jesus, raise us from the dead.)

Did Life stir in caverns dim,
Whilst patient eyes were fixed on him?

None so merciful as he, ...
He sets them free, he sets them free.

He opens every cage of pain,
He will not have the oxen slain.

The sheep as his own people seem,
He leads them to the living stream.

The birds have heard the story now,
It shrills and thrills from bough to bough.

Lord, of Thee the skylark sings,
Give Life, more Life, unto all things.

ΤΕΤΕ☐ΕΣΤΑΙ

'He failed,' I said; 'the deed he came to do
Two thousand years ago is still undone;
There is no mercy yet under the sun,
And Love lies dead beneath God's gentle blue.'

It is not true; the Doer knew the Deed.
A million years is but a little thing,
The sunshine and the sap of a short spring,
To raise the tree of Life out of its seed.

Safe buried under our fierce dreams of power
The tree's deep roots grow, sheltered from the wind,
For there is One, greater than all mankind,
Who in the soul of each man waits his hour.

Yea, even to our broken world of clay
The Son of Man in Man shall surely come,
Then will I cry to Love who now am dumb,
'Dear friend, I heard thy footsteps yesterday.'

1   'It is finished.'

MERCY

Mercy came wandering through a man's mind,
Out of the deeps there arose a wind
And a bitter cry, 'Here doth Justice dwell,'
Then Mercy knew herself in hell ...
'Where shadows dwell,' she said, 'I cannot stay,'
For she is God and bides in Heaven alway.
Robed in the blessèd human form divine,
She offers all men living Bread and Wine.

A SUNLIT CLOUD

A sunlit cloud touches the mountain peak
Where brighter gleams the light of sunlit snow,
White clouds and blue air
Are all about us everywhere,
The blue of heaven leans down as if to seek
The lake's blue waters lying far below;
    So near, so dear,

The Eternal Beauty leans towards my soul
Till Life and Love are merged in a great shining whole.

THREE-IN-ONE

The Spirit of Love moved on the face
Of the world's blind waters, and man uprose,
And Paradise was his dwelling-place,
Where a River of living water flows.

The Spirit of Truth moved on the face
Of the world's blind waters, and Christ came down,
And the hills were too low for his dwelling-place,
And the stars of heaven too dark for his crown.

The Spirit of Life moved yet again
On the face of the waters deep and fair,
And Love was a-glitter with sun and rain,
And the waves were a song and the winds a prayer.

THE ANGEL IN THE GARDEN

An Angel in a Garden: what bright dreams
Of lilied Gabriel, and rose-petals flung
By spirits wandering amongst living streams,
With golden harps on silver willows hung,
Do those fair words bring to the dreamer's mind?
Ah no, the terrible truth to tell,
The Garden where the Angel stood
Is no stream-blessed and fragrant dell,

But a forlorn and sorrow-shadowed place,
A leafless waste, a flowerless, haunted wood,

Where even dying daisies find no grace,
Shrunk in the dry and bitter wailing wind;
Blood lies upon its grass like dew.
Yet some will understand
That here the Faithful and the True
Has bid his fairest Angel stand.
Far stars shine near above the leafless trees,
Capella, Syrius, and the Pleiades ...

SYMPATHY

When Christ was about to die,
In the deeps of his separate soul
The vail of the Temple was rent in twain
Between the known and the Unknown,
Between the part and the Whole.
Surely he felt their pain,
His enemies' pain, as his own;
Did he not cry their cry,
The cry of the sorrow of them who love forsake,
And cannot find what they have cast away,
   Though their hearts break?
O Love, who feels men's sorrows as Thine own,
   All human pain
Of murderers, and priests with hearts of stone
Was in Thy heart that day,
When the lost slayers' cry came from the slain.

THE ANSWERED PRAYER

A man prayed, with eyes grown dim,
Tears hiding the blue sky,
'A friend has come to me

In bitter, evil poverty;
My house is empty, I have nought to give,
No bread that one may eat and live.

Give me, that I may give to him,
Water of Life to raise the dead,
The Everlasting, Living Bread.
Give me one loaf for my poor friend.' ...
God gave him all things without end.

THE SINGER
(AFTER ST AUGUSTINE)

Father of all things, crowned
With Mercy, ever blest,
Save Thou the linnet's young
That has fallen out of its nest
On to the hard ground,
Lest it die ere its first song be sung.

THE TRAVELLERS

As we sped on in our crazy boat
From the moon a little cloud did float,
Out of the darkest waves of thought
A ladder of Light was wrought.
Behold, the sudden gleam sufficed
To cut a path over the sea,
A silver Road of Mystery
And Highway for the feet of Christ.

EDEN AND GETHSEMANE

Everything sang together from every month of the year,
When the Lord walked in the garden in the hushed
evening cool,
All the daffodils were dancing for joy that He was near,
And lilies gazed up in His Face out of a little pool;
But the man went away and hid himself in rage and fear.

The Lord smiled, a rout of roses came rushing to His side,
Then the mobs of queer-faced pansies began to laugh and
run;
When through the young green grass they saw a sudden
brightness glide,
The daisies knew that theirs at last was the far-shining
sun;
But the man crouched low in the thicket the better to hide.

Then the Lord knelt down in the garden, where four rivers
meet,
The daisies blanched as they saw Him cover His Face with
a cloud;
He wept, and His tears fell down on cowslip and meadow-
sweet,
The flowers were still like dead things, each wrapped in a
dreadful shroud;
But Adam came out of the thicket, and knelt at His feet.

BARTIMEUS

Down the inner Road of Dread,
Between the living and the dead,
On through the starless night and storm,
The Light of the World, passing silently,
For a moment paused behind my soul,

And I beheld the whole
Of that mysterious lost and sightless form
Reflected on the outer air ...
Jesus of Nazareth, passing by,
Hear thou the blind man's prayer,
Echoing out across the night –
'Lord, that I may receive my sight.'

NAZARETH

Unto the greater Lights
Small is this earth of ours,
Short are its days and nights,
Soon dead its passion flowers.

Unto Rome's marble pile,
Her Lords of Life and Death,
Small and low-roofed and vile
Seemed remote Nazareth.

Yet not through Rome's high gate
Came singing the Divine,
But that small Door of Fate,
Nazareth in Palestine.

For size is man's demand,
And smallness the earth's doom,
But the Infinite can stand
In a narrow room.

And This that made the sea,
And the great stars above,
Lived suddenly for me
In a word of Love.

Yea, this small earth of ours,
Shut in by narrow bars,
Is crowned with passion flowers –
The Nazareth of the stars.

THE MOON AND A LAMP

A lamp burning in the window on a dark night
Said to the travellers, 'God is Light';
But the Moon, blazing whitely, on the heavens above,
Wrote in shining letters, 'Light is Love.'

THE INNER HILLS

I cannot paint the loveliness of things,
Pouring clear colour into gracious form,
Yet in my soul beat the caged skylark's wings,
And the huge mountains tower above the storm.

Gleaming they stand, cloud-haunted, near the sky,
Oh, shall I do the Divine Hills a wrong?
Hardly I dare, in wildest ecstasy,
Drag their great glory into my small song.

CONSIDER THE LILIES

Beyond the Evil and the Good,
Deep in the purple-shadowed wood,
White and red the lilies stood.

In rain-soaked grass on faery hill
Grows the primrose pale and still,
Knowing neither good nor ill.

We who toil upon our way,
Greedy, lustful, prone to slay,
Hating, fearing, all the day,

Praising right, and doing wrong,
In a blind bewildered throng,
Catch a note of some far song;

Dream of one long dead, who stood
With the lilies in the wood,
Beyond the Evil and the Good;

See across our pathway gleam,
Like a sudden silver stream,
The lustrous shadow of his dream,

Who knew not any good or ill,
Powerless to force or kill,
The Will of God being his will.

Beyond our region, dark and dire,
Of oppositional desire,
Burnèd his life's clear fire.

Like the lilies was his will,
Or primroses on faery hill,
Growing patiently and still,
Standing where the lilies stood,
Deep in the purple-shadowed wood,
Beyond the Evil and the Good.

FLORENCE (1920)

Back to the Lily town, the exile dreaming
Of Peace long sought for, and the end of pain,
Where delicate faces from dim arches gleaming,
Colour the world with kindness once again.

Here shall one stand in fair and holy places,
Where, amongst Angels, tired shepherds smile,
And crownless kings, with ivory-lighted faces,
Grow gentle-hearted for a little while.

Here, in the arms of a pale girl reclining,
Glimmers the answer to the whole world's prayers,
And underneath the Eastern stars clear shining,
Light of a Truth more radiant than theirs.

Here to my soul I clasp the humble-splendid
Dream of an exile, battle-broken, blind,
Love that is Truth and Life, in beauty blended,
The one Light's rainbow in a storm-swept mind.

THE GOSPEL OF JOHN

Christ, knowing all things, knew
There were two of his friends who understood
The deeps of his inner mind.
With his last breaths he gave them to one another,
John and Mary, to be the witnesses of the Inner Truth.
The rest might found churches, preach,
Spread the news of his presence through the world
　From city to city;
　To these two was given
　The inner witness.
They, in their life together, were soon surrounded

By all the women and the quiet ones.
Doubtless it was to them that the Samaritan came,
And told her story of the Living Water,
To quench the thirst of all men for all time,
And the Spirit in us by which we know
The Holy Spirit that is God;
Whilst Nicodemus brooded silently,
Thinking of the wild wind that blows where it listeth,
And how the tree-tops rustled in the moonlit garden.
Then Mary of Bethany, the gentle and patient one,
Would doubtless tell of all that she heard
When she gave to Jesus ungrudgingly
The hospitality of her mind.
But it must have been from Martha there came
The story of the Resurrection and the Life.
How Lazarus must have listened when there was a sudden
hush,
And Mary Magdalene told once more
Of the Voice she heard, long ago,
In the darkness of the early morning amongst the olives.
And out of talk like this,
And the long pondering of John and Mary,
And the love of the woman who was a sinner,
And perhaps too of that one who was so nearly stoned by
the Jews in the Temple,
    John's Gospel arose.
That was the greatest gift anybody ever gave the world,
    For in it is the Inner Knowledge of Christ.

    THE PILGRIM PSYCHE

I launched my ship again last night,
This poor old wreck of the world's gales,
Swung out on seas of rainbow light ...
I was too sad to hoist the sails ...

Then she and I crept near the shore,
Where coral shone beneath the wave.
She asked what I was seeking for,
Yet I but sought to cheat my grave.

Then out beyond the wave-swept bar,
Where the green lawns of earth grow gray,
I steered by a strange-coloured star ...
God grant we do not lose our way.

IN OXFORD STREET

A little idle, lonely song, secret and far away
Haunted the roads of all the world, and fled along the
shore;
It laughed in rustling corn that grows high up on
Knocknarea,
And sang along the sunset waves at windy Mullaghmore.

It darted in and out among the trees at Lissadil,
And whispered in the twilight what the quiet primrose
meant,
And flung a sudden call from every green enchanted hill,
And faded far away o'er silver miles of sand and bent.

The little streams have fled from me aghast with broken
cries,
As through the din of Oxford Street I walk cold ways of
death,
Yet in my soul a sudden wave of starry silence sighs,
Under my storm-swept roof of dreams the singer entereth.

IN THIBET

The masked gods danced on painted feet of clay,
Harsh music muttered, thundered, shrieked aloud;
Demons and ghouls and ghosts made holiday.
Yet one man stood alone in the wild crowd;
He swung a coloured rattle round and round,
His face was strange with love and holiness,
On his closed eyes the peace of God was shed,
And all the while his lips moved without sound,
Yet all the while my heart could hear his prayer,
But who should answer him I could not guess.
Then from the whiteness of a long-set sun
There came the echo of a Voice that said,
'When all men pray to false gods, and but one
Has found the One Eternal, I am there ...'
I fell down at his feet as one dead.

APOSTLES OF ETERNITY
'Certain women of our company.'

First came, with profound eyes and clear,
Mary, poet and seer;
To the cradle and the cross,
Bitter gain and radiant loss,
She brings strange wisdom, deep and still,
The white Peace of Goddes' will;
She dreams, and waits, and understands,
Bringing a message to all lands.

At sunset to the well there came
A woman without name or fame,
Water of life for every man
Christ gave to the Samaritan.
She unto her neighbours went

On the mysterious errand sent,
Her living water she outpoured,
Many she brought unto the Lord.

To her whose soul was steeped in sin
Christ gave the light of heaven within,
Forgiveness, righting every wrong,
And Love's soul-shattering song;
Yea, to the sinner at the Feast
He gave the Star in the East;
On us, in darkness wandering far,
Still shines in Love the sinner's star.

To Martha, weeping o'er the dead,
His death-defying words were said.
Unto the world his words she gave,
Annihilation of the grave,
Peace amid all our grief and strife,
The Resurrection and the Life.
John from her lips the strange words took,
And wrote them down in his great book.

The twelve still dreamt of thrones and power ...
Mary of Bethany knew his hour;
She, who on the Truth did gaze
At his feet in other days,
Knew the strange rune of measured breath,
The inner will of pain and death;
Her spikenard ointment, rare and sweet,
She poured o'er his death-destined feet.

When all men thought that he was dead,
The Light of his new Life was shed
On Mary Magdalenè, sent
Forth with the news of a wild event, –
The first to pierce Death's bitter night,
Apostle of our deathless Light,

Strangest speaker since time began,
Bearer of Christ's great gift to man.

She told how the whole world's friend
Unto his Father could ascend.
There, where all true desires and fair
Can breathe their own eternal air,
Where the wild winds of the Spirit go,
From whence the Living Waters flow,
Where Life trails starry robes divine,
She bade men drink of the new wine.

THREE WAYS OF LOVE

Love that would have and hold,
Jealous and full of wrath,
Cruel as hate, and as old, –
The Love of the Flame for the Moth.

The yearning passion that flies
On the giddy wings of Desire,
The Love of the Unwise, –
The Love of the Moth for the Fire.

Love that is Life and Light,
Radiance, reflected far
From the million mirrors of night, –
The Love of the Sun for a Star.

RAISING THE DEAD

No, not by fierce concentration
On a belovèd human form,

Or the toil of the imagination,
Shalt thou find what was lost in the storm.
Ah piteous, Death gives thee back for thy faith
But a beautiful image, a phantom, a wraith.
But a gift thou hast given to another,
And a prayer thou hast prayed not amiss,
For the sake of a human brother,
Shall bring down from the stars thy bliss.
This Messenger holds all heaven in his hand ...
Alas, who will understand?

A MADONNA BY BOTTICELLI

The Divine Sorrow in her human eyes
Out of the heaven of heavens looks down
On blood-drenched countryside and burning town,
Dark with the old incalculable pain,
The torment of the Slayer and the Slain,
The worm at the earth's heart that never dies.
Lo, in her eyes' moon-haunted gloom
A million armies meet their doom.
The sorrow of the whole world is there:
The torment of all prisoners doomed to die,
The criminal's broken heart, the dreamer's prayer,
The ignorant judge's unfeared agony;
The pain of little struggling lives that pass
From life to death unnumbered in the grass,
The voice that failed among the choirs of spring,
Yea, even the brown owl's broken wing,
All desolate cries that wail along the wind
Pierce with sharp swords this virgin's inner mind.
From these she knows not respite or relief,
The Eternal Beauty, and the ancient grief.
On earth the road to Calvary she trod, ...
Hers still the Sorrows of the Son of God.

REALITY

Thou who hast filled the blue bowl of the sea
With beauty, and the gray bowl of the shore,
Who with the living ecstasy
Thus fillest all things golden to the brim,
Giving to all men what they labour for;
My little cup of metal dim
Can yet hold a burning coal:
Cast Truth into my soul.

DYSMAS

Oh, great among the blessed Angels sent
By the strange Mercy of Eternal Truth,
This man, who was a robber from his youth,
Has lit for us the Light Magnificent.

Haunter of desert roads, the thief who stole
From the slow caravan amber and gold,
Has given back to the world a hundredfold,
Has given Light to the human soul.

'If this poor lost one found the Life Divine,'
Men say, 'shall I, even I, not dare to pray?
Shall I not meet Christ on the Dolorous Way?
Better than amber this, or gold most fine.'

Of those who wept beside the Crucified,
Three messengers have brought the world relief:
Mary the harlot, and the unknown thief,
And John whose words unto the end abide.

THE GLORY OF GOD

Beyond the sunset, over the sea, a pale green luminous ray
was shed.
'Lo, this is the very gate of Heaven, the ultimate Glory of
God,' I said.

When silver the moon rose out of the darkness, serene and
stainless and white,
The Glory of God seemed to fall like a sword on the waves
of the night.

But a voice of past agony in the inner deeps of my spirit
stirred,
And the sun burnt cold, the moon hid her face, in fear of
the spoken word.

'Father, forgive them who torture me thus,' – the great
words glitter and shudder and shine;
And this was the ultimate Glory of God, the Gate of the
Kingdom Divine.

IN THE DOCK

'There sit my judges,' said the prisoner,
'Bitterly throned, so high above
Mercy and Christ and Love
That their pulses do not stir
Or throb to God's great beautiful song,
Forgiveness of all wrong.'
But Truth in his own soul answered, 'Nay,
Judge not; but for thy sins, and God's grace,
That brought thee to this place,
Thou wouldest have been as they.'

PEACE

Fret not thyself, nor make great argument
With other men on other light intent,
For they too love the Perfect One, who praise
The Vision and the Glory in strange ways.
The lark knows not the song the linnet sings,
The thrush gains heaven without the eagle's wings;
The lake unto the mountain cannot rise,
Yet it reflects the blueness of the skies;
No daisy's beauty does a snowdrop wrong,
Each sings to God her white and golden song;
The fragrance of the mignonette divine
Is foolishness unto the jessamine;
The pale sea-thrift, growing among the rocks,
Sings not the great song of the hollyhocks;
What shining lily or blue violet knows
The secret of the colour of the rose?
These neither strive nor cry, into the air
They lift their lovely forms, their colours fair,
Each pouring forth into the sun's clear rays
Her answering rhythm of love and praise ...
What matter if one does not understand
Or see the lamp held in a brother's hand?
Anger and argument are the dead things
That Love into the Lake of Fire flings;
Orange or white, or green, or rose, or blue,
The shining vision of each flower is True.

WATER

What light doth water hold,
Beautiful water, clasping to her heart
All things divine, remote, apart,
Stars and rainbows manifold ...

Thus doth the midnight swimmer float
At ease in the moon's boat,
Thus doth she plunge through the fleece of the Lion,
Dipping her head in the gleam of Orion,
Wild to clasp in far-off seas
Arcturus or the Pleiades.
Yet stars must pale, and the night end –
Water is still our friend,
For all the livelong day
With heaven you may play;
Blue sky, the clouds, and the great shining sun,
All things luminous and dear
  She bringeth near:
  This, this hath water done.

DAISIES

Green trees against the sky's blue,
'Twas all the world they knew.
Would it not be well for us
Sometimes to see the whole world thus?

TULIPS

How the May-flowering tulip lifts its cup
To the strong sunlight, and the crashing rain!
Immortal flower, no heart thus lifted up
To hold God's will could live and die in vain.

LILIES OF THE VALLEY

Sweeter than chimes of silver, stronger to compel
Than melodies of bronze haunting the air
From all the marble belfries of the world,
In living rhythms of joy each fragile bell,
Out of its green and sunlit tower unfurled,
Rings in my soul a delicate call to prayer.

THE WINDS

Through all our pallid sea and skies
The wild breath of His presence flies,
Like the way of the wind through a field of corn,
Or the pathway of Light on a living stream,
His footsteps waver and flash and gleam.
His Three Winds, since time began,
Are Love that shakes the soul of a man
As the wind shakes a rose on a summer morn,
Till the raindrops fall on the grass below
Where the little thirsty daisies grow;
And Truth that shakes the human mind
As the sea is shaken by the wind;
And the wind of Life that blows where it wills,
Over cities and deserts and valleys and hills.
They who would know God watch the breeze,
Listen to the rustle in the trees,
See the snow on the mountains above,
Follow the winds of Truth and Love;
Fear not the stony water-course,
Tracing the stream of Life to its source
Amongst the Everlasting Snows
Find the Wind that shakes the Rose.

A GARDEN GRAVE

Men, poetic wise,
Tell me the bluebells are her eyes,
Tulips the lips once clear and red,
And cold cheeks of the dead,
Whilst her white hands and her brow
Are arum lilies now.
Oh, foolish dream and cold!
Her body was burnt, I know,
Gray ashes all her countenance,
   Flame her hair's gold.
But bluebells, chiming, whisper low,
   'Perchance, perchance ...
She is not very far from our frail towers;
Though her heart crumbled in the far-off years,
Her faithful spirit tends all lost and broken flowers
With the new love and the old human tears.'

TO A LADY – NOW DEAD

When first I saw your curved and gracious face
With noble gentleness of beauty shine,
I thought of starry music and blue space,
And then of colours, long lost, Florentine.

The sculptured splendour of your moving form
Was shepherding my thoughts to light-crowned Greece,
But suddenly you walked above Life's storm,
Shining upon me from far hills of peace.

And now my heart was lifted up with dread
And exaltation to a Light above
The rainbow's, where life rises from the dead,
And Beauty walks in Everlasting Love.

AMEN-RA

The Daisy in her heart the sunlight holds,
Each golden disc with its white petal rays
Tells of the Great Light that the flower beholds,
Lifted above earth's green and living ways.

So shall our minds hold the strange Image Bright,
The glory of the Spiritual Sun unseen,
In rays of Love round the great Disc of Light,
Supported by frail shapes of living green.

THE FAIREST

In this dark world how great and fair a throng
Of shining things hold lamps to guide our feet,
Music and lovely forms and frozen song,
And cowslips most compassionately sweet.

But there is one thing fairer far than all,
Dearer than dawn-lit waters deep and clear,
The Perfect Love that answers every call,
And from the coward heart doth cast out fear.

'HE THAT WONDERS SHALL REIGN'

Surely he might have fled
Quietly into the hills that night
With his little band of friends, leaving far behind
The angry city on its wind-swept height,
Walls and bright towers and shivering olive trees,
A silver glitter on the dawn wind;
He might have known safety and friendship and ease ...

He did not go,
By any fear or longing shepherded,
But kept his tryst with Judas, 'that all men might know
He loved the Father,' even so he said.
I who stand so far below
The first rung of this ladder, in the humblest place,
Consider with wonder the things that are above,
The radiant wisdom that is Love's face,
The courage that is the golden heart of Love ...
Often I dream, though the world is wide,
And full of great and beautiful things,
Nothing can lift me to his side,
Nothing can give my spirit wings ...
Yet a Voice whispers in my heart all day,
And Light shines through its phantom terrors grim,
Bringing strange dreams to weeping eyes of clay,
Saying, 'Arise and follow him,
Fear not at all, he is himself the way.'

COLOUR

Secretly out of the earth one night
Slip yellow and white;
Suddenly, without a sound,
Blue rises out of the ground ...
What happy person ever sees
Green steal out of the trees?
Red is on us now and gold;
Which of us saw a rose unfold?
Who watched the gradual brightness creep
Like a dream out of sleep?
Unseen, unknown, beautiful, dumb,
Colour into our world has come,
Blue, and Gold, and Green, and Red –
The Love of God – our daily bread.

THE CONSOLER

Not when he dwelt at peace under bare skies,
Nor when he came at dawn down from the height,
With the night's prayer still shining from his eyes,
And all the world was bathed in a new light;

Not when the shouting people branches spread,
And garments, on the ground as he rode past,
Nor when he healed the suffering, raised the dead,
Did God send forth an Angel from the Vast.

But when the stars above the olives gleamed
On Love that reached the ultimate goal of pain,
And his friends slept, whilst only Mary dreamed
That hardly should they hear his voice again,

Yea, even in that Agony of prayer,
When his soul rocked, and every star grew dim,
Charged with strange rapture none but he could bear,
God sent a Messenger to comfort him.

GOD IN THE TREES
(AN UNREAD BOOK)

Oh, beautiful singing thought,
The very poem I sought;
I don't want to read this book,
I want just to sit by the brook,
I want to fall on my knees
And worship God in the Trees.

THE TULIP TREE

Under the moon last night
The Tulip Tree shone white,
And the bluebells looked as blue
As in the very woods they do;
Yea, even on our tiny lawn
A blackbird sang at dawn,
And then a thrush took up the cry
In sudden clamorous ecstasy,
Till God smiled, looking gently down,
To see such joy in London Town.

TO A LITTLE BOY

Oh, how can you want to know the time?
   Surely you know
It's time for the fern leaves to uncurl,
It's time for the May to blow,
It's time for the lark to arise with a song
   In the blue sky;
It's time for flags to furl,
It's time for Death to die,
It's time for us all to play and sing the whole day long.

TO M. L'E

You sit so still in your invalid chair,
In the quiet room, day after day.
Nobody hears your step on the stair,
Nobody sees you flying away.

You hypocrite, you can't hide from me,
I've seen you flash down a moonlit lane,
I've watched you dancing over the sea,
I've met you on mountains again and again.

Last night I caught you in a wild rout,
Far, far away, where the old world ends,
I watched you tossing the stars about ...
I know, I know who are your friends.

WRATH

Once men thought,
Foolish and blind,
The thunder was the wrath of God,
Terrible with lightnings shod,
Judging and punishing mankind
For evil deeds in darkness wrought.
Now do we know the thunder rolls
Only in our own souls,
And lightnings flash but from the eyes
Of the unwise.
Yea, we, soon angered, must confess
That God is Joy in Gentleness.

JUDAS

What all men share all men must execrate,
The mournful sin of Judas, whose despair
Shines out a sign for watchers everywhere,
The target of the world's most shallow hate.
What holy soul austere, invincible,
Treading strange heights on mortal feet of clay,

Has not at one time sold
The gift God gave him but to give away,
  Receiving not silver or gold
In payment for the Light Invisible,
But glory, for scant skill
In the task perilous and hard
Of pointing the way over the hill,
The path of Light on the sea,
The moonlit road through vine and olive yard,
Into the shadows of Gethsemane.

SIZE

The Wise and Great do tell us every day
How gloriously those great worlds in the skies,
So many million billion miles away,
Spread out Infinity before our eyes.

Yet does my heart forsake the starry wild;
Quite close to-day I saw the Eternal shine,
Pouring out Light from the eyes of a child,
Huge and remote, beyond the stars, divine.

Yea, you may rake the heavens from pole to pole,
And weigh the moon, and probe each star and sun,
But you will find Love in a human soul.
A little space holds God, when all is done.

MOONLIGHT

This moon, so lonely fair,
That thrills the midnight air,
Shone thus two thousand years ago

Into the silver-shadowed gloom
Of that wide upper room,
Built high above the narrow street,
Where Jesus with Truth strange and sheer
To all men's hearts drew near ...
But his friends knew him not,
Nor whither he must go,
Nor why, thus utterly alone,
He knelt down on the cold stone
Gently, with love, to wash the feet
Of Judas, called Iscariot.

MUSIC AND WORDS

Music says, 'Awake, listen, attend, arise,
Something is calling from a far shore;'
And the words answer, 'Follow the True and Wise,
The One who went before.'
Music cries out with a wild chord,
'Lift up your hearts, behold, a Dream, behold;'
And the words answer, strange, and clear, and cold,
'We lift them up unto the Lord.'

THE ROADS OF MYSTERY

The road of a new rose, delicate, white,
Up from its roots, deep buried and blind,
   Down in the earth's night;
The way of the sunlight over the sea;
The path of a thought from the soul to the mind –
   Are the Roads of Mystery.

THE MEEK

Oh, what is the old promise worth?
When shall the weak
And pitiful meek
Inherit the earth?
Nay, in that distant day,
When wrath and pride
In me have died,
And fear has passed away
With its monotonous distress,
I doubt not that this star shall roll
Nearer to its bright goal,
When Gentleness
Inherits my own soul.

THE SINGING BOUGH

Yes, I was born in May.
The first of lovely things
That blessed my sight,
Before even the swallow's wings,
Was a wet bough flashing white,
Swung out against the radiant blue,
Singing the first notes of the great song
Of Orpheus, the Beautiful ... the True,
The Loveliness that crowns all life with flowers,
Through good or evil chance
Of soul or circumstance,
And holds my hand and lifts my heart the whole day long
...
Oh, rapturous sunlit Melody Divine,
Soul-shaking Dream of mine ...
Now I am growing old, yet to this day
I still must worship God in the White May.

THE WRITING ON THE GROUND

I read in the ancient book,
'He stooped to write on the ground.'
I thought, 'What he wrote who can tell,
Some truth, austere, profound,
Mysterious, inscrutable, –
But why did no one look?'
Then I went out after the rain;
Water like liquid sunlight ran
Over the grass and down the lane,
Singing as only water can,
How he who runs may read
What God writes everywhere,
On the grass in flower and weed,
With white clouds on bright air,
Or a blue haze on a far hill ...
Love's beautiful will.

THE DIVINE IMAGE

No one can tell
How he looked as he stood on the marble stair,
In the purple robe with the thorns in his hair,
All is forgotten now.
No one can say
Whether eyes of gray,
Smiling in opalescent light,
Or peaceful pools of radiant brown,
(As in Luini's memories dim
And dreams of him)
Looked down
From under the torn bright hair and the great brow,
As he stood there,
Pouring Love on the fires of hell ...

No one can tell ...
Nay, even in these late days,
Those whose keen gaze
Can pierce through Mercy's thin disguise
Shall see the colour of his eyes,
And those who worship Love's grace
Know the strange radiance of his face.
Yea, they who find Truth's pearl most rare
Shall see him standing on the stair.

NEMESIS

In a past life he lied to men, with foolish tales
Of God's great wrath, and men believed his lies;
Now he has grown more wise.
This is his bitter lot,
To speak the truth whilst men believe him not.

GENTIANS

At Sils Maria, on a June morn,
When I caught in the grass a glint of blue,
It seemed that the earth's green vail was torn,
And Heaven was breaking through.

CHRIST IN THE LANE

This morning, through the gold and green,
Christ walked, by men unseen,
But the blue flower in the lane
Said as he passed, quite plain,

'Speed well, speed well, O Strange and True,
We have waited long for you.'
His robe in a bramble caught and frayed,
Thorns shrank, by memories dismayed,
Till from his garment's tattered hem
Peace flowed on them.
To hold his Love was lifted up
The celandine's gold cup.
The small green fronds uncurling cried,
'We thought you had died, we thought you had died.'
Like Mary's ointment, golden sweet,
The gorse spilt fragrance on his feet.
Whilst like that Angel long ago,
Whose garments were as sunlit snow,
Joyful and splendid the White May
    Proclaimed the Resurrection Day.
O Christ, a burden of gloom
May haunt the wallèd room,
But the blue shining out of doors
    Is yours, is yours.

THE SEER

A rainbow shines in my mind,
I weep with the joy of its gracious form,
Made of water and colour and air, on fire
With the song of a skylark, singing high
In a blue dazzle of sky.
    Men lost in the storm
Dream that all vision is empty desire;
    Men say I am blind,
They see not my great arch built out of air,
    Belovèd and only Fair.

OLD AGE DRAWING NEAR

'What will you do when you're old?'
'I'll dance with joy on the starry wild,
I'll sing to the moon,
And shout to the sun,
And mock at the languid afternoon,
And steal fruit from the brambles, and run
To plunder the rainbow's gold,
I'll be again as a little child,
That's what I'll do when I'm old.'
'But if you're helpless grown,
Weary, in pain?'
'All the gay world divine
Still shall be mine,
Sunshine and rain,
And wild roses blown
In my dream, in my prayer.'
'But when the twilight ends?'
'Shine out, O friend of friends,
Give Life's new glittering whole,
Love strong as the swallows' wings,
All wild truths and beautiful things,
To a child's frightened soul
That peers through the secret door, the door in the air.'

THE WONDERFUL HOUR

Under a high-set tree
I spent a wonderful hour,
Dreaming of the green life,
The long growth, the difficult strife,
The strength and balance hard to attain,
Through joy of the sun and life of the rain,
The unconquerable ecstasy

And triumph of the white flower.
Then the new adventure high and rash,
The tree's life, undaunted, upward-soaring, mute,
Culminating in the Red Fruit,
The berries of the Mountain Ash.

PRAYER

Shadows and lights o'er the mountains pass,
The wind sweeps over the flowery grass,
Till the forms of the flowers pass away
Into a host of coloured gleams,
With a sound as of rushing streams ...
We go to Church every seventh day,
He went up into the hills to pray ...

THE SUNSHINE FALLS

The sunshine falls in mystery
On the white clouds and snow more white,
It is a glory on the sea,
And in the meadows light.

O Love, cast not thy rays alone
On the High Spirit's snow-clad towers;
O'er dark seas build thy great white throne,
And be our Light among the flowers.

SALVATOR MUNDI

I gave up all things, and behold all things came and
begged to be mine,
Mine is the life of the rainbow, the river, the corn, and the
vine,
I shine from stars, I flow in streams, I rise up from the
earth in trees,
My vision, enthroned beyond all dreams, shines over a
thousand seas.
My writing glitters in cloud and shower, the blue skies are
my scroll,
My face is mirrored in every flower, my mind in every
man's soul.
My Spirit is that thin golden air, still brightness, or
wandering wind,
Love that flows o'er the wild seas in prayer, or life that
enfolds the mind.
It shelters the lonely dreams of men, and holds up the
skylark's wing,
For deep in my boundless heart is the heart of every living
thing.
I give my Dream to the outcast, the slave, or the king on
his throne,
I give my soul to the beggar, I go forth from myself alone.
The sun and the moon and the stars I give, and I grudge to
none,
I give the whole Glory of God to every man under the sun;
For through my soul there flows the Love that has built up
the earth and sky,
And set in the heart of dust and stone a glory that cannot
die,
And made a road for the tides beneath, and the wonderful
moon above,
And the wind-driven hearts of foolish men, in the calm
Heart of Love.
Sunlight and starlight are my dreams, and the twilight

deep and still,
For I have given my will to God, and mine is God's dear
will.
Mine is the Dream and the Splendour, the broken parts
and the whole,
For I have given my love to God, and my soul is Love's
wild soul.

SECRET WATERS

Lo, in my soul there lies a hidden lake,
High in the mountains, fed by rain and snow,
The sudden thundering avalanche divine,
And the bright waters' everlasting flow,
Far from the highways' dusty glare and heat.
Dearer it is and holier, for Christ's sake,
Than his own windy lake in Palestine,
For there the little boats put out to sea
Without him, and no fisher hears his call,
Yea, on the desolate shores of Galilee
No man again shall see his shadow fall.
Yet here the very voice of the one Light
Haunts with sharp ecstasy each little wind
That stirs still waters on a moonlit night,
And sings through high trees growing in the mind,
And makes a gentle rustling in the wheat ...
Yea, in the white dawn on this happy shore,
With the lake water washing at his feet,
He stands alive and radiant evermore,
Whose presence makes the very East wind kind,
And turns to heaven the soul's green-lit retreat.

EVERYMAN'S GLIMPSE OF HEAVEN

I have been Fear, and Desire, and Hate, caught in Earth's
flying zodiac zone,
Endlessly treading the wind-swept path, driven from sign
to flaming sign,
I have been Vanity, Pain, and Death, changed and builded
and overthrown,
Yet once for a moment I, even I, was Love; steadfast this
light doth shine
For him who would stand in truth beyond earth's
glittering zodiac way,
A branch of the Tree of Life eternal, the changeless and
star-laden vine,
Truth, Beauty, and Love, for ever and ever, to-day and
yesterday.

'YET A LITTLE WHILE'

So long ago, so far away,
Such weary lengths of time and space
Between this day and the other day
When the world saw thy face.

Such sighing winds, such wells of tears
Such centuries of fear and pain,
Such sandy miles of desolate years,
Before we see thy face again.

'A little while,' oh, promise strange,
The Love that in our souls once shone
Has vanished down dim ways of change,
We know not whither thou hast gone.

Some say a bright and distant star
Thou shinest in the heavens above;
Nay, there is no more near nor far
In God's enfolding soul of Love.

There is the Mystic Garden Fair,
The Tree of Life, the shining stream,
By crystal waters thou art there,
Close to our hearts, it is no dream.

There is the place from whence Life came,
There is the fire Prometheus stole,
There is the little holy flame
That burns in every living soul.

And there are rainbows and sea-shells,
And light, and wings, and flowers,
And every blessèd dream that dwells
Wistfully in this world of ours.

Oh, glorious divine ascent,
And simple secret marvellous,
This is the Place to which he went
That he might come again to us.

For Love is that Diviner air,
The Breath of Life, the Rainbow Fire,
The goal of all things unaware,
God's soul, and purpose, and desire.

And Love is his eternal fate
Who takes Love for his guide.
Lo, at his touch the barrèd gate
Of heaven opens wide.

Thus very near our eyelids dim
The central Glory flames and swings,
And Cherubim and Seraphim
In emerald splendours bathe their wings.

Here in God's Love alone we live,
This is the key of the lost door.
Yea, he who knows how to forgive
Shall wander down the years no more.

And he who clasps on earth the hand
Of one who might have been his foe,
Does for a moment understand
Whither he too must go.

Deep in his soul Light whispers clear,
From the struck rock the torrent flows,
All streams are living waters dear, ...
All deserts blossom as the Rose.

A little while, – soon, soon, perchance,
The Road of Dust and Tears may seem,
In the Glory of Love's countenance,
But a dark tunnel through a dream.

THE HOUSE OF THREE WINDOWS
(1926)

THE HOUSE OF THREE WINDOWS

Lord, in thy glamoured house of sun and shining air,
When all the green built walls are white with the white
may,
And wandering bluebells weave bright carpets
everywhere,
Whilst overhead where the blue ends no man can say,

Strange Builder, let me not forget thy windows three:
Whiter than may boughs, bluer than blue skies, high set
Are thy three shuttered lattices of ecstasy:
Open the windows for me, let me not forget.

THE CRUCIFIX

Listen, O Jove of the thunder,
Hermes with light wings shod,
Osiris, Isis, Serapis,
Children of power and delight,
Zeus in the ether hiding,
Cynthia, goddess of the night,
Aphrodite, queen of bliss,
Was there any need of this?
The white brow pierced above,
The helpless feet nailed under,
The poor hands in pain abiding,
Nothing holding, motionless –
Zeus, come to his aid –
Cast o'er the sun one tiny cloud,
One little gentle clinging shade –
Ah, was there any need for this
That man to man has done?
The broken body's last distress,
Those fading eyes, those bloodstained locks,

To show the world that God is Love,
And Love, dear Love, is God –
Is God then weaker than the sun?
Oh, who shall understand
Love's dreadful paradox
And wild heart-breaking song,
All potent mind and helpless hand,
Feet of ice and wings of flame,
Darkened eyes and shining soul,
Truth with a new name,
Life that is Love's goal,
Love that resents no wrong,
Love that answers every call,
Losing all, forgiving all,
Waiting with a quiet will,
Till death climb the hill.
Listen, O Jove of the thunder,
Hermes with dark purpose shod,
Osiris, Isis, Serapis,
Children of power and delight,
Zeus in the ether hiding,
Cynthia, goddess of the night,
Aphrodite, queen of bliss,
Was there ever dream like this,
God in a human heart abiding,
Emptied of all human bliss,
Bereft of joy and wonder?
Can this blood spilt on the stones
Have shaken your bright thrones?
Is this, then, wisdom's high reward,
The fragrance of her secret rose –
The hidden meaning in her eyes?
'Trust Love in all things, turn the other cheek,
Into its sheath thrust thou the sword,
Resist not evil, love thy foes,
Dare to be numbered with the weak.'
Oh, terrible logic of the unfaltering skies

That shrinks not from this dreadful gain,
Life, a shrieking storm of pain,
Love surrounded by derision,
Truth crowned with thorns –
Was this the goal of the wise star?
Is this the way divine?
Can any heavenly splendour shine
Thus far, so far
From the bright roads men's dreams have trod?
Yea, this is the power and the glory
And the everlasting story;
Yea, this is the Light and the Vision,
This is the Image of God.

THE HIDDEN ONE

He is so silent that I can always hear him,
He is so beautiful that I could never fear him,
So beautiful that I cannot see him at all:
He is so selfless that he is everywhere,
He does not deny himself to any sparrow's call,
He cannot forget to answer even my foolish prayer.

A ROUND PEBBLE FROM THE BROOK

These submerged stones how still they lie
    Under the stream,
Whilst the bright torrent hurries by,
The rushing waters flow and gleam
Like the white garments' swaying hem
Of Him who lit the starry sky,
For ever passing, moulding them,
Amid the rhythmic chorus of all things,

And shouting suns and planets whirling fast,
And the great stream of dancing singing change,
Till they become at last,
As years and centuries swing by,
One with the meteor and the thunder-stone,
One with the One who cannot dream alone.
And when the Flute-player, the Fair, the Strange,
Calls life out of her wallèd Garden of dim years,
To dance her way into the lightning-wingèd spheres,
And the green earth sings clear with all her lands
'Death is no more,' and the trees clap their hands,
And the flowers cry, 'Now there are no more graves,'
But, 'Glory to God in the highest,' thunderous ocean sings,
Till the Mountains rise in a great giant throng
And fling wild Rhythms to the winds and waves,
'Peace and goodwill to men and we as they,'
Torrent and tide rejoice, high rock, steep waterfall
Join in the chorus, answer to the call.
Through the wide world, thus whirling to and fro,
Strophe and antistrophe echoing go,
'Glory to God, peace and goodwill to all' –
In that far day when Life waves flaming wings,
No smallest step in the dance shall stumble or fail,
No note be lost in the scale,
No little silence do the Music wrong,
Yea, even the stones, least of Immortal things,
 Shall join that song.

NEW YEAR (1926)

I have come forth from dark distress
Into the singing light again,
The ancient lilt of loveliness
Pours onward flooding through my brain.

A dweller in dim corridors
And caverns of a twilight land,
Now have I found the windy shores,
The living waves, the yellow sand.
Great treasure in my hand I hold,
A bright shell found in that dark cave,
Sea splendour built up fold on fold
By rushing tide and breaking wave.

I run, I sing, I swim, I dive,
I fly along the dawnlit wind,
I am alive, alive, alive,
High tide and sunrise in my mind.

THE RECONCILER

Startled we were, arrested, strange, aghast,
Following the coffin down the churchyard way,
Beneath our feet the abyss had opened vast,
And clay was horrified, looking at clay.

But suddenly a flower arose and sang
And all the grass was full of crocus blooms,
Down in their roots the very bluebells rang,
And horror fled away among the tombs.

Then Spirit took dear Beauty by the hand,
And wandered through our souls in joy and grace,
And lo ... white sunrise over a dark land,
And Spirit gazing into Spirit's face.

TO E. G. R.

All lights are quenched, all joys in darkness drown,
The fog lies heavy on the breathless town,
Ah, come with me and breathe the sunny air
In Jacob Boehme's Garden of roses fair.

Behind the smoke bright towers soar up sublime,
Entombed the unborn flowers wait their time,
Gabriel doth hold a Lily, not a sword,
Are we not guests at the mysterious board?

The River of Life is running strong and free,
White is the May, and all the hyaline sea
Shines suddenly with Christ's mysterious smile ...
Sit by this window, let us watch awhile ...

A MUSICIAN
(Parsifal)

The shadow of Christ lay heavy on the wall
Of his mind's secret-haunted inner cave,
As on an Atlantic cottage hearth might fall
The shadow of a sunset-lightened wave ...

O subtle rhythm, shadow woven spell ...
O wandering wave from the lost ocean vast,
Singing the dream his lips could never tell ...
Unveil, strange music, the forgotten past.

THAT THEY MAY BE ONE

With all the joy of the world I rejoice,
With all the sins of the world I repent,
With all men's dear forgiveness I forgive,
With all the light of the world I give thanks,
With all the longing of the world I pray,
With all the love I love, with all life I live:
Lo, we are all one heart, one soul, one voice.
Rejoice, rejoice, free of the shining ranks
That breathe together God's bright mutual air,
Dull soul that could be lonely yesterday.
Now have I found, far down beneath my mind,
God's utter friendliness in all mankind.
There is the sound of many waters heard
In the one voice, as I stood in a dream,
Men's souls like waves the sea of being stirred,
And lo, beneath the ripples' glint and gleam,
Translucent unity was everywhere.

THE DISCIPLE

To stand at his side on the grass,
To take from his hand the broken bread
Of Beauty, and give it to all who come,
Crying out to the folk that pass,
'Here are the hills and the seas,
The fair flowers and the tall trees:
Take the Bread that all dreamers crave,
Waste not one delicate crumb,
Let not a rose-petal fall' –
Nay, better to say, 'In his name
I give you the spirit of all these things,
Here is love that is flowers, love that is wings,
Life like a dancing flame,

Life like a singing wave,
Truth strong-rooted as hills and trees,
All these are love, all these,
God over all, and in all.'

LIMITATIONS

I can hear but one dream crumble, one voice cry, one
sparrow fall,
Yet I can see a flock of birds, I can watch a hundred wings
–
Is there no man can feel each sorrow, and answer every
call?
Why can one hear but one thing at a time, and see a
hundred things?

There is peace in the sun's still shining, but Truth in the icy
blast
Shatters the heart of the hungry, passing the fortunate by –
He whose soul is pierced by the arrow that flieth out of the
vast
Shall hear each sparrow fall, each mourner weep, each
dumb thing cry.

THE SECRET SHARER

O coloured torch of sea-born poetry that falls
Into the hidden deeps unlit by any sun,
The ultimate and blind abyss of a man's soul,
Showing how love and pity once broke the prison walls
Of personality, and love was strangely one
With the belovèd outcast, the dear murderer.
Amid the surge and solitude of the sea's strife,

Where beneath wind and wave wild tides of being stir,
These travellers of the world have found their goal.
Deep in submerged and hidden caverns of the heart,
These lovers of the sea have found the Life of Life ...
We thrill to the great truth, we children of the night,
And cannot see the Light of Light, and call it 'Art.'

THE CRIMINAL

Nought do we know of all his wandering
Save that he did some dark and dreadful deed
And suffered death for it; and this strange thing,
This Rapture, for a criminal was decreed,
Of all the millions dying and the millions dead,
On him alone should fall the sun's last ray,
Only to him in human words be said,
'Thine the lost garden ere the close of day.'
Whilst still there fell before the set of sun
On Golgotha long shadows of cross bars,
Behold the Sinful and the Sinless One
Together trod strange roads beyond the stars.

THE LAST KISS

Strangely the Scripture saith,
But one of his friends did Love allow
To go straight to his death
With Christ's last kiss still shining on his brow,
  For all the world to see ...
By that crown of thorns in his hair,
The Angels everywhere
Guessed at the traitor's inner tragic loyalty.

LOVE

Love goes the whole world round,
  Knowing no bound
    Love comes in the end to all:
Christ went to prepare a place
  In God's beautiful grace
For Judas and for Pilate as for
    John and Paul.

ENEMIES

One cried for justice in God's name.
Into God's presence we came,
  The injurer and the injured ...
Which was which I know not,
For when together we prayed,
Together we both forgot.

MYTHS

Once Orpheus wandered o'er the plains of Thrace,
Through field and wood his lovely Lyre rang,
Till shyest folk and wild in every place
Heard and took courage from the song he sang.

Once Hermes like a shepherd led his sheep,
The souls of men, by the dark river bank,
Where vengeance rose out of the muddy deep,
And life and joy through those dead waters sank.

Thou Orpheus, all life answers thy wild call,
Thou Hermes, to thy piping shepherd wise,

The dream of Love, the fairest dream of all,
Out of thy living waters shall arise.

The Lyre of Orpheus doth in heaven gleam,
The staff of Hermes in the ancient scroll,
But lo, thy voice in every wind and stream,
And thy great deed in every living soul.

HIGHER CRITICISM

I

So Mark thought this of him, reading in an older book,
And Luke read Mark, and John perhaps read all,
And made a beautiful story out of his mind ...
Ah, what does it matter, Matthew, Mark, Luke, John,
Catching the gleams that from his splendour fall,
Whilst his clear voice is still in every wind
Of this sad world; to know him you but look
Into the Love of God. Deep in my spirit and yours
Burns the One Light; surely there are open doors
Between man's soul and God, surely he is not gone
From us, he is as near, as known, as wildly dear
To you and me, as to John, Luke, or Mark.
That image in their minds, mysteriously fair,
Is but a lovely picture painted on the dark
Wall of a cave, a human heart like yours or mine.
What then are all our images?
Love that can dare
The supreme hardihood, the great adventure, knows
The friend invisible to mortal eyes,
The strange land gleaming in the sunset skies,
The unknown harbour for the battered sail,
Beyond men's dreams of anger and rebuke,
The secret of the white unfaltering snows,

The opened gate of heaven, the lifted veil ...
What more had Matthew, Mark, or John, or Luke?

II

Yet must we love these pictures painted on the wall
Of every brother's mind, however worn or faint.
For everywhere he passed and let his shadow fall
Some flower grew, some dream arose, some light was
shed.
Ah, how shall we restore lost outlines, fading paint –
How shall we know which were the words he really said,
Entangled in men's fancies, memories, faults, desire
That turns all things to its own likeness, foul or fair?
As easy tell the moonlight shining on the waves
From the sea's darkness, or the stars' far-coloured fire
From broken shadows wandering in night-haunted caves.
Where love is perfect, full, unfaltering, he is there.
Love fills the lost and broken outlines of his face,
Yea, all the light in all this world of ours is one.
Mercy is his whole soul, God has no other grace,
Do we know Light from darkness, we who have seen the
Sun?

THE MOURNER

I met a curious philosopher
Who said, 'Men vainly dream themselves bereft, forlorn.
Black clothes, not sorrow, makes them weep,
And weeping makes them mourn.'
I could but smile at her,
For when I heard that one I loved was dead,
My clothes were russet red,
I did not weep or sigh,
I still walked smiling in the light,

But grief, like a great iceberg, piled up mountains high
On an unspent volcano's broken crown,
Did choke and freeze and smother down
Back to the darkness of primæval night,
The underground abyss from whence it came,
An inner fount of flame.

SYMBOLS

In a vision of delight
I saw heaven last night,
And all the people of the earth were there –
Golden harps by the golden air
Swept into rhythms of light and flame
Rang out the everlasting name,
    All names above;
And every soul was casting down
The Crown of Life, the Victor's Crown,
Before the great white throne of living Love.

IF ONE KNEW

Ah, if you only knew
Who walks among the flowers
Through the long night hours,
Makes the poppies' dreams come true,
Paints the gentian that strange blue,
    Pours out the dew.

Ah, if you could but know
Who it was last night who came
And lit the acorn's flame,
And bid the lark by moonlight sing,

You would know almost everything,
  And see the wind blow.

Ah, if you could but see
Who calls the birds at dawn,
Who waters the green lawn,
You would find out in the end
Who is the flowers' friend,
  The comrade of the tree.

NOVEMBER

The leaves have fallen on the grass, whilst overhead
The winter wind wails through dry boughs and sere,
All greens have faded, everything is dead,
  With the dead year.

Nay, see on every bough the unborn buds vibrate,
Already their hearts flame with life's most vivid hue,
Already Spring is waiting at the gate,
  All things are new.

THE POET TO HIS AMBITION

O vanity, who diggest in my soul
For those lost words and splendid, go thy ways,
Take with thee thy shrill trumpet, thy bright scroll,
I will not sell my life for any praise.

Behold another digger sighing stands
Beside me, she shall have thy spade.
Dear Love who digs for Truth with humble hands,
All Life and Light are thine, come to my aid.

POSTHUMOUS

O faded leaf, what is it to you
Though men should say
This is the flower the sun shone through,
Living gold and translucent blue,
  But yesterday?

Rather a dream of the Voice Divine
On some far day,
'O little branch of the great Vine
Your soul is my sunshine,'
Might not God say?

A LONDON FOG

Black night is over all, the sun
  Is seen of none,
Veiled by the soot from our own chimneys sent
Lost the Bright Firmament ...
The fog has reached my mind.
Alas, the wild desires blazing high
Have filled with smoke that sky
To hide from my inner sight
  The Light of Light.

Yet far from here, great golden-wingèd gleams
Shine upon shining waters, and palm trees
Cut the clean sunlit air radiant with dreams
That haunt the shores of coral-ringèd seas.
Oh, the green branches and the golden air
For those who dare, for those who dare ...
O God, send a great wind ...
A strong heart and a voyage fair,

Some day I shall be there,
And sunlight in my mind.

THE MIRACLE

Dry and dropped on the road I found
A violet root: I dug a hole
With my hands in the loose ground
By the wayside, and planted it
Near where a wild white strawberry grew.
I said 'I leave it dear to you.'
I said 'God's light is in its soul,
Soon we shall see a shining flower ...'
All dry sticks mocked my little wit ...
To-day I found a violet, sunlit.

AT PUDSEYS

All night the waves of darkness broke about my head,
I prayed for sleep in vain, none seemed to hear my words.

Yet God who knows all deepest needs gave me instead
Dawn in the primrose garden, and the songs of birds.

THE MAY TREE

Where my feet pass
The celandine shakes in the wind.
'O golden dream of the grass,
Thou art dear to my mind.'

But where the may tree fills the whole
Of the blue sky with her frail flight,
White petals fall into my soul
In a new cradle song of light.

'Thy trunk hath many storms withstood,
Sharp thorns have thrust thy leaves apart,
O thou white dream of the green wood,
Thou hast broken my heart.'

SAINT SEBASTIAN

Bound to a tree he stands,
Riddled with arrows raining thick and fast,
From the fierce hands
Of his own legion sped,
Yet by the inner Light, the radiance vast
Uplifted, comfortèd;
  So doth the Soul
Writhe in agony, stabbed by darts
Of its own judgments, angry deeds, and hate,
Life's armoury for piercing other hearts.
  But all the while
The Spirit calm, unpierced, and whole,
Gazes into heaven with a smile
Invincible, beyond the avenging fate,
In regions where no dream has ever trod,
  Seeing the open space,
And the dear human face,
Through Love and Pity near, so very near to God.

HOLY ROOD

Love is the strong upright beam,
Truth and Life the Cross bars;
Strangely, oh strangely, these seem
To hold up the Sun and the Stars.

POETRY

O song what art thou, fairest of earth's things,
Thou skylark of the mind's inviolate sky,
Thou child of falling waters, rushing wings? ...
'Nay, but the echo of a voice am I,
The silent voice that haunts the inner mind,
The immortal soul of every mortal dream
That waves in corn, and cries in the wild wind,
And sings like sunlight on a mountain stream.'

THEY WENT FORTH

At the twilight hour when snow was falling,
Falling silently over the town,
The Pied Piper came calling, calling,
Calling quietly up and down.
He played his pipes of wind and cloud
Till they all came rushing down the stairs,
My dreams, my hopes, my prayers,
Rushing down with cries of delight
They vanished into the silent night.
There was no sound of footsteps in the street,
They vanished into thin air ...
They did not stop to say good-bye,
For a moment you heard their voices calling,

Then the old silence settled down ...
They went alas who knows where,
Beyond the hills in a huddled crowd,
Through the thick snowflakes into the sky.
Who knows, who knows
Where the Pied Piper goes
Whilst the snow is falling, falling
  Over the town?

THE CROSS

Talk not of Justice and her scales of woe,
We know no justice, weighing gain and loss,
Save the balancing arms of love held wide
That cannot sway or falter to and fro,
Mercy on this side and the other side,
The adamantine justice of the Cross.

JUSTICE

To please the Gods great Agamemnon slew
His daughter, raising a swift wind of war
He burnt Troy town, and with his pirate crew
Sailed home in triumph from that alien shore.

In vengeance for the slaying of her child
Fierce Klytemnestra slew that cruel lord,
Doubtless believing, in her frenzy wild,
Justice had armed her with a shining sword.

Orestes slew his mother, in his soul
The Furies rose against his bitter deed,

He clung to the God's Altar, the safe goal
Of those whose sin is by just powers decreed.

Behold, he had done but as they dreamed and willed.
Gladly the Slayer rose up from his knees,
The Voice of Light in his dark mind was stilled
And the Erinnyes were Eumenides.

Thus the old story doth of Justice tell,
And we yet dream of Judgment and of Sin,
See Justice opening wide the gate of hell
And hasten still, dear God, to enter in.

'To please the Gods,' 'for Justice sake,' how long
Shall life and love and joy be still denied,
Whilst in the midst of an indifferent throng,
Mercy, the Beautiful, is crucified?

AN ILLUMINATED MISSAL

Here all men come to the centre of things,
Angels, and shepherds, and travel-worn kings.

Such a bright procession never was seen,
Amongst the Kings there's a crownèd Queen.

Long hair falling on a brown dress,
In the midst of the shepherds a shepherdess.

Breathless and joyful in rapturous awe
All the grand people kneel down in the straw.

Ivory sceptres and robes of pride,
Humbly the kings have cast them aside

To journey o'er miles of desert sand
Into the heart of the Beautiful Land.

By the light of a star they found their way
From what far country no man can say.

But the shepherds were humbler, light shone on them,
For they pastured their flocks near Bethlehem.

And the Ox and the Ass were the humblest of all,
So Christ himself has come to their stall.

Dumbly they gaze with round eyes undismayed
At the Radiant Love in their manger laid.

Whilst Mary smiles in her robe of blue
And whispers 'The Lord has need of you.'

Round the border, primroses blossom sweet
And a grasshopper lies at the Virgin's feet.

There are bees and roses and berries red,
All crowding into the little gray shed,

Where under the Light of the New Star
The Child smiles Peace on All Things That Are.

TO AN UNCIVIL ACQUAINTANCE

Once did you do, oh, years and years ago,
Down in the deeps of time, a deed most kind
And pitiful; now you have a hard mind,
You have forgotten, but I know, I know.

The centuries in my magic glass stand still,
Your scorn has left me cold, for evermore
I see you kneel near that mysterious Door
And watch a white flame burn under your will.

THE DIVINE LISTENER

Everything sang to him always, for to him all things were
dear.
The lilies I think sang of sunshine, God's light in the inner
mind.
As I wander o'er field and hill, I stoop down and try to
hear
What the grass sang of the endless and mystical way of the
wind.

I'm sure the dewdrops sang of the rainbow in heaven
above,
Where light in a dream of colour gives itself to the rain,
The waves of the lake sang of danger the cradle-song of
love,
And I know that the shining corn is the song of the buried
grain.

But at night when the rain fell down from fathomless gulfs
of air,
In vain did the tempest shriek, in vain did the thunder
roll.
As he stood on the shuddering hillside wrapped in the
silence of Prayer,
No sound he heard save the Morning Star singing deep in
his soul.

THE QUESTION

You say, how can you know there is a God at all?
O friend, how do you know what poetry is for,
How do you know the snowdrops and the waterfall
Are lovely, or that silver waves break on the shore
At twilight, bringing a great peace with the high tide
Into men's souls: in this mysterious world and wide
How do you know that there is beauty anywhere,
Who know not that you know the one and only Fair?

THE PHILOSOPHER

Life came to him, 'Whence art thou, oh untrue?'
'I come from God' – there is no God, he knew.

Truth came to him, 'Whence comest thou, Most Fair?'
'I come from God.' 'No God is anywhere.'

Love came to him, 'Whence comest thou?' he cried,
'I come from God.' 'There is no God.' ... Love sighed.

Of all these three, Love only answerèd:
'But I am God,' Love said.

SACRAMENTS

For Music's ecstasy thy name I bless
Drinking thy wine and eating thy strange bread,
I pray thy living force of holiness
May raise my earthbound spirit from the dead.

At sunset kneeling near dim waves I pray,
Where dream-entranced with Beauty wet sands shine,
O Hidden Heart, give me thy gold and gray,
Bright Valour, silver lowliness Divine.

But where the rustling cornfields front the sun,
Deep in my soul with that blue sky above,
I only pray, O thou Belovèd One
The wind doth sigh for thee, give me thy love.

VISION

'All beautiful things,' I cried in grief, 'turn brown and fade
and pass,
Even the wind dies with spiritual sighing infinite ...'
Then the sun shone on a wet leaf lying sodden in the
grass,
And lo, the hyaline sea a-glitter with the Light of Light.

HEAVEN

Men say it is a selfish soul
That makes of heavenly bliss
Her vision and her goal.
Nay, heaven is but this,
To shake off the earth's dust
And be the invisible wind,
Content in unseen ecstasy to bear
God's sunlight everywhere,
To the just and the unjust;
And carry gentle showers,
Pouring the spiritual rain
On the earth's parchèd flowers,

Unthanked, unseen, unpraised, yet not in vain.
To be the unknown servitor of the blind,
The nameless unguessed thrall of love and prayer,
The drudge, the slave, the lover of mankind.

LUX UMBRA DEI

Blue and red and yellow still
Paint the sky and climb the hill,
Whilst the wind whispers to the trees
'All the earth and sky are made
Out of the shadow of a shade,
But from the shadow of God are these.'
When primroses are in the grass
And the blue waves of bright air
Are touched with the sunset's rose,
Wrapped in three colours everywhere
We see the shadow of God pass
And know what each trancèd dewdrop knows,
What pilgrim glory through the ether flows.

THE ECLIPSE

The shadow of the earth lies on my soul,
'It is but a cloud,' one said,
'Soon it will fall from the air
In silver waters running fair,
Unfurling its life-giving shining scroll.'
'Nay, nay,' I said, with parchèd lips,
'It is my life's eclipse,
Striking the moonlight of my dreaming dead,
The shadow of the earth lies on my soul ...'
A star sang, wise from her long wandering

Through leagues and leagues of blue light unfathomable,
'I who live free in ultimate space do know
The shadow of the earth so small a thing,
The soul of man so great, ah who can tell,
Pent up behind your narrow prison bars,
Into what sea of Light all living waters flow,
What pilgrim you shall meet beyond the stars.'

ASK, AND YOU SHALL RECEIVE

Alas, my dream sings and soars
But my Love lies on the ground;
I shall come back from the wars
Uncrowned – forever uncrowned.

Stoop down from thy inner light,
Thou art Love, give me all things,
Thou art the secret of flight,
Thou art the swiftness of wings.

THE IVY LEAF

Only an ivy leaf blown in,
Lying helplessly and still
On my bedroom floor:
Nay, a gift from the bright Kosmos flung
At my feet, a song in a strange tongue,
A beacon from a far rock-guarded shore,
God's token thrown across my window-sill.

ANIMALS

You really think thy cannot feel like you or I?
Ah me, I know not; yet one said, so legends tell,
'Alas for him who cannot hear the dumb things cry,
How shall he see the Light Invisible?'

THE LEGEND

The Legend tells with a strange naïve surprise
When Jesus from the earth had gone,
And his friends were a weeping scattered band
Fearful, distracted and unwise,
How on one soul his gentle spirit shone,
Old, and an exile in a far land,
'A partridge running in the sand'
Could still give joy to the Belovèd John.

THE PENALTY OF PERCEPTION

O joyless knowledge, tale that must be heard
For thy brother's sake ... 'Imagination
Makes mortals suffer for a stranger's pain,
Thus Pity dwells never within a fool,
But in wise men; not without penalty
Too great a wisdom in the mind abides.'

THE VISION OF ISAIAH

Wonder, wisdom, and might,
Faith holding a great light,

One by one singing through my mind,
I watched the great procession wind,
Then some one bade the singing cease.
Amid the hush of folded wings
The glory of the Everlasting Father came
Crowned with a new name,
The Star of Bethlehem, Peace.
Oh, the last and the best,
Fairer than all the rest,
Fairer than all things,
Into my soul came Peace.

THE TEST

An ancient song I sing, a thrice-told tale I tell,
Deep in the secret places of the human heart,
So near, so brotherly entwined, lie heaven and hell,
How shall we know the frontier holding them apart?

Bright vanity fills hell with flames of rapture wild
And shapes of dancing light that seem divinely fair,
Yet thus we know the truth, when God but says 'My
child,'
Hell shrieks and fades away, and heaven is everywhere.

INTERROGATIONS

Poor patient words, 'when,' 'where,' and 'who' and 'why,'
Earth's little sighs of loneliness are they,
Idly they drift beneath our cloud-hung sky,
Clay whispers them eternally to clay.

Poor mortal words shut out from heaven, for there
'Who' matters not, into Love's image grown ...
'When' is 'always,' and 'where' is 'everywhere,'
Our passionate 'why' unheard, undreamed, unknown.

THE MASQUERADE

O Mystic Christ, how often dost thou speak
From lips that do deny thee, hearts that scorn thy heart;
How often in the soul as yet too weak
To bear the brightness of thy countenance,
Hiding thy face behind the magic vail of Art
Thou speakest with the voice of all Romance.

THE SOUNDLESS MELODY

Pan heard in the hollow reeds beside the stream
The unborn music of his unmade flute,
The willows bowed and whispered in his dream,
The grass stood silent, all the birds were mute.

There was a Listener wiser than Pan
Who stood by a dark stream, where willows are,
And dreamed in the hard hollow heart of man
To hear the music of an unborn star.

SOME DAY

The frost has melted, for the earth's hard heart is broken,
Released, relieved, the gentle grass lies glittering in the
sun.

Shall it not come to pass one day, by the same token,
Earth-frozen spirit shall melt in love, God's shining will be
done?

THE VISION OF GOD

Into the passionate heart
Of one who dreamed apart,
Out of the blue waters' brightness,
Out of the stars' remote flame,
And out of the dawn winds' whiteness,
The sense of the Holy came.
But to a soul in despair,
Out of the grief-laden air,
Out of the black-hearted city
Where Beauty has never trod,
In a rush of Love and Pity
There came the Vision of God.

ALL SOULS

I

Who loves the blossom better than the bud?
Unto our hearts does not the brown root tell
The secret of the flower invisible?
Who dreams the low tide lesser than the flood,
Or sees no comeliness in a child's face?
   Is dawn less fair
Than the bright colour noonday sunshine paints
On the same seas and mountains everywhere?
All souls, you say, what are they but all saints

In the making, theirs is the twilight's grace
Dim haloed in the early morning air.

II

This is the saint's day of my heart, here I say we, not they,
Without presumption, humbly claiming a high fellowship.
All saints shine far above me, all too nobly great
For one whose heart fails and whose footsteps slip.
Rather I cling to all souls, sinful, blind, or sad
As I, yet beautified with great desires and strange,
Weeping or smiling, childish spirits glad,
Men of wild words, dumb things that stand or crawl or fly
'Neath the cold northern lights, under the tropic sun,
Slaves of the earth, yet sons of God, children of change:
All you who breathe the air with me – to you I cry –
Who care not what you have done or left undone –
You living souls be near me, with me, when I pray.
Ah then, no saint in heaven will still be far away,
And God is only one with us when we are One.

THE RIVER AND THE WIND

I prayed, but silent were the starry skies,
The answer came to me in this wise,
The sound of many waters in my mind –
The spiritual sighing of the wind
Opened the closèd lids of thought,
To see the Light I sought.
Through the valley sang the stream,
But the wind was part of my dream.

LEAVES

Like leaves on the Autumn wind,
All seen things wingless must ride
On the invisible tide
Of an unthinkable Mind.

STORM

A great wind rushed out of the sky,
It fell on a branch set high
That held a yellow leaf and sere,
It shuddered and shook in the lightning's glare,
Swung to and fro, straining to hold
The little trembling shadow of gold,
It writhed and clung to the helpless thing,
Sap cried to sap with a wild cry,
In vain, in vain, in the fall of the year,
Weak and faint was the tree's will ...
Letting go, surrendering
  Silently,
Beauty fell out of the air,
A dead leaf lay on the grassy bank,
Then slowly the wind sank,
As the moon rose over the hill.

THE TRUE WITNESS

He witnessed to the truth, for this he was born,
For this he trod our sun-enchanted world,
For this he raised the dead, and healed the blind,
Hearing God's Spirit when men heard the wind,
Seeing the sunlight in shut petals furled.

He witnessed to the truth, thus his alone
In each man's soul that mystery divine
That is the kingdom of the coming day.
The Tree of Life was in his garden grown,
He is the thing he has, the Truth, the Way,
The Love that turns life's waters into wine.

THE PUZZLE

They walked with Christ along a weary road
And strove against a sense of mystery
And begged to know the house of his abode,
But all he said to them was 'Come and see.'

O God, unseen, unknown, where dost thou dwell,
Shall not my soul find all her purpose there?
This is the mystery no tongue can tell,
The elusive spiritual city far and fair.

Yet through the ever shifting clouds of change
The answer in my heart still gleams the same,
Homely amid thought's stormlit rainbows strange,
Simple and shining as the dawn's white flame.

I walk with Love on through a weary land,
And strive against the sense of mystery,
And beg to know the goal ... to understand ...
Love only smiles and whispers 'Come and see.'

THE ONE

'Twas a poet who said,
    'Truth and Beauty are one

In star, flower, or clod.'
  And Love answerèd,
'As the rays so the sun –
  The One is God.'

MOUNTAINS

Down in the plains, out of a million doors
A million lives do issue, countless hands
Clutch at the world's heart, grasp and faint and fall,
Turning to dust in many crowded lands.
Up in the hills the one life sings and soars,
The one voice echoes from each mountain wall,
With open hands the one light downward pours
Sunshine and flowers and wings and fragrant air.
I wept to leave the mountains, and come down
From Life's high battlements and snow-heaped towers
Unto a place of darkness and great mills ...
Yet every joy on earth is everywhere.
But yesterday, prisoned in a dull street,
I found Christ walking through the armoured town,
And in his soul the glory of the hills,
The mountain torrents and the humblest flowers,
The fragrance of all springtime meadows fair ...
The joy of his great message winged his feet.

EPITAPH

I

'You took away my childhood' – 'But to give you youth ...'
'You took away my youth' – 'To give you the wise years.'
'You took away my life' – 'Yea, but to give you Truth,
Life without falsehood, Love beyond these tears.'

EPITAPH

II

My cup o'erflowed with joy and thankfulness,
God said it is too small to hold the wind
 Of the Spirit's flight,
Or the sun or the stars or the birds' wings,
I will give you one that will hold all things,
Life for the dead and light for the blind ...
 For this his name I bless.
The cup he gave me holds his wind, his wings, his Light.

THE DISILLUSION OF EURIPIDES

Once did I dream of the immortal fight
For Helen, golden glory of the world,
Song against song, light against shining light,
By laurelled heroes in the conflict hurled.

Now do I know the Victor's dear-bought joy
Is out of empty air and a cloud made,
For Helen never really sailed to Troy,
And Menelaus, conquering, clasped a shade.

FUGITIVES

As Orpheus fled from Hades long ago,
With my dear love I fled out of the town
Where wild winds blew hot ashes to and fro,
And all my hopes and fears were burning down.

'Eurydice, fear not the perilous road.' –
'Alas, I fear these towers of singing flame.' –
'Dear friend, we have the stars for our abode,
Light without fire, the Light from whence we came.'

THE END OF THE STORY

'Dream not to minister to the unwise,
Though but a drop of water is his need;
Between the good and bad a great gulf lies,'
Said Abraham, yet this was not Love's creed.

'Though one from death arisen to him was sent,
God's messenger out of the dark unknown,
Yet would he not believe him or repent ...'
Love cried to Lazarus out of Light's white throne.

Then Lazarus looked across the chasm and smiled,
To one greater than Abraham he prayed,
'O Love, our God, look down on this thy child,'
And plunged into the dark waters unafraid.

And Dives, seeing hope where Hate once trod,
Knew suddenly the heavenly beggar dear,
Lifted his heart in a great prayer to God,
To save his friend from the wild waves of fear.

At once the blest soul battling with the tide,
The damnèd praying on that baleful shore,
Before the only God stood side by side,
Together in light they dwell for evermore.

But Abraham dreaming his old dream austere
Heard the great song those happy angels sang,

And wondered if the Judgment Day was near,
And why the crystal bells of heaven rang.

'By Love the gulf is dried, the chasm filled,'
So Lazarus sang, and Dives answerèd,
'To tell men love is all that God has willed
Jesus, who loved, has risen from the dead.'

JESUS AND MARY

Life's wine was spent, Life's Light burned low,
'They have no wine,' she cried
   To Love at her side ...
In her heart spake the voice divine –
Ungrudging, letting all things go,
Love answered, 'What is mine is thine.'

She had been with him from of old,
To the servants (the humblest and least
   Who wait at Life's feast)
She poured out her witness true,
The secret of Love she told ...
She said, 'Whatever he tells you, do ...'

Vessels of stone with water filled,
Great pitchers filled to the brim
   They brought to him.
No word of his shook the air,
Yet suddenly, as Love willed,
The Wine of Eternal Life was there.

THE UNCONSCIOUS

A hot dull room, great crowds and flaring lights,
And yet a growing vision of clear sky,
Palm trees, and a far wind-swept mountain range,
Till all at once a girl's voice fell from heights
Serene and unemphatic, effortless,
And melody, like a smile, stole suddenly
Over the music's face, the notes fell one by one,
Cool hyaline dewdrops shining in the sun,
'I know that my Redeemer liveth,' strange
That every heart did answer unaware,
Before a man had time to think or doubt,
From regions dim where sunken rivers flow,
Out of some deep lost knowledge buried there,
That rose up with an inner soundless shout;
The air shook with that hidden resonant 'Yes, I know.'

THE GOOD DEED

'What have you done for me?' God asked the soul of a
child:
'I was not good or brave,
There was little I could do,
But a cup of cold water I gave
To the cowslips, and sometimes bread
To the sparrows, because of you
   And because of him
Who dwelt with wild things in the wild ...'
'Was it not enough?' sang the Seraphim.

THE SOUL LIKE A WATERED GARDEN

God made each shell and flower and tree
And granted all life's prayers ...
Alas, what secret enemy
Stole in and planted tares?

THE MAGIC WELL

There is a story that men tell
How watering their camels on the height
Not far, not far from Bethlehem,
The wise men found their Light of Light
Deep mirrored in the waters deep
Of this mysterious mountain well.
On the same star-enchanted night
Here too the shepherds brought their sheep,
Where drownèd dreams and shadows are
Far from the stars they found their star,
Out of the deeps it shone on them,
Not far, not far from Bethlehem.

THE THIRD ANGEL

When Abraham met the Angels near his tent
Clear eyes and wings divine shone out on him.
Therefore the Rabbis named them Cherubim
And Seraphim, God's life and truth divinely sent,
And to their children's children told the tale
How the great light shone through the mystic vail.
These were the Two, but ah, the third, the third,
His was the name ineffable, unknown,
Not in the tabernacle was that strange word

Whispered, the name all names above,
The Angel known to Christ, and Christ alone,
The third great word divine, and strangest – Love.

SABBATH

As he stood to hear
Lake water murmuring softly far away,
The song of the wind rustling in the corn,
Men asked: 'Why dost thou not go up to pray
In God's House on this blessed Sabbath morn?'
Waves of blue air went whispering crystal clear
Through his deep soul, he only said aloud,
'Something greater than the Temple is here,'
His strange eyes fixed on a white sunlit cloud.

THE THIRD POET

Hardly the dim church can the fresco hide
Of life by wrath and judgment overcast,
Yet have I found the Church door open wide
Into the sunny cloister, smiling passed –
O Soul of great adventure, thine at last
The light to Byron's bitterness denied,
The pain of Dante's pilgrimage of pride,
Like starlight in the sunshine fading fast.
What though thy weakness broke thee, held thee down
Whilst men tore off thy crown –
Who loves the sin does most the sinner hate,
Therefore it is written over hell's gate
By fiends, 'Cast hope aside who enter here.'
    Runs not the world's doom thus?
Deep in the soul is graved the answer clear –

'New life for Dante as for Lazarus,
For him to whom all lovely things were dear,
A crown of life thorn-starred, mysterious.'

WITHIN

Thou source of every river, and thou sun
And centre of all light, yet hidden away
From the outside world and the light of day,
In vain we seek through earth, and sky, and air,
For never a passionate soul has found thee there,
In vain we search the fields of day and night
Flower starred, sunlit, for Him whom Christ called Light,
And seek through years of struggle and of strife,
Clutching at straws, the Life that is our Life –
In vain we look for Thee in Heaven above,
    Whom Christ has callèd Love ...
Strange Father of that inner life that flows
Deep down beneath the colour of the rose,
And lifts the hills to heaven and lurks unseen
Within the trees' bright aureole of green,
And hides behind the sunset's blue and gold,
And sings in shining rivers manifold,
And waves of the wild air, give us to see
And know ourselves, that thus we may know thee,
To dig deep down beneath our thoughts and find,
Haply each son of man in his own mind,
Thy hidden light, far from the cosmic din,
Where Love walks free of wrath, and death, and change, –
O country starry fair and silver strange,
    The Kingdom of that heaven that is within.

THE METHOD AND THE END

We who love beauty truly, yet can sometimes speak
In words harsh and unbeautiful of our true friend,
(Adoring a far flame to our own souls denied),
We flatter her wild light in foolish language weak,
Lost in the heart's desire, we know not the hearts' guide,
Nor dream to find the method hidden in the End.

Thus many talked with Christ, yet did not understand
Those words that sounded simple spoken by a friend,
Familiar words and homely, heard thus every day.
Christ help us all who will to follow, hold his hand,
Yet know not the great road of love, the truth, the way,
Nor dream to find the method hidden in the End.

FORCE

The light burns low, ended the endless feast,
The rose-leaves' withered petals are all shed,
Gone are the kings; those tyrants of the East
Who live for ever are for ever dead ...
Augustus, where is now thy golden throne?
Ashes the emerald-crownèd brow sublime,
No more before thee prostrate nations moan,
Whilst he who had nowhere to lay his head
Has made the very winds and streams his own
And conquered Life and Death and space and time.
Augustus, where is now thy golden throne?
Who lives for ever is for ever dead.

OPPOSITES

That pain hunts joy, and pleasure follows pain
  To Socrates was plain;
Mourn not the dreams that fade out of your heart,
  When these depart
Their opposite Reality shall stand
  At thy right hand.
Grieve not for Time's pale brood of years that fly,
  When these have drifted by,
Their unknown opposite thy friend shall be
  Thrice-vailed Eternity –
Nay, that which gives will surely take away,
  Day follows night, night day.
Chained to a flying wheel, a whirling ring
  That to and fro doth swing,
Slave-owner change round the wild circle drives
  Our tortured fettered lives,
Shall we rise up then but to be flung back
  On the old foot-worn track,
The play of whirling opposites down hurled
  To this death-haunted world,
The butterfly become a worm again
  And joy inherit pain?
Shall those who walk in peace heaven's flaming round,
  Sink back to the old ground?
And he who passes the Eternal Door
  Starve in our streets once more? ...
Nay, by masked guides out of the tumult led
  We leave the circle dread,
The milky way, the long unending road
  That leads to no abode,
Casting aside dreams and hates and fears
  And tumult of the years,
Breaking the bonds and strong magnetic bars
  Of sun and moon and stars,
Forsaking summer's heats and winter's cold

Time's mansions manifold,
The Opposite of Opposites to find
  In love and life and mind
And clasp the Absolute beloved and strange –
  Bright Opposite of Change.

STAGE OR STABLE

In every human life in every age
A solemn play is played mysteriously fair,
Great kings and priests go strutting up and down the
stage,
Reflected in a host of mirrors everywhere ...
Till suddenly, in the lost stable of the inn,
Where captive souls gaze humbly from dim eyes,
All the lights fade and all the drama's din
Into a rustling silence and pale darkness dies;
Gone is the painted majesty of throne and law,
Here where the poor folk dwell, and ox and ass abide,
The Son of Man, Reality, lies on the straw
And Mary kneels in peace and rapture at his side.

THE UNBORN

Lilies once murmuring your ancient rune
Deep in the earth's heart, all your buried sheen
Folded beyond the sight of the most wise,
Now russet sheaths hold balls of living green,
Still veiled you whisper you are coming soon,
To bow your heads beneath the sunlit skies,
And lift your silver ladders to the moon.

THE REVOLT AGAINST TIME

Oh I am tired of thought, weary of memory's grind,
　Now the lost past,
Life after life unveiled, menacing lives in my mind,
The terrible load of time inexorably vast ...
Like a sea-seeking stream that cannot pause or stay,
Crowned with dead leaves, the future flows away
Into the past – the present – ah, the present disappears.
There is no present at all in all the weary years,
And yet I dream and dream; in heaven amongst the
flowers
Shall we not find the present hidden in the dead end,
Yea, when the future is past, the present shall be ours,
And we shall know Eternity, Life's only friend.

YOUTH AND AGE

This Phaedo that I work on, glad, but weary eyed,
(As ever and again,
With care and pain,
I search the heavy word book at my side)
I read such years ago on summer eves
Amongst bright flowers, under swaying leaves,
Held by new magic in the translated page,
And magic in the bluebells round me grown,
And magic in each gray and high-placed stone
That marks the Cairn of Maeve above the sea ...
Dark book of memories and mystery ...
Round wheels the whirling dance
Of life and circumstance ...
This strange delightful labour of my age
Was my youth's wild and rainbow-lit romance.

MY CREED

There is no man can walk the narrow way
Of heaven alone, with a great multitude
Of secret sharers come we to that feast.
Rejoice, rejoice, beside the way of peace
The homing swallow has builded her nest.
Beyond the great gateways of the new birth
Shines the high road that Isaiah trod,
No ravenous beast shall go up thereon,
The rage of the lion is faded and gone.
A lamb shall be born with a golden fleece,
No murderous deed shall be dreamed or done,
No jealous fury tear Thyestes' breast,
No more shall Atreus' rage affront the sun
Or blast the glory blazing in the West ...
The very serpent has hatched her brood
Fangless and poisonless, green and gold.
The children of men and the sons of earth
Are brothers at last and the children of God.
Where love is the heart's wall, love the soul's array,
There is nothing living left out in the cold ...
   When all is said and done
There is room for every man and every beast,
For the Life Eternal is One.
'Behold we have seen his star in the East.'

THREE CONSOLATIONS IN ILLNESS

I

Veiled was the face of the unfaltering guide,
The long dark hours were on me, not a spark
Lightened my heart, there was no joy nor hope,
Ashes the glow that once was life's desire ...

Yet near my soul did something stir and grope,
A little flame sprang up in the spent fire,
A human hand outstretched reached down into the dark,
I knew a friend was watching by my side
Holding in her strong heart through the long night
As in a lamp that dark and hidden light,
Just visible to tired eyes and dim
That wept their loss of the clear sight of him
Who is dear Love Eternal Infinite.

II
Parsifal

The clouds came down amid a storm of pain,
There was no word from heaven, no word, no word.
   Then a friend came
And played this music, till once more I heard
The singing rhythm of the inner flame,
The darkness in my spirit paled and stirred,
And showed the gentle light of God again.

III

Oh God is good, even when he hides his face
He shows his love in many skilful arts –
   Flowers all light and grace,
   Roses that blazed out everywhere
Cried of the kindness hidden in human hearts,
And human words made bright the darkened air.
Yes, God is good, from his great heart there flows
Hands to relieve, and gentle souls of friends;
O wonderful friends, your patient deeds and kind
Are the bright petals of the Mystic rose
That grows where the world ends,
The tree of life a-glitter in the wind.

AFTER THE STORM

Suddenly everywhere
  Clouds and waves are one,
The storm has cleared the air,
  The sea holds the sun
  And the blue sky –
There is no under, no above,
  All is light, all is love –
Is it like this when you die?

UNPUBLISHED POEMS
From Poems of Eva Gore-Booth: Complete Edition
(1929)

THE WORLD IS ROUND

There is no edge to the sunshine nor the wind nor the
driving rain,
There is no bound to the courage that holds the whole
world in its grip,
No sheer abyss divides our soul from the souls of the
slain,
Softly out of the frozen ground the delicate snowdrops
slip.
So we have found that the world is round;
And if you sail far enough on the outward-bound ship,
The wind and the sea and a brave heart will bring you
home again.

A SYMBOL

I saw Blind Justice o'er the Nations reign
Blood sated, leaning on her stupid sword,
And in her hands the scales of sin and pain,
By all the Lovers of the world abhorred.

I dreamt the Spirit of the Fair and Wise
Broke down those hideous scales of Right and Wrong,
Tore the foul bandage from her starry eyes,
Shattered the Sword of Justice with a song.

THE TRIBUNAL

For the Hidden One in every heart,
Lost star in the world's night,
Fire that burns in the soul of art,
The Light within the Light –

For the gentleness of Buddha's dream
And Christ's rejected truth,
The treasure under the world's stream,
Pearl of pity and ruth –
Before six ignorant men and blind
Reckless they rent aside
The vail of Isis in the mind ...
Men say they shirked and lied.

A MOMENT'S EXPERIENCE

Ah, push aside the vail of hate and strife
And gaze if but for a white moment's while,
Beyond the meagre bitterness of strife,
Into Eternity's most secret smile,

Catching a glimpse of that mysterious hour
When the world's purpose shines beyond its plan,
The sunset palace and the ivory tower
Of him who shall be called the Son of Man.

HEIMWEH

In Florence, my heart's city, far away,
A tower springs to heaven marble-wrought,
Pale rose and ivory heal this world of gray
And Gabriel's lily shines through dreamlit throught.
But here in this dull land of uncarved clay
In a dark snare my weary soul is caught,
Through fogbound streets day follows yesterday,
Beauty and life and light are brought to naught.
Peace: in the mind of him who wills in Deed
The ivory sculptured thoughts pace to and fro,
The tree of life springs out of scattered seed,

Amid the thorns and nettles lilies grow;
And sudden in the sunset glitters clear
The marble tower of hope austere.

TRUTH
'I am the Bright and Morning Star.'

Spirit patient and wise,
Soul at the heart of things,
Out of whose broken deeps arise
Colour and form and beauty herself in a rhythm of
flashing wings –

Soul of each dim fir-wood
And green rain-haunted lawn,
Dream by the world withstood,
Vision of pilgrim and poet and seer, and song of the birds
at dawn –

Spirit mighty to mould
Into beauty the sorrowful will
That fashioned the gods of old
Out of a dream in the hearts of men, and the marble heart
of the hill –

Shalt thou not build anew
Out of sorrow and sighing and tears
In all men's souls, of the heavens blue,
The rainbow-lit lily of peace that grows on the far-away
edge of the years?

Pity for friend and foe,
Love between foe and friend,
Out of the dreamlit caverns flow
Of the God of the Buried River of Stars, who is all men's
God at the end.

MAGNA PECCATRIX

What a man does for Christ he does for all,
Even the least of us; each fair deed done
Doth on all men in light and gladness fall,
The whole world's rainbow from the whole world's sun.

Once through the blackness of primæval night
A huge star burned deep in this sinner's mind;
Great as her sin the Lamp that held the Light,
The everlasting Light of all mankind.

Thus patiently through the long shadow years,
For many a one content her light to share,
Her deed is done again, she kneels with tears
To wash men's feet and wipe them with her hair.

BOREDOM

How dull is this vain talk, thought the Wise Guest,
Reclining at the Feast, rose-crowned, full-fed;
But to the servant, waiting on the rest,
Offering to each man holy wine and bread,
Alert and humble, working all the time,
No talk could matter, stupid or sublime.

A CONVICTION

Where is the road out of this world of strife?
Mercy is the Rhythm of the Divine Song.
  Who can forgive
Shall be forgiven, who can love shall live,
All-conquering prayer forgiving every wrong
Is the absolute Truth that is Eternal Life.

THE THREE CHORDS

Music affords
In every key
Three common chords:
Foundation stones are these of all our harmony.

Through heaven vibrate
Three common chords,
Beyond all life and fate
And dreams of flaming agonies and fair rewards.

To pity and ruth
The great harps thrill,
Love, Life and Truth,
The very self of God and song of unknown Will.

In the soul of man
The echo rings,
Faith, Hope and Love
Are the Pilgrim's staff and the Angel's wings.

The Way ascends
Out of the strife,
And the road ends
In Love, where faith is truth at last and hope is life.

Oh Christ most wise,
With fire shod,
May we dead arise
To life in the soul and spirit and mind of God.

PRIMROSES, WIND AND RAIN

Beautiful dawn, thou far-flung radiance white,
May our minds be as primroses in spring,
Giving their coloured Beauty back to Light
That calls from earth their lovely blossoming.

Oh, rustling in green trees, great Voice of Life,
May our souls be like birds in the wild air,
Floating and darting, whirling in strange strife,
Wind-blown, swift flashing, singing everywhere.

Thou gentle Rain of Love compassionate,
Fall on waste spaces, in bright fountains rise,
Bearing our spirits beyond Love and Hate
Into the soul of the Eternal skies.

JOAN OF ARC

No, not in visions or fierce ecstasy
To her the spirit came,
But when from the high-set stake
She turned to the kindly monk who by her stood
Begging him for the comfort of the Rood,
Moaning in fear the Everlasting Name –
Then self-forgetful, with a sudden cry,
She warned him of the swiftly mounting flame
And bade him leave her unconsoled to die,
Thrusting him into safety for Christ's sake,
Lest he should share her lonely agony.

CATERPILLAR TO BUTTERFLY

Oh Bright One shining in strange light
Beyond my earthbound sight,
I, living without joy,
In darkness creeping to destroy
The rose's heart, in heavy haunted hours
Of sorrowful greed among green-sheathed flowers,
Sometimes I dream that some far day
I too may flit from height to height
Where the Buddlea hedge on the south slope grows,
Or, folding o'er the great gold rose
My wings of coloured light,
May harmless drink of her full cup,
Scarce stirring chaliced petals fine.
Nay, could I be like you divine,
In one long rapture lifting up
My wings to the blue sky,
I would fly as you fly ...
Worms dream that once, from the enfolding gloom
Mysterious of a chrysolitic Tomb
Where a dead caterpillar lay,
A Glory rent the shroud and fled
Waving blue wings above the dead,
Scaling the inaccessible skies ...
But worms are grovelling creatures without eyes ...
These are but dreams ... no one can say ...
I have seen many caterpillars die ...
I know not, I ...

CRUCIFIXION

In the crowd's multitudinous mind
Terror and passion embrace,
Whilst the darkness heavily blind

Hides face from horror-struck face;
And all men, huddled and dumb,
Shrink from the death-strangled cry
And the hidden terror to come
And the dead men hurrying by.
White gleam the limbs of the dead
Raised high o'er the bloodstained sod,
And the soldier shuddered and said,
'Lo, this was the Son of God.'
Nay, but all Life is one,
A wind that wails through the vast,
And this deed is never done,
This passion is never past.
When any son of man by man's blind doom
On any justest scaffold strangled dies,
Once more across the shadow-stricken gloom
Against the sun the dark-winged Horror flies;
A lost voice cries from the far olive trees
Weary and harsh with pain a desolate cry: –
'What ye have done unto the least of these
Is done to God in Heaven, for earth and sky
And bird and beast, green leaves and golden sun,
Men's dreams, the starry dust, the bread, the wine,
Rivers and seas, my soul and His, are one.
Through all things flows one life austere, divine,
Strangling the murderer you are slaying me,
Scattering the stars and leaves like broken bread,
Casting dark shadows on the sunlit sea,
Striking the swallows and the seagulls dead,
Making the red rose wither to its fall,
Darkening the sunshine, blasting the green sod –
Wounding one soul, you wound the soul of all,
The unity of Life, the soul of God.'

ACKNOWLEDGEMENTS

It is an outrage that the poetry of such a prolific poet as Eva Gore-Booth has been, in the main, out of print for nearly ninety years. Although outrageous it is, unfortunately, not surprising. In October 2015 when Ireland's national theatre, the Abbey, launched their programme to commemorate the centenary of the Easter Rising that programme was overwhelmingly male focussed. Arts manager Lian Bell initiated a vibrant media campaign which emerged under the hashtag #WakingTheFeminists, a term coined by Maeve Stone. The movement gathered immense support and led to the board and the director of the Abbey Theatre publically committing to a policy of gender equality. My thanks and appreciation to the numerous feminist voices in Irish theatre for their dedication to this campaign which continues to highlight the gender-biased nature of Irish publishing and cultural production.

Throughout his term in office, President Michael D. Higgins has been a steadfast supporter of gender equality, including measures to create gender balance in Irish cultural memory. In his keynote address to launch The Theatre of Memory Symposium in the Abbey Theatre, Higgins noted how 'centenaries offer us: opportunities to add, to restore, to revise; opportunity to recollect the excluded, such as Eva Gore-Booth.' I wish to thank President Higgins for his unwavering promotion of my work to restore Gore-Booth to her rightful position in literary and political realms. It is the greatest honour to have President Higgins' endorsement in his foreword to this volume. I am also indebted to Dan Mulhall, who during his time as Irish Ambassador in London, was keen to promote and endorse this restoration project.

Alan Hayes has been dedicated to ensuring that the writings of Irish women remain in print; he relaunched the feminist press, Arlen House, with this very objective in mind. Many thanks to Alan for inviting me to compile a selection of Gore-Booth's poetry and for being supportive when that initial idea ballooned into this publication of her entire poetic works. I compiled this volume while based at the School of Irish Studies in Concordia University. Many thanks to all of my colleagues there who ensured that my time was productive, engaging and most of all enjoyable, especially to Michael Kenneally, Rhona Richman Kenneally, Siobhán Ní Mhaolagáin, Matina Skalkogiannia, Emer O'Toole, Susan Cahill, Jane McGaughey and Gearóid Ó hAllmhuráin.

I am indebted to my home institution, Liverpool Hope University, for their support of my research and for providing necessary financial aid to help towards publication of this volume, especially to Professors Nick Reese and Kenneth Newport. Also to my colleagues John Appleby, Fiona Pogson and Karen Quinn. My thanks to Katherine O'Donnell who advised me on readings of poetry during my PhD research at UCD. When I first began recovering the work and literature of Gore-Booth I could not imagine that her legacy would inspire so many. My work has been supported and encouraged by so many who deserve special thanks. To Maureen O'Connor for not only supporting my work but for her invaluable contributions to recovering and re-imagining Gore-Booth's literature. To Lucy Keaveney, who co-founded the Countess Markievicz School, for her continued dedication to honouring Irish women including Gore-Booth. To Joy Ní Dhomhnaill, a talented artist and a valued friend, for drawing the striking image of Gore-Booth for the cover of this book. Thanks are always due to my many friends and my family who continue to encourage my research especially my brother Barry and my parents Chris and Marie Tiernan for their endless love and support. Finally but by no means least, my thanks to Charlotte Hall, a truly inspirational Manchester woman.

Eva Gore-Booth was born on 22 May 1870 into a wealthy Anglo-Irish family in the West of Ireland.[1] The Gore-Booth's owned Lissadell House, a seventy-two roomed Greek revival mansion situated on a 32,000 acre estate in County Sligo. Eva's parents were conscientious landlords and when a second wave of famine swept across the area, during the winter of 1879–80, they opened their food store for any tenant in need. This sense of responsibility for others less fortunate was to have an impact on the Gore-Booth children old enough to appreciate this event. The eldest of the Gore-Booth children, Constance, later Countess Markievicz, was to become a significant figure in the fight for Irish independence and a most accomplished Minister for Labour in the first Dáil Éireann.[2] Eva's older brother, Josslyn, became an influential advocate of co-operative farming in Ireland and worked closely with the agricultural reformer, Horace Plunkett.[3] Eva rejected her aristocratic lifestyle and moved to the industrial city of Manchester in 1897 where she lived and worked amongst the working classes, many of whom were Irish emigrants.

While in Manchester Gore-Booth became a successful and resourceful trade unionist and social reformer. She established unions for women workers previously ignored by mainstream organisations. In particular, she supported women in occupations thought to be morally precarious such as barmaids, circus performers, flower-sellers and pit-brow lasses. In her most infamous campaign, protecting the rights of women to work as barmaids, she orchestrated the defeat of no less an adversary than Winston Churchill. Due to her determined political campaigning she ousted Churchill from his Manchester constituency at a 1908 by-election, at a time when women had no entitlement to vote in general elections. Gore-Booth worked tirelessly for women's suffrage and played an instrumental role in achieving votes for women. As well as her union work and suffrage campaigns, Gore-Booth authored nineteen volumes of published poetry, philosophical prose and drama. She was a persistent contributor to newspapers and journals as well as writing, sometimes politically contentious, pamphlets.[4]

During World War I, Gore-Booth became a militant pacifist supporting conscientious objectors and publishing highly-controversial condemnations of the war. Adopting a pacifist stance in England at this time was a particularly defiant act. Gore-Booth was at risk of appearing unpatriotic or worse labelled as a German sympathiser. She was a dedicated champion of Irish independence and in the wake of the Easter Rising, she supported the families of men killed during the insurrection, most notably Michael Mallin's wife, Agnes, and Francis Sheehy-Skeffington's wife, Hanna. Gore-Booth launched a campaign for the reprieve of Roger Casement's death sentence, which although ultimately unsuccessful, gained international attention.

Gore-Booth became particularly concerned about capital punishment in the wake of the Easter Rising. Her concerns were realised in 1920 when the Restoration of Order to Ireland Act was introduced to quell the Irish War of Independence. The Act resulted in an alarming rise of execution rates in Ireland the following year. Gore-Booth remained politically active until her death in 1926 at the age of 56. She died at her then home in Hampstead, London with her partner, Esther Roper, by her side.

NOTES

1 For a full account of her life see, Sonja Tiernan, *Eva Gore-Booth: An image of such politics* (Manchester, Manchester University Press, 2012).

2 For the most recent scholarly examination of Markievicz's life and politics see, Lauren Arrington, *Revolutionary Lives: Constance and Casimir Markievicz* (Princeton, Princeton University Press, 2016).

3 Sonja Tiernan, 'Sligo Co-operative Movements (1895–1905): the birth of an Irish political activist,' *Founder to Shore: Cross-currents in Irish and Scottish Studies*, edited by Shane Alcobia-Murphy, Linsay Milligan and Dan Wall (Aberdeen, AHRC Centre for Irish and Scottish Studies, 2010), pp 189–96.

4 For a complete collection of Gore-Booth's political writings see Sonja Tiernan (ed.), *The Political Writings of Eva Gore-Booth* (Manchester, Manchester University Press, 2015).

ABOUT THE EDITOR

Sonja Tiernan is an Associate Professor of Modern History and Head of the Department of History and Politics at Liverpool Hope University. Sonja is from Dublin and was awarded her PhD from University College Dublin; she has held fellowships at the National Library of Ireland, Trinity College Dublin, the Keough-Naughton Institute for Irish Studies at the University of Notre Dame and was the Peter O'Brien Visiting Scholar in Irish Studies at Concordia University. She is a Council member of the Record Society of Lancashire and Cheshire and an editorial board member of *Breac: A Digital Journal of Irish Studies* and of *Feminist Encounters: A Journal of Critical Feminist Studies in Culture and Politics*. Sonja has published widely on aspects of Irish and British social history. She is a contributor to the *Dictionary of Irish Biography* and to *Century Ireland*. Her books include *Eva Gore-Booth: an image of such politics* and *The Political Writings of Eva Gore-Booth*, both published by Manchester University Press. Her most recent articles re-examine the legacy of Irish women and are published in numerous volumes including *The Shaping of Modern Ireland: A Centenary Assessment*.